WebEx® Web Meetings For Dummies®

Cheat Sheet

The Meeting Center Environment

The Meeting Center is where you host and participate in WebEx meetings, so you'll spend a lot of time th~~ ~~ get you comfortable fast, here are a few of the tools and features you'll use

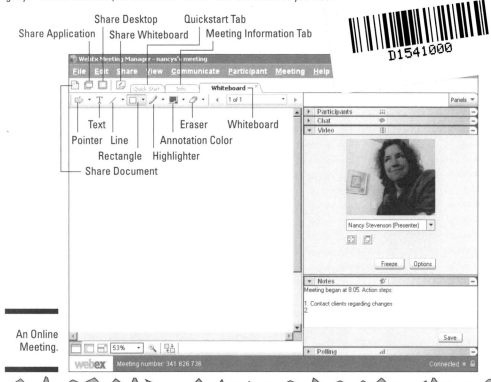

An Online Meeting.

Meeting Center Shortcuts

From within Meeting Center, you can use shortcut keystroke combinations to invoke certain actions, as shown in this table.

Shortcut	Action	Shortcut	Action
Ctrl+W	Close Meeting Center	Ctrl+Alt+N	Display whiteboard
Ctrl+T	Transfer files	Alt+Enter	Display full screen
Ctrl+Z	Undo last action	Ctrl++ (plus sign)	Zoom in
Ctrl+Y	Redo last undone action	Ctrl+− (minus sign)	Zoom out
Ctrl+Alt+F	Display Font Formatting dialog box	Ctrl+Alt+M	Pass microphone
Ctrl+Alt+O (*oh*, not zero)	Share presentation or document	Ctrl+M	Mute/unmute your microphone
Ctrl+Alt+A	Share application	Ctrl+F	Find participant
Ctrl+Alt+D	Share Desktop	F1	Help

WebEx® Web Meetings For Dummies®

Cheat Sheet

My WebEx Menus

My WebEx is where you control all your user settings. Display My WebEx by clicking the My WebEx tab on your WebEx site. This table summarizes what you'll find there.

My WebEx.

Menu Name	What You Can Do
My Meetings	Display all your scheduled meetings; access to One-Click Meetings setup
My Computers	Set up computers to be accessed remotely
My Files	Store files for use in presentations; access recorded event archives
My Contacts	Enter, import, export, and view WebEx contacts
My Profile	Enter/edit your name/contact information, Personal Meeting Room settings, and default session type

Menu Name	What You Can Do
My Reports	Access usage reports, attendee reports, archived file reports, and so on
Preferences	Set your home page, time zone, language, and locale
Training	Access information on WebEx training options
Support	Access information about WebEx support
Feedback	Send feedback to WebEx Customer Care

Copyright © 2005 Wiley Publishing, Inc. All rights reserved.

Item 7941-X.

For more information about Wiley Publishing, call 1-800-762-2974.

For Dummies: Bestselling Book Series for Beginners

WebEx® Web Meetings

FOR

DUMMIES®

by Nancy Stevenson

WILEY

Wiley Publishing, Inc.

WebEx® Web Meetings For Dummies®

Published by
Wiley Publishing, Inc.
111 River Street
Hoboken, NJ 07030-5774

For general information on our other products and services, please contact our Customer Care Department within the U.S. at 800-762-2974, outside the U.S. at 317-572-3993, or fax 317-572-4002.

For technical support, please visit www.wiley.com/techsupport.

Wiley also publishes its books in a variety of electronic formats. Some content that appears in print may not be available in electronic books.

Library of Congress Control Number: 2004117105

ISBN: 0-7645-7941-X

Manufactured in the United States of America

10 9 8 7 6 5 4 3 2 1

1O/SY/QS/QV/IN

WILEY

About the Author

Nancy Stevenson has had careers in arts administration, the software industry, and publishing. In the last 11 years she has authored almost 50 books on topics ranging from distance learning to e-commerce, desktop applications to wireless technology. She makes her home in the beautiful Pacific Northwest, where she spends her non-writing time acting in community theater productions, walking on the beach, enjoying her wonderful family, and occasionally writing novels nobody has (as yet) published.

Dedication

To my partner in life, Earl, who makes life so rich and happy.

And to my brother, Greg, wishing you peace at last.

Author's Acknowledgments

Thanks to all the folks at WebEx who helped me discover the ins and outs of their excellent service: Lisa Villasenor, Matt Ceglia, Dan Simmons, Janine Robinson, Ed Wong, Jeff Roberts, Sangeet Saurabh, Sanjay Dalal, McCario Naymie, Shikha Mathur, Eric Vidal, and Kari Lopez. Thanks also to Wiley Publishing and the contributions of their always-professional crew, including Greg Croy, Chris Morris, and Andy Hollandbeck; they make my words work.

Publisher's Acknowledgments

We're proud of this book; please send us your comments through our online registration form located at www.dummies.com/register/.

Some of the people who helped bring this book to market include the following:

Acquisitions, Editorial, and Media Development

Project Editor: Christopher Morris

Executive Editor: Gregory S. Croy

Copy Editor: Andy Hollandbeck

Editorial Manager: Kevin Kirschner

Media Development Manager: Laura VanWinkle

Media Development Supervisor: Richard Graves

Editorial Assistant: Amanda Foxworth

Cartoons: Rich Tennant, www.the5thwave.com

Composition Services

Project Coordinator: Adrienne Martinez

Layout and Graphics: Carl Byers, Andrea Dahl, Denny Hager, Joyce Haughey, Barry Offringa, Julie Trippetti

Proofreaders: Laura Albert, Leeann Harney Jessica Kramer Joe Niesen TECHBOOKS Production Services

Indexer: TECHBOOKS Production Services

Publishing and Editorial for Technology Dummies

Richard Swadley, Vice President and Executive Group Publisher

Andy Cummings, Vice President and Publisher

Mary Bednarek, Executive Acquisitions Director

Mary C. Corder, Editorial Director

Publishing for Consumer Dummies

Diane Graves Steele, Vice President and Publisher

Joyce Pepple, Acquisitions Director

Composition Services

Gerry Fahey, Vice President of Production Services

Debbie Stailey, Director of Composition Services

Contents at a Glance

Table of Contents

Introduction

●●

*W*ebEx is part of a quiet revolution. This revolution affects the way you connect with other people, the way you share information, and the way you interact with your employees, customers, and partners. That's because WebEx provides a cadre of Web meeting applications that enable your organization to enter the brave new world of on-demand business.

By using WebEx, you tap into the power of a comprehensive suite of specialized multimedia applications that help you do everything from supporting customers to launching a worldwide marketing event. With WebEx, you can train employees and customers or tap into the power of your sales organization in ways you never dreamed of.

This book helps you understand just what WebEx services are, what you can do with them, and how you can empower your organization and its communications by taking your interactions online.

About This Book

For Dummies books are here to make your exploration of a new topic easier. In this book, I point out the benefits of the WebEx Web meeting services and tell you how to use specific features. Of course, some features may be more relevant to your organization than others. I haven't written this book assuming you'd read it from beginning to end, so feel free to find the topics that are of most interest to you and jump around to get yourself up to speed.

If you're new to the whole concept of Web-meetings, read over the first few parts first. If you know which service of WebEx is of most interest to your organization, you can go directly to the relevant chapters. This is a flexible introduction to WebEx, its services, technology, and features. Take what you need today, and come back if you need more tomorrow.

Foolish Assumptions

I haven't assumed much in writing this book, except that you have heard of the Internet, that you or your organization holds meetings, and that you have an interest in holding meetings and other events on the Web.

You may have an interest in Web meetings because you want to save all those travel bills that result when you send employees around the world for sales calls. Or perhaps you want to keep your customers happy in a more efficient way. Perhaps your training budget could be trimmed if you had prerecorded online sessions that could form the basis of a self-paced tutorial library. Whatever your online communications need, WebEx has a solution for you.

You may be an on-the-go professional who'd like to hold a pay-as-you-go Web meeting with a client. Or you may be an organization with its own network that wants to find an enterprise-wide solution to communications and collaboration. Whether you are a lone professional or a company with global presence and thousands of employees — or something in between — this book is for you.

How This Book Is Organized

I've organized this book into parts for a few reasons. First, that's what my publisher told me to do. Second, organizing information into bite-sized chunks helps you understand new concepts and facts more easily. Finally, each part starts out with a cartoon, and I know you love cartoons.

Here, then, are the parts I've broken this book into.

Part 1: Meet Me on the Web

Discover just what WebEx Meeting Center is, and what solutions it offers to you, in this part. I provide a broad overview of the benefits of meeting online, the technology that underlies WebEx and keeps your meetings secure, and the various purchasing options available to you. In addition, this is the part where I share some of the essential setup options for your WebEx services, and some of the ways you can get support from WebEx as you get going.

Part II: Always Be Prepared

Before you can start a meeting, you have to schedule a meeting, choose your audio options, invite people, set meeting options, and assign privileges. That's what Chapter 4 is all about. If you need to access information on a remote computer from within your meeting, now is the time to set up your remote computer with this ability so it's available to you when your meeting starts. I show you how in Chapter 5. Finally, in Chapter 6 you explore the ins and outs of preparing for a marketing event using Event Center.

Part III: Let the Meetings Begin

In this part, you finally jump into running your own multimedia Web meetings. You discover how to start and run a meeting in Meeting Center. I show you how to share things during a meeting, such as documents, applications, Web content, and a remote desktop. You also explore the features of the Web meeting space, such as chat, the whiteboard, polls, notes, and session recordings.

In Chapter 8 you jump to the other side of the fence, experiencing what it's like to attend a WebEx meeting.

Part IV: Selling, Supporting, and Training with WebEx

Three other great uses of WebEx are holding sales meetings, supporting customers, and training anybody you want to train. This is the part where I take you through the ins and outs of using Sales Center, Support Center, and Training Center. Each has its own unique features and benefits, and each offers brand new ways to connect with people to sell, support, and train.

Part V: Taking WebEx Further

When you have mastered how to set up and hold various Web meetings and events, it's time to explore more advanced WebEx topics. In this part, you look at all the reporting capabilities of WebEx that help you monitor your online meeting activity and maximize your use of WebEx. I also provide a chapter that gives you an overview of what's involved in administering your WebEx site, should you opt for an enterprise-level solution.

Part VI: The Part of Tens

What would a *For Dummies* book be without this section? Here's where you get those neat lists of ten great things you can do with . . . whatever. Here I tell you about ten things you can do with WebEx on an enterprise level, ten ideas for using WebEx for your small business, ten tips from WebEx's own technical support folks and ten ways that companies have benefited from WebEx.

Icons Used in This Book

What are those little things in the margin, you ask? These handy graphical icons are there to draw your attention to useful information.

The Tip icon is there to draw your attention to handy shortcuts, useful advice, and tidbits of knowledge that enhance your WebEx experience.

Oops. Heed this icon. It tells you of pitfalls you might avoid if only you heed this sage advice. These pitfalls might be economic, technological, or even social, but they're worth paying attention to!

This icon points its finger to handy pieces of information that you'd be wise to keep in mind.

Where to Go from Here

When you bought this book you may have already tried out a few WebEx meetings through your company or an online demo at webex.com and be ready to sign up. If so, you might want to jump to Chapter 4 to get some ideas on setting up meetings of your own. If you are interested in discovering more about a particular service go to Part III to explore Meeting Center, or Part IV: Chapter 9 covers Sales Center, Chapter 10 explores Support Center, and Chapter 11 gets you up to speed on Training Center. Finally, if you might have to administer a WebEx site, check into Chapter 13: it's your introduction to site administration.

Part I
Meet Me on the Web

The 5th Wave   By Rich Tennant

"For thirty years I've put a hat and coat on to attend meetings and I'm not changing now just because I'm meeting on WebEx from my living room."

In this part . . .

You've got to start somewhere, right? In this part, you get an overview of what WebEx is and how you can begin to familiarize yourself with its features through online demos and training. You take a peek at the online meeting environment and cozy up to various support options available to you. Finally, you hear about the benefits of meeting online, from cost savings to security and everything in between.

Chapter 1

What's a WebEx?

*W*e've come a long way from the first meeting, which probably occurred when a few cavemen sat around a fire discussing the pros and cons of hunting saber-toothed tigers. We've replaced their grunts with sophisticated language (sometimes several languages in a single meeting). We've found ways to visualize our ideas with whiteboards and bullet point presentations. Companies have utilized all sorts of technologies, from conference phones to video conferencing, in search of the perfect meeting.

Yet for most of us, there are still a few obstacles to effective meetings. Organizing a meeting can be a nightmare in itself, with a wide variety of schedules and locations to accommodate. The cost of getting to and from a meeting, both in terms of time and travel expenses, can be prohibitive. If a meeting is held on the phone or even online, concerns about security and reliability ("Hey, Johnson just got disconnected . . . again!") abound.

Enter WebEx. WebEx offers a comprehensive suite of Web meeting applications designed to improve collaboration and increase your productivity. Simply put, WebEx has found solutions to many of the problems you face in setting up and hosting meetings. The solutions work for any meeting, from a handful of people holding a spontaneous problem-solving conference across the corporate campus, to a CEO delivering a report on corporate profits to 3,000 employees located around the world.

Look, Ma, No Software!

The first thing you need to understand about WebEx solutions is that there is no box to open. Customers simply access WebEx applications with a common Internet browser. WebEx offers a set of applications, and those applications are Web-based. That means you access your meeting online. So if you're on the road, you can tap into the meeting as easily as the nearest Internet connection. It also means that you don't have to do much of anything to set up and maintain your WebEx applications, and you don't have to fool around with hardware to deliver a presentation (which beats having to fool around with connecting your laptop and that darn overhead display thing like you did at the last Dallas sales conference, huh?).

It's Not Software . . . So What Is It?

WebEx has developed a comprehensive suite of Web meeting applications because not all meetings are alike. It offers you a very flexible approach to purchasing one or more meeting applications that make sense for your business. WebEx's Web meeting applications are designed to fit a specific meeting need, such as running a medium-sized project meeting, launching a global marketing event for thousands of people, or holding a one-on-one customer support session. You can mix and match the applications you need, and add new ones at any time. You can even customize your meeting applications to, for example, sport your own company logo in every meeting.

You can take the plunge and get a whole slew of these applications by buying WebEx Enterprise Edition. This includes Meeting Center, Sales Center, Training Center, Event Center, and Support Center in a single, easy-to-deploy interface for the company with a broad range of meeting needs.

Taking a look at all WebEx has to offer

Using WebEx, you can expand the reach of everybody in your company, from Jack the CEO to Jill the sales manager, to tap the potential of real-time collaboration.

WebEx currently offers the following Web meeting applications (what you have available depends on what your company buys):

  ✓ **WebEx Meeting Center™:** This is for those garden-variety meetings that make up so much of our work days. From project or team meetings to impromptu brainstorming or troubleshooting meetings, this is where you'll conduct your business on a day-to-day basis. You can see a Meeting Center meeting in progress in Figure 1-1.

✔ **WebEx Event Center™:** This is specifically designed for larger scale events, which can easily involve thousands of people in diverse locations. New product introductions, strategic business announcements — anything that requires that you really make a splash — work great in Event Center.

✔ **WebEx Training Center (see Figure 1-2):** Do you want to supercharge your training programs with an online component? Does your training require you to set up hands-on computer labs, register students for a training session, hold interactive discussions, or demonstrate how a software product works? If so, you need Training Center.

✔ **WebEx Sales Center:** Looking to get an edge over the competition? Using Sales Center, salespeople can improve their win rates by holding sales calls online.. Here you can demonstrate applications, share presentations, bring in experts on the fly, and discreetly view the whole meeting from your sales prospect's point of view.

✔ **WebEx Support Center:** With desktop control, remotely resolving technical problems is a snap. Hold one-on-one meetings (or one-on-one plus experts you call in to help out) with customers or employees to troubleshoot problems and provide personalized assistance.

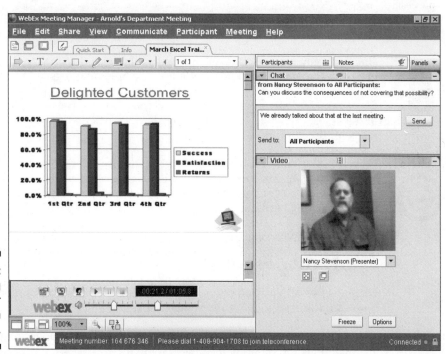

Figure 1-1:
A Meeting Center meeting in action.

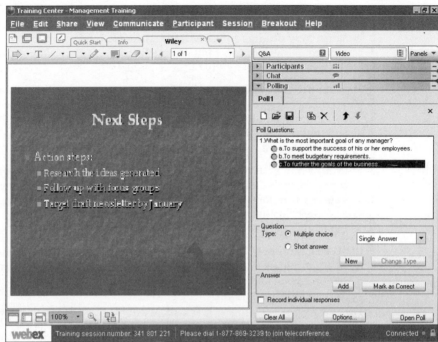

Figure 1-2:
Training via
WebEx.

One thing you'll get used to as you get familiar with the service is that WebEx calls different meetings different things. You hold meetings in Meeting Center and Sales Center, run events in Event Center, and hold sessions in Training Center and Support Center. I may refer generically to *meetings* in some places in this book, but when I get into the meat of a particular application, you'll discover the appropriate lingo.

Do you have to buy a bunch of services to simply meet online? No. You can get your feet wet with the WebEx Pay-Per-Use service, which allows you to hold meetings as you need to and be charged one at a time. See Chapter 2 for more about Pay-Per-Use.

What do you get?

Each meeting application offers different features. But, on a broad level, here's what the various WebEx solutions provide:

✔ Tools for scheduling meetings, including Instant Meetings and One-Click Meetings for initiating meetings on the fly. You'll learn more about these in Chapter 4.

✔ An online meeting environment (see Figure 1-3) with features for sharing files, giving sophisticated multimedia presentations, interacting with attendees, annotating presentations, incorporating video, recording meetings, and even sharing Web pages and applications. Chapter 7 gives you specifics about many of these features.

✔ A secure, reliable network based on a platform called WebEx MediaTone,™ which supports a full range of real-time data, audio, and video communications in several languages. You discover more about this technology and how it does what it does in Chapter 2.

✔ Tools to help run a meeting (there's even an eject feature to get rid of that uncooperative attendee — there's one in every bunch), poll attendees to check their understanding of material or get their input (see Figure 1-4), and generally ensure that everybody has a productive, pleasant meeting experience.

✔ A centralized command center called My WebEx™ (see Figure 1-5) where you can configure settings, view all the meetings you have scheduled and their status, and generate reports about your meeting activities.

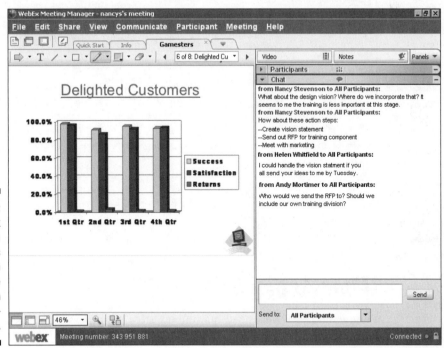

Figure 1-3:
A WebEx meeting in progress (shown in the Macintosh environment).

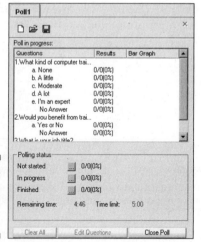

Figure 1-4:
The polling
feature in
use.

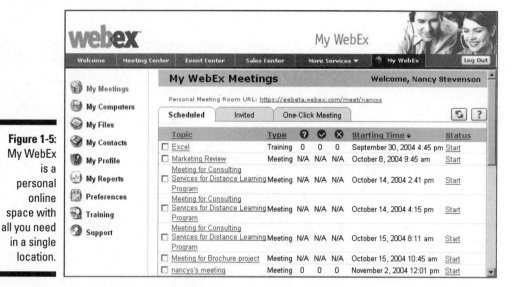

Figure 1-5:
My WebEx
is a
personal
online
space with
all you need
in a single
location.

What do you have to do?

Though you can add some bells and whistles, here's essentially what you
need to make use of most WebEx meeting features:

✔ A computer (desktop or laptop) or wireless device with an Internet connection.

✔ The WebEx client downloaded to your computer (this takes seconds to do and is pretty much automatic; I take you through it in Chapter 4).

✔ A connection, which can be either through a WebEx teleconference (see Figure 1-6) or an Internet Phone connection using something called VoIP (which you'll hear more about in Chapter 4).

A Plethora of Multimedia Communications Options

Great. So WebEx provides all these tools for online interaction and communication. But just what are people out there doing with the service?

Just about anything you can imagine, actually . . .

Putting meetings in their proper places

WebEx began with a focus on online meetings, so meetings are a lot of what people use WebEx for. But meetings can mean different things to different people.

With the WebEx solution, you can

✔ **Hold events with up to 5,000 attendees in Event Center.** Think annual meetings. Think new product announcements to a global customer base. Think of informing your employees that you've just been taken over by a huge conglomerate. WebEx Event Center supports this type of enterprise-wide event.

✔ **Call impromptu meetings on the fly with the Instant Meeting feature.** Meeting Center, and Training Center offer this instant option, and all centers offer a One-Click Meeting option you can run to enable you to launch meetings quickly from your desktop or even Office software. This quick access to meetings or sessions is great for brainstorming, solving problems across time zones, or announcing a shift in project priorities that requires quick action.

✔ **Use integrated audio to keep conversations flowing.** Take advantage of integrated audio services to monitor and control audio activity from within the WebEx meeting environment. All WebEx Web meeting applications are available with your choice of audio services. Choose toll or toll-free global teleconferencing (see Figure 1-6) with call-in or call-back options or VoIP.

> ✔ **Run meetings that involve people in geographically diverse locales.**
> These may be training sessions for employees in three or four countries, for example. You can easily share files and document your ideas on a whiteboard during a sales meeting with international customers. In fact, anything you can do in a face-to-face meeting can be done in a WebEx meeting or session (except passing around the coffee and donuts).

Presentations with an attitude

Meetings may get lots of people talking, but for those times when your meeting is more of a presentation, you'll be glad to hear that making presentations is easy with WebEx Meeting Center, Training Center, Sales Center, and Event Center.

With WebEx presentations, you can create multimedia-rich presentations with PowerPoint animation and transition features with high-speed streaming of multimedia. This simply means that you can fly slides in from the right or left, twirl bullet points around in space, and add neat special effects without painful glitches and delays on the user's computer. Figure 1-7 shows such a presentation in progress. (By the way, Chapter 6 provides some wonderful tips for building great online presentations.)

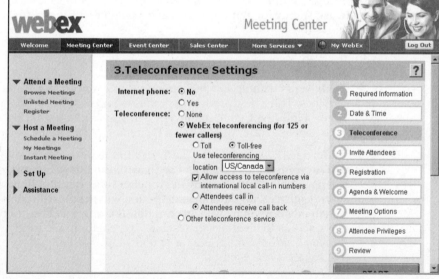

Figure 1-6:
The WebEx integrated audio services within a meeting.

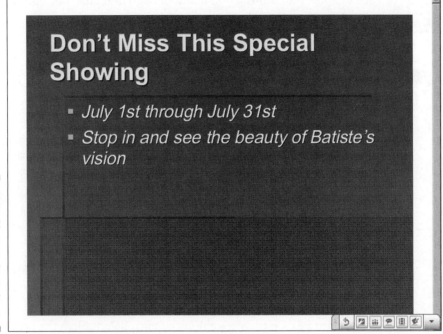

Figure 1-7:
A Power
Point
presentation
in Full
Screen view
helps you
make your
point.

Sharing things

One of the great strengths of the WebEx experience is the ability to share things, from single documents to your whole desktop. This makes an online meeting truly interactive.

Here are a few ways that you can share in a meeting (but remember this will vary depending on which WebEx Center you are using):

- ✔ **Allow attendees to browse the Web with you and explore Web sites you direct them to.** You might acquaint your customer service people with the online ordering process on your own Web site, or have your Web design and marketing people explore the competition's Web sites together to get ideas about how to differentiate your site, for example.

- ✔ **Enable attendees to share an application without having it installed on their computers.** What a great way to demonstrate your new software product to customers or train employees on a new data-processing system!

- ✔ **Share your customer's desktop so you can troubleshoot a setup problem in a support session.**

See Chapter 7 for information about both shared browsing and shared applications.

Getting Started

I could describe a football game to you all day, but unless you've seen one, you don't really know what the experience is like. In the same way, now that you have an idea of what WebEx's suite of applications is and what you can do with it, it would probably help you to jump right in and play around with it.

WebEx offers an amazing array of ways to get into the WebEx experience and lay the groundwork for using the service. These guys practically hold your hand through the entire experience of learning about their services and setting up your first meeting.

Attending a demo

One of the best ways to experience WebEx is to go through its online demo (see Figure 1-8). Go to www.webex.com and click the Join the Live Demo link. You'll be greeted by a real live host who demonstrates just what a WebEx meeting is all about. Ask questions or just sit and watch — it's a low-stress, user-friendly process, and you can duck out whenever you need to.

Experiencing the free trial

Are you the type who thinks nothing worthwhile is free? Well, in this case, you're wrong. If you want more time one-on-one with WebEx, you can try the free, 14-day trial. You get unlimited online meetings for up to three people for two whole weeks.

You can also use various support and training features, as well as the Meeting Assist feature. Meeting Assist gives you the services of a WebEx support person for 20 minutes as you run your first online meeting. You can use this help during a live meeting, or, if you want to do a dry run instead, your WebEx helper will spend time one-on-one to get you up to speed on the WebEx meeting environment.

Just follow these steps to sign up for the free trial (did I mention that it's absolutely free?):

1. **Go to** www.webex.com **and click the Take the Free Trial link.** A sign-up form appears. You can also find a link here to sign up for the free trial of Support Center.

2. **Enter your name and e-mail address and click the Register for Trial button.** An additional form (see Figure 1-9) appears.

3. **Enter information in the fields in the Tell Us About You and the Tell Us What's Important To You areas and click the Submit Registration button.**

   A message appears explaining that an activation e-mail has been sent to you, directing you to the demo, and informing you that you also get one free Meeting Assist session to help you learn the ins and outs of running a WebEx meeting.

Reading this book is, of course, your best bet for discovering all about WebEx (she said modestly). But if you're documentation-happy, WebEx provides quite a bit of help on its own. When you sign up for the free trial, take advantage of the links on the confirmation page that appears. They include a Quick Start Guide, User Guide, and Guide to Successful WebEx Meetings. There's even a How Do I? link that takes you to free online tutorials about setting up and running meetings.

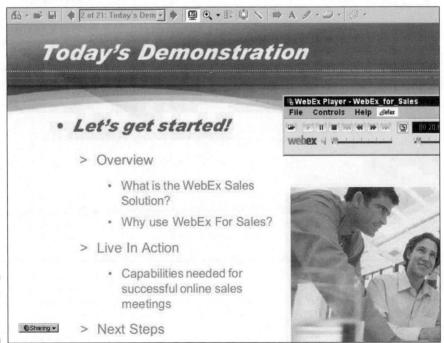

Figure 1-8:
The WebEx demo.

Figure 1-9:
Registering
for the free
trial.

Performing a needs assessment

If you're interested in the possibilities of WebEx, you might want to contact one of the WebEx Solution Specialists. Go to www.webex.com/solutions/online-marketing-solutions.html and click the Solution Specialist link. Fill in information such as your name, company, and the number of people who will use WebEx and with what frequency, and then click the Submit button. A specialist will contact you by e-mail to discuss your specific needs.

Chapter 2

The Ins and Outs of Meeting Online

In This Chapter

▶ Understanding the technology behind WebEx meetings

▶ Understanding security issues

▶ Exploring the components of My WebEx

▶ Saving money with WebEx

Security, savings, superior reliability — these are a large part of WebEx's benefits picture. But WebEx can also help you proactively build your business and increase your revenue. So what's the first step to getting on board with WebEx?

Whether you need to convince a board of directors to sign up or just want to feel comfortable as you use WebEx for your meetings, it's useful to first understand how the technology behind WebEx makes it secure and reliable and scalable to your individual needs.

In this chapter, I tell you about WebEx's exclusive underlying technology (called *MediaTone*), help you understand how WebEx keeps your meetings secure, introduce you to the key components of Meeting Center, and give you an overview of the various WebEx services and costs.

Consider this your briefing on just what makes WebEx tick.

The Technology behind the Scenes

There's no reason for you to go under the hood and take apart the technology that makes WebEx work, so I won't go there. But it is helpful to have a basic understanding of the technical foundation of WebEx so you can appreciate its unique features and reliability.

If you really care . . .

If you're the techie type, you'll want all the techie specifics. Here they are:

The MediaTone Network leverages the T.120 standard, which supports platform-independent, multipoint data communications. T.120 was originally developed by leading telecommunications providers to promote Integrated Services Digital Network (ISDN) service. T.120 is the first well-defined switched architecture for real-time data communications. This standard addresses multimedia technology issues with attention to both voice and data requirements.

WebEx has built upon the T.120 standard by adapting it to a Web-native infrastructure and enhancing the T.120 Presentation and Application Layers. WebEx has also extended the T.120 protocols for scalability, fault tolerance, security, and manageability, while assuring PSTN (Public Switched Telephone Network) integration. By basing the MediaTone Platform on an enhanced version of the T.120 standard and by creating a set of integration toolkits, WebEx has created a highly scalable and open information-switched network.

The T.120 protocol that MediaTone uses for switched real-time data communications focuses on a portion of the OSI (Open Systems Interconnection) communication model (Layers 5–7, if you must know). Why should you care? Because the OSI model is a standard that defines how messages should be transmitted between any two points in a telecommunication network. (Now that you know what it is, you can forget the OSI acronym entirely. . . .)

Okay? Moving on . . .

There are essentially two parts to the MediaTone technology: the network and the platform.

The underlying architecture: The MediaTone Network

Just as a building is built on a foundation, WebEx meeting technology is built on a worldwide network architecture called the *MediaTone Network*. WebEx has set up network switches around the globe to provide access points that allow you to have secure online meetings, from Timbuktu to Tallahassee. Furthermore, there's an automatic fail-safe capability built within the network architecture so your WebEx services are always there for you. This private network is the most reliable available, and it's unique to WebEx.

One important thing about the MediaTone Network is the security it offers. Some other meeting services use a database-centered model, in which meeting data is stored and retrieved, but MediaTone relies on carrier-switching technology — the same thing your phone company uses to switch phone communications instantly around the world. Although you can connect to WebEx from anywhere, at any time, your meeting contents are never stored in somebody else's database. Instead, they are immediately switched through the MediaTone Network.

You'll hear more about security in the section titled "But Is It Secure?," later in this chapter.

Communicating in real time with the MediaTone Network

MediaTone provides the suite of meeting applications that WebEx offers with many features and a rich set of multimedia communications goodies that make online meetings and events happen. The technology offers fast performance, while being reliable, scaleable (meaning you can invite a few people to attend or invite a few thousand) and secure.

The MediaTone Network gives you the following perks:

- ✔ Whiteboarding
- ✔ Application sharing
- ✔ File transfer
- ✔ Support for HTTP
- ✔ Vector-based graphic format for sharing documents and formatting
- ✔ Sharing and synchronizing rich media
- ✔ A set of APIs (application program interfaces) and other programmer-type tools that allow Meeting Center to be integrated with Web and desktop applications

I explain how all of these capabilities, made possible by the MediaTone Network, translate into Meeting Center features in the section titled "Exploring a WebEx Site," later in this chapter.

Mac or PC? No problem!

Do you love your Apple? Or does the Windows opening music make your feet tap and put a smile on your face? Wherever your loyalties lie, you'll be happy to know that the MediaTone Network plays well with other platforms. No matter what kind of computer you use, from Windows or Linux-based PCs to

Macs, WebEx provides a cross-platform solution. MediaTone even allows you to use many wireless devices, such as PDAs, to access your online meetings.

Sharing presentations with UCF

Universal Communications Format (UCF) is the part of the MediaTone technology that makes interactivity possible, so it's worth a special mention.

UCF includes a portable document format (Adobe Acrobat's `.pdf` format is an example of this that you may have used before) that allows you to share and annotate any kind of document, whether it's created in a software that meeting attendees have available on their computers or not. UCF is what makes it possible to share PowerPoint presentations (see Figure 2-1) that include animations and transitions, Flash animations, video, audio, and even Web pages with others in your meeting.

Figure 2-1:
A
PowerPoint
presentation
in a Meeting
Center
meeting.

But Is It Secure?

In a word, yes. The MediaTone Network keeps private data private by encrypting all the contents of your meetings with 128-bit Secure Sockets Layer (SSL) technology. This protocol, created by Netscape, uses a private key to encrypt data before you send it over a secure SSL connection in the course of running a meeting.

And most importantly, none of your data is ever stored automatically on a WebEx server, so you can rest assured that what's yours is yours. Although the attendees can save shared documents from a presentation if the host has granted them that privilege, those documents are saved to the attendees' local computers. Another important part of the WebEx architecture is that it's entirely owned by WebEx. Your data never goes through some third-party facility run by a guy named Archie in Lower Slovenia. All communications go through WebEx hubs located around the world.

Exploring a WebEx Site

WebEx offers a whole suite of Web meeting applications, including Meeting Center, Training Center, Sales Center, Support Center, and Event Center. Each has its own unique features and tools. You access them all from your WebEx enabled site.

Welcome!

The services you purchase from WebEx dictate what you see when you go to your WebEx site. For example, if you purchase Meeting Center and Training Center, you have tools for accessing those applications on your site. However, a WebEx site always contains a Welcome Page and a My WebEx page plus whatever meeting applications you've purchased. The Welcome Page shown in Figure 2-2 is for a company that has purchased the Enterprise Edition of WebEx, which pretty much provides the full suite of bells and whistles.

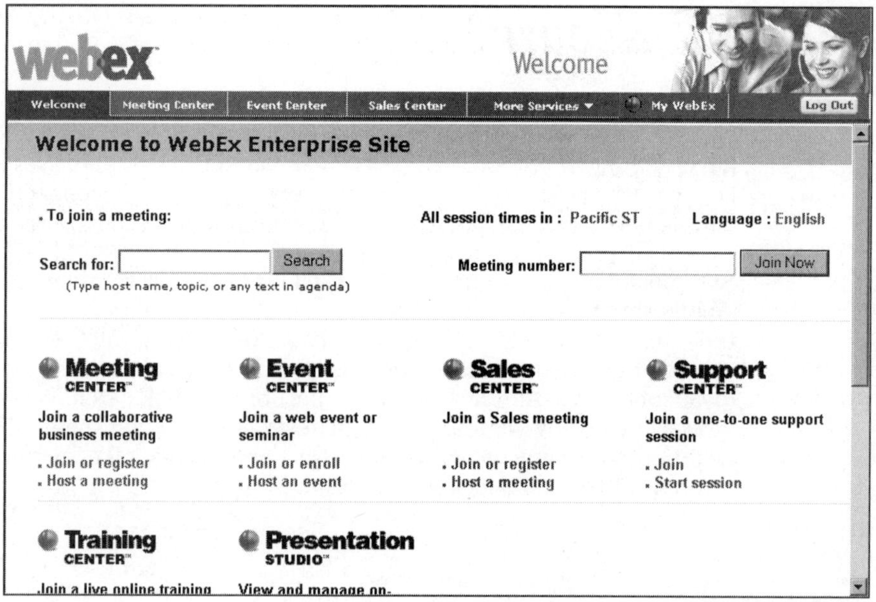

Figure 2-2:
A WebEx
Enterprise
site with the
Welcome
page
displayed.

On the Welcome page, you find the following:

- ✔ A search feature to search for meetings by host name, topic, or any text included in the meeting agenda.

- ✔ A text box in which you can enter a meeting number and click the Join Now button to join instantly.

- ✔ Items for each center you have access to. Click the name of the center and that page is displayed. Or, click the various links to join, register for, or schedule a meeting, session, or event you will host.

- ✔ A Navigation bar you can use to move to individual centers, to the Welcome page, or to your My WebEx pages.

Pick your center

The various centers offer different things on their pages. Because it's the backbone WebEx meeting application, I'll start with Meeting Center. Think of Meeting Center as a virtual version of that conference room down the hall, but without the long walk, the funny spider-shaped conference call device, or the hot popcorn.

On the Meeting Center page shown in Figure 2-3, you can see a set of tabs that you can click to display scheduled meetings for the current day weekor month. This listing includes the Starting Time, Topic, Host, Duration, and

Status of each meeting. Use the links in the Status column to join the meeting. To see more detail about any meeting, just click its topic.

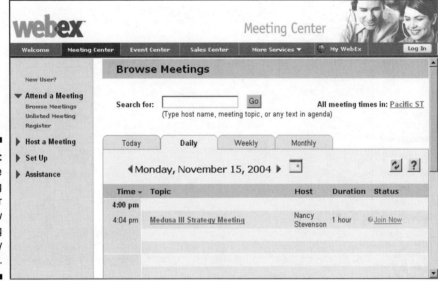

Figure 2-3:
The
Meeting
Center
window
showing
daily
meeting list.

You also find a set of menus along the left side of the screen, including

- ✔ **Attend a Meeting:** This includes commands to find and register for a meeting.

- ✔ **Host a Meeting:** Here you can schedule a meeting, see a list of all the meetings you've scheduled, and access the Instant Meeting feature to set up a meeting on the fly with only a few steps.

- ✔ **Set Up:** These tools allow you to install Meeting Manager (a simple software client you download to your computer so you can utilize WebEx meeting features). There are also Set Up features for Preferences such as your time zone and home page, as well as My Profile, which contains your name and contact information.

- ✔ **Assistance:** This gives you access to help, training, and support.

Event Center, Sales Center, and Training Center have a similar look and feel as Meeting Center; however, there are features unique to each (which you learn about in detail in Chapters 6, 9, and 11). Support Center, which you can see in Figure 2-4, looks a bit different because there aren't a bunch of prescheduled sessions to list. Instead, you see two buttons you can click: one to join a support session and one to start a session. You can also use the links on the left side of the screen to start or join a session, to control setup and preferences, or to get assistance, as with the other centers.

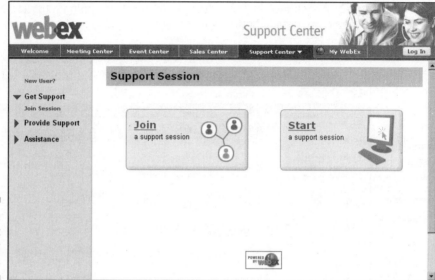

Figure 2-4:
The Support
Center
page.

You discover more about using Support Center features in Chapter 10.

Getting productive with My WebEx

My WebEx Meetings page (shown in Figure 2-5) is actually *your* WebEx Meetings page because it contains your user profile, your address book, a list of your meetings, your contacts, and more. It's your personal user account control room, from which you can manage all your account settings.

The My WebEx Meetings page contains a list of all the meetings you have scheduled and all meetings you've been invited to. It also has a tab you can use to set up One-Click Meetings; this feature places a shortcut on your desktop or in certain applications so you can instantly start a meeting even when you're not on your WebEx site. There's also a menu bar along the left side of the page.

Collaborating with Meeting Manager

WebEx itself isn't a software product; it's an online meeting environment. However, you do have to download some software to use WebEx. These are simple clients that take a minute or two for you and your attendees to download. (*Clients* are software programs that run on your desktop computer but that have to interact with a server to perform a particular function.) Don't worry: It's all pretty much automated and painless.

Figure 2-5:
My WebEx
Meetings
page
with its
personal-
ized user
settings.

A few clients are available: Meeting Manager, Training Manager, Sales Manager, and Event Manager. The one you need to download will vary based on the type of session you want to run or attend.

Each client has a similar look and feel but provides features specific to the center it's used with. But to give you an idea of the type of features that the software provides, here are the capabilities that Meeting Manager provides:

- ✔ A participant list to help you keep track of who is attending
- ✔ Document and presentation sharing
- ✔ Multimedia presentation and rich media sharing
- ✔ Automatic presentation and document sharing
- ✔ Application sharing
- ✔ Desktop sharing
- ✔ Web browser sharing
- ✔ Remote computer sharing
- ✔ Web content sharing
- ✔ Video
- ✔ Audio

✔ Chat

✔ Note taking

✔ Whiteboard sharing

✔ Meeting transcript

✔ Polling

✔ File transfer

✔ Integrated recording

Integrating WebEx with other applications

There's a reason that superstores that stock it all are so popular: Life is easier if you don't have to run in and out of different buildings to do what you need to do. In the world of business, the equivalent inconvenience would be having to go in and out of numerous software programs to get your work done. WebEx thinks that's a bad idea, so it was designed to integrate seamlessly into your existing business processes and software programs you may already have running on your machine. WebEx has provided integration to some of the most commonly used scheduling programs, including

✔ **Microsoft Outlook:** You're in and out of your e-mail and scheduling program all day long, right? By installing an add-in program for Outlook, you can schedule, start, and join a WebEx meeting from within Outlook. To install this program from the My WebEx Meetings page, click the Support menu item, display the Downloads page, and click the My WebEx Integration to Outlook link.

✔ **iCalendar-based calendar programs:** With any calendar program based on the iCalendar standard, such as Lotus Notes, you can add a meeting that you've scheduled through Meeting Center to your calendar.

In addition to setting up calendar programs such as Outlook, you can use the One-Click Meeting feature to place a shortcut button that starts an Instant Meeting in the applications you hang out in everyday:

✔ **Microsoft Office:** The One-Click Meeting feature supports integration with Office. This means that from within any Office application, you can instantly start a meeting and share the application you're in at the time with others.

✔ **Desktop:** Hop from your desktop (whether it's Windows- or Mac-based) into a One-Click Meeting (see Figure 2-6). Then share any application on your desktop just by right-clicking it and choosing a sharing option.

✔ **Web Browser:** You can place the One-Click Meeting button in your Web browser to instantly start a meeting while browsing the Web.

✔ **Right-click menu:** When you right-click an application or file icon on your desktop, if you run One-Click setup and choose this setting, you see a One-Click Meeting command you can use to get a meeting going

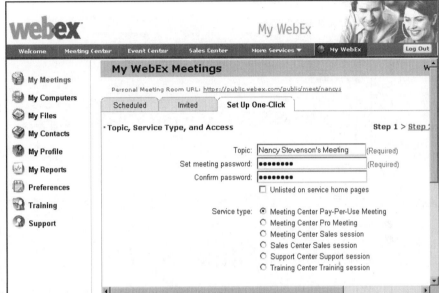

Figure 2-6:
A One-Click
Meeting.

Use the Set Up One Click tab on the My WebEx Meetings page (see Figure 2-7) to customize all the settings for One-Click Meetings, including where you want to place shortcuts for One-Click Meetings. The setup process includes these five steps:

1. Enter a topic, provide a password, and choose the meeting application service (such as Meeting Center or Training Center) that you want to start with the One-Click shortcut.

2. Set Voice Conference options, such as whether to use Internet Phone, the WebEx teleconferencing system, or another teleconferencing service. (You hear more about these options in Chapter 4.)

3. Choose Meeting Options, including whether to use chat, video, file transfer, or other features for your online meeting, event, or session.

4. Adjust Attendee Privileges, such as whether attendees can save, print, or annotate shared documents.

5. Choose where you want the One-Click button to appear (see a previous bullet list in this section for possible locations).

Figure 2-7:
The One-
Click
Meeting tab.

The Economy of Meeting Online

You have a few ways to go when signing up for WebEx services, from buying a single session to getting a customized subscription. Choose the right one and you'll save money for your organization in a variety of ways.

Pay-Per-Use

Are you the kind who dreads commitment? No problem. Just pay for meetings as they come up with a Pay-Per-Use arrangement. You can schedule a single meeting at a cost of 33 cents per minute per person attending. So, for 3 people to attend a 20-minute online meeting, you'll pay about $19.80. Not bad if that meeting closes a huge sale, huh? And if you need only teleconferencing services (voice only), you'll pay only 20 cents a minute per user.

As with any service or product, prices do change occasionally. Go to www.webex.com and click the How to Buy WebEx link (see Figure 2-8), or call 1-866-863-3910 to speak with a customer care person and check out the current pricing.

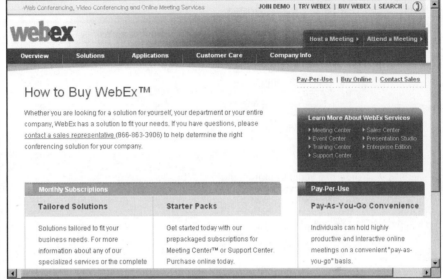

Figure 2-8:
Clicking the
How to Buy
WebEx link
on the
WebEx
home page
takes you
here.

Buy a package

Don't you just love packages? They usually hold happy surprises. WebEx thought so, too, so it created two prepackaged subscriptions for Meeting Center Online:

- **WebEx Express** is the economy package. You get 5 meeting "seats" with unlimited usage and 200 total minutes of audio conferencing for $375 a month.

- **WebEx Meeting Center Pro** is the next stepup. For $995 a month, you get unlimited use for 5 seats and a total of 500 minutes of audio conferencing along with support for rich media communications.

Table 2-1 compares the features you get with each package in more detail.

Table 2-1	WebEx Express vs. Meeting Center Pro	
Feature	*WebEx Express*	*Meeting Center Pro*
Price	$375/month	$995/month
Seats	5	5
Audio Minutes	200	500

(continued)

Table 2-1 *(continued)*

Feature	WebEx Express	Meeting Center Pro
Presentation Sharing	Yes	Yes
Share Any Document	Yes	Yes
Share Multiple Documents	Yes	Yes
Rich Media Sharing	Yes	Yes
Integrated Audio Conferencing	Yes	Yes
Internet Audio Conferencing	Yes	Yes
SSL Encryption	Yes	Yes
Unlimited Meeting Size	Yes	Yes
Application Sharing	No	Yes
Record & Playback	No	Yes
Video	No	Yes
Web Sharing	No	Yes
MS Office Integration	No	Yes
Interactivity Tools	No	Yes
Access Anywhere	No	Yes
Meeting Transcripts and Notes	No	Yes
File Transfer	No	Yes

Note that you can get additional seats and audio conferencing minutes beyond your monthly package for additional fees ($10 per person and 20 cents per minute at the time of this writing).

There are other packages available, such as small-business and marketing packages and support packages. See Chapter 3 for more about buying packages and what they contain.

Note that some of these features are optional; check with your site administrator to be sure which are available to you.

Customize!

If your meeting needs are huge (or just unique), you need a huge solution. A customized subscription is the way to go. With the custom approach, you work with a WebEx representative to determine which packages and services are best for you. By using the Enterprise Edition of WebEx, you can fashion an integrated, organization-wide Web communications and online meeting service.

The kinds of special bells and whistles you can get with a customized solution include a localized Meeting Center available in any of seven languages, unlimited Training Center access with self-paced training, a personalized interface, and a dedicated 1-800 support line.

You can call a Solution Specialist at 877-509-3239 and have a heart-to-heart about your needs to set up a custom subscription.

Bottom line: WebEx saves you money and increases your productivity

Now that you know what WebEx costs, it's worth reflecting on how it saves you time and money. With an online meeting service in place, you

- Don't have to travel to meetings. Sure, some meetings just have to be face-to-face, but for those that don't, do you really want to spend hours in a car or airport to attend them?

- Have the potential to close more sales faster, and get online with One-Click Meetings to instantly respond to a question or solve a customer problem.

- Experience less costly document sharing and distribution, along the way sparing the copier some wear and tear.

- Access lower-cost training and support options, again saving time and money by not sending people to a remote site or having to support the cost of a computer lab — just share applications online or even set up a virtual hands-on lab through Training Center!

- Get the convenience of letting people access recorded sessions or run through self-paced training any time they like.

- Have the ability to use a single meeting service enterprise-wide instead of bouncing around through a hodge-podge of separate conferencing and meeting systems.

- Avoid burdening your IT folks with another layer of software inside your walls because WebEx is a completely hosted service.

Chapter 3

Getting Started with Meetings

*O*kay, you've been through the demonstration on webex.com and the WebEx 14-day trial, you've learned a bit about the ins and outs of meeting online, and you're psyched. You're ready to sign on the dotted line and start meeting 21st-century style. That's what this chapter is all about.

Here's where you discover how to get started: I'll show you how to log in to your WebEx account and set all your personal preferences. I'll tell you about downloading the Meeting Manager software (yes, it's a Web-based service, but there is a little software involved) and explore the many different options for support so you're not all alone out there.

It's time to enter the brave new world of online meetings. Trust me, this won't hurt a bit . . .

Logging In: Beam Me Up, Scotty!

After signing up with WebEx, you will be provided with a Meeting Center Web site address (usually in the format your_company.webex.com). This is where you go to schedule and start meetings and to manage various user settings.

Follow these steps to log in to Meeting Center:

1. **Enter your Meeting Center URL into the address box of your browser and press Enter.**

2. **When your WebEx site appears (see Figure 3-1) click the Log In button on the Navigation bar.**

3. **Enter your username and password and click Log In.**

Log In button

Figure 3-1:
The Log In
button on
your WebEx
site page.

Want instant login? Click the Remember User Name and Password check box on the page and you'll never have to log in again. However, remember that any joker who can get his hands on your computer can also log in and run meetings. (I grant you, roving meeting thieves are not rampant, but there is a security issue you should consider when setting up an automatic login.)

To log out (I bet you can guess this one), just click the Log Out button.

Setting Up WebEx to Suit You

WebEx offers several ways to customize your WebEx experience. On the WebEx Meeting Center Welcome page (an Enterprise Edition Meeting Center is shown in Figure 3-1), notice that there are four items that you can use to instantly join or host an Event, Sales meeting, Support session, or Training session: The applications that you see in your WebEx site will vary depending on which applications you've purchased. There's also a My WebEx button: Click it to go to My WebEx to begin setting up your personal control center.

Click the My WebEx button, and you'll see the options offered in Figure 3-2.

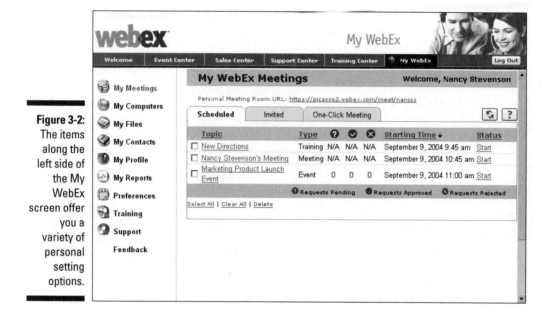

Figure 3-2:
The items
along the
left side of
the My
WebEx
screen offer
you a
variety of
personal
setting
options.

Editing preferences

Preferences aren't rocket science; in fact, if your company hasn't purchased localized versions of WebEx for use in different countries, the only setting here will be your home page when you enter Meeting Center. But if you have a localized solution in place, there are some settings here that are important to take a look at before you start meeting. For example, simply changing your locale setting will affect all your listed meeting times, dates, currency used, and numbers.

When you click the Preferences button in My WebEx, you see the four simple settings shown in Figure 3-3 (remember, if you haven't purchased localized versions, you will only see the home page item).

The four settings you can adjust here are as follows:

✔ **Home Page:** You can set one home page for your WebEx site; this is the page you will go to when you open the site. You can choose from five items by choosing from the Home Page drop-down list; then make a selection from the drop-down list to the right of your choice to specify exactly what will be displayed on that page. For example, you can choose to make Sales Center your home page with the Browse Meetings Monthly view displayed, rather than the default Browse Meetings Today view.

✔ **Time Zone:** This one's pretty self-explanatory: from this drop-down list choose the time zone from which you're hosting the meeting

✔ **Language:** WebEx has several localized versions. If they are available to your account, you can choose the appropriate one from this drop-down list.

✔ **Locale:** Choose your country. This choice will have an impact on how information about your scheduled meetings is displayed.

When you've finished adjusting your settings, click OK to save them and return to the My WebEx page.

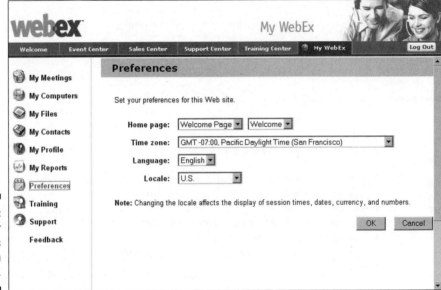

Figure 3-3:
Set up your
preferences
quickly from
this page.

Modifying My Profile

You and WebEx are meant to be good buddies, but you can't cozy up to a new friend without knowing something about him or her, right? The My Profile settings in My WebEx allow you to tell WebEx all about yourself (no, WebEx doesn't need to know your favorite color or most embarrassing moment). What you enter in My Profile is basic contact information such as name, address, and phone numbers; and the default type of session you'd like to set.

If you own the My WebEx Pro solution you can also set any welcome message or image you want to display on your Personal Meeting Room page here.

To modify My Profile, follow these steps:

1. **Choose My Profile from the My WebEx Navigation bar along the left side of the page. The form shown in Figure 3-4 appears.**

Figure 3-4:
The My
WebEx
Profile page.

2. **Enter your personal information, including name, address, phone, e-mail address, and so on.**

3. **In the second section of the form, enter any welcome greeting you'd like to appear when people enter your Personal Meeting Room.**

   Remember this is only available if you have purchased the WebEx Pro version.

4. **If you'd like to post an image on your Personal Meeting Room page, you can do that here.**

   To do this, enter the location of the image in the Upload Image text box, or click the Browse button to locate the image and click OK to select it. Click the Upload button to complete the upload. There may be a slight delay while the image is uploaded.

5. **In the Session Options section, select the radio button for the type of session you'd like to be your default.**

6. **If you'd like to give others who have a user account on your WebEx site permission to set up meetings for you, click the Select from Host List button and select the name of the person you want to include. (If you haven't yet set the person up on your Host List, enter his or her e-mail address in the Scheduling Permission box.)**

7. **Click Update to save your settings.**

If you have purchased Support Center and you want to rearrange the order of tabs in the support dashboard, click an item in the Order of Tabs area and click an up or down arrow key to move it up or down in the order. Discover more about Support Center in Chapter 10.

Downloading Meeting Manager

Remember those prerequisites you had to deal with when you signed up for classes in college, like when you couldn't take the Advanced Chemistry Lab until you took First Aid 101? Well, a WebEx meeting has an important prerequisite as well: You must download the manager software client before you can host a meeting, and all attendees must download the client before attending as well. Don't worry: They'll be asked to do so and given an easy link to do it in the e-mail that invites them to your meeting.

To download this client yourself, follow these steps:

1. **Click the appropriate button in your WebEx site for the kind of session you want to run.**

2. **Click the right-pointing arrow next to the Set Up menu in the left-hand pane.** Setup items are displayed.

3. **Click the software link (Event Manager, Training Manager, or Meeting Manager, depending on the page you've displayed).**

4. **Click the Set Up button.** A dialog box appears (shown in Figure 3-5) telling you to wait while the file is set up.

5. **Wait a minute or so: That's really all you have to do.**

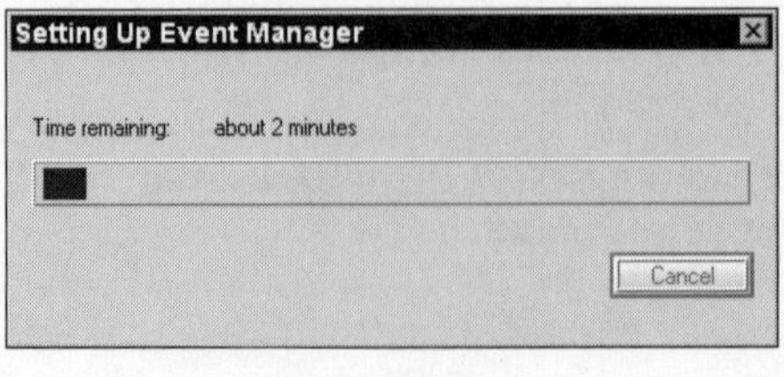

Figure 3-5:
Download-
ing WebEx
software.

Setting Up Event Manager	☒
Time remaining: about 2 minutes	
▮▬▬▬▬▬▬▬▬▬▬▬▬▬▬	
	Cancel

Note that Meeting Center installs Meeting Manager automatically the first time you start or join a meeting, but it can take a couple of minutes; you and your attendees would be wise to follow the steps above to preinstall it so you're not late to the meeting. You may also notice Meeting Manager downloads occurring from time to time even after you've installed it. These are just small automatic updates being made to your software.

You Are Not Alone: Getting Assistance

WebEx isn't hard to learn or use, but it does exist in the unpredictable world of technology, and that means unexpected problems can come up when using your WebEx applications. People have different network configurations, different operating systems, different peripheral models. You could need help from time to time.

All of the pages for Centers (Meeting, Event, Sales, Support, and Training) in the Meeting Center include an Assistance menu on the left side of the screen. When you click the right-pointing triangle next to Assistance, three links appear: Help, Support, and Training (Sales Center lists Support, Training, and Sales Assists).

Here, then, is the lowdown on WebEx Assistance, starting with Support.

How supportive they are!

The Support link takes you to a Support page (see Figure 3-6). Here you'll find a few different items:

- ✔ Information about the version of the center (each application is updated separately).
- ✔ Contact information for self-service support, live support, and training, as well as a feedback form to help WebEx continually improve services based on your experience.
- ✔ Documentation for using WebEx and the specific center you're in at the time.
- ✔ Downloads for essentials, such as Meeting Manager, or add-ons you might like to try, such as the Access Anywhere Agent for accessing a remote computer.

Going for technical support

If you want a WebEx expert (in database or human form) at your beck and call, try the two technical support options:

✔ You can e-mail self-service technical support, an automated support system, by clicking the support@webex.com link.

✔ Find live technical support by clicking the http://support.webex.com link, or by calling the support phone number, 1-866-229-3239. You can also click the International Toll Free Phone Number link to look up toll-free support numbers in any country.

Grabbing documentation

The Documentation section of the Support page is made up of brief descriptions and links to documentation. Find the document that looks helpful and click its link. The document opens in Adobe Reader (see Figure 3-7).

If you don't have Adobe Reader, you can download it by going to www.adobe.com.

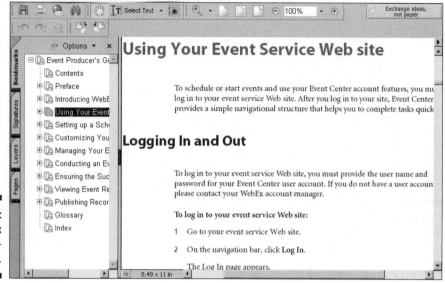

Figure 3-7:
WebEx
documenta-
tion.

Help!

If you click the Help link under Assistance in any of the Centers, the Help page shown in Figure 3-8 appears. Here you can do three things:

- ✔ Click on an item on the Contents tab to see a listing of major topics; click on any of these to display help information on the right side of the page, often containing links you can click to display additional details.

- ✔ Click the Index tab to display an alphabetical list of topics and sub-topics. Click any of these to display help information.

- ✔ Click the Search tab and enter a search term and click the Go button to find what you need. A list of topic links appears. Click on to display help on that topic.

You can also access help at anytime while running an online meeting or session.

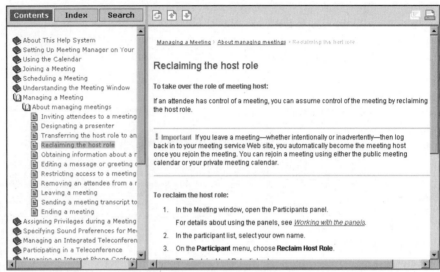

Figure 3-8:
WebEx Help
Contents.

Following the training link

The third item under Assistance in the Meeting Center is Training. When you click this link, you see the following:

- ✔ **Attend Training:** Here's a link to allow you to quickly register for online training sessions. Clicking that link takes you to the Web University Login page. (Read more about Web University in the next section.)

- ✔ **Take Advantage of All Our Training Services:** This section includes links to the Training and Education section of the WebEx Support Site, Web Service Assist and Consulting for personalized hand-holding type help, and Specialized Training Programs.

- ✔ **Contact Us:** There is both a link to e-mail WebEx Training and a list of support phone numbers.

Links provided here will get you started, but WebEx has lots to offer in the training area, so in the next section I go into the various offerings in more detail.

Gaining Training

There are several ways to get training on WebEx, some of which don't even require that you have a WebEx account.

First, you can click the Service Offerings item on the WebEx Web site (www.webex.com) and choose any item, such as Event Center or Training Center, from the menu that appears (see Figure 3-9). In the page that is displayed, click the Quick Tour link to view information about that specific WebEx service. You can click the screen images to enlarge them in order to help you get a feel for the environment and features of each WebEx application.

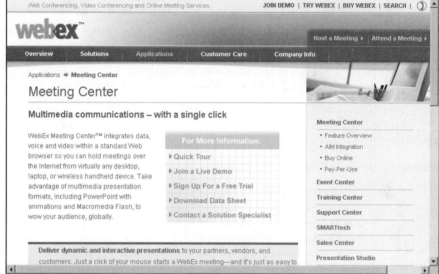

Figure 3-9:
The Training Center offers a couple of introductory tours.

Get your seminars free!

WebEx also offers ongoing free online seminars, which go beyond basic WebEx training (though you pick up something about meeting features by osmosis as you participate in the online event). They cover topics such as Increasing Customer Satisfaction, Selling Online, and Marketing Online.

Follow these steps to sign up for a seminar:

1. **Go to** https://webexevents.webex.com/webexevents **for a listing of upcoming seminars (see Figure 3-10).**

2. **Click the Enroll link for a seminar you'd like to attend.**

3. **Enter information in the enrollment form that appears.**

4. **Click the Submit button. An e-mail confirmation will arrive shortly with instructions for attending the event.**

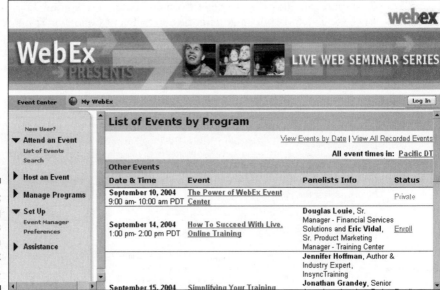

Figure 3-10:
Seeing
what's
available in
free WebEx
seminars.

Nervous about running that first online meeting? WebEx gives you 20 free minutes of coaching to help you run your first meeting after you sign up for a WebEx account or 14-day free trial. You have to give 48 hours' notice, and WebEx recommends that you limit attendance to 25 people. Go to http://try.webex.com/mk/get/WEB_MEETINGASSIST to sign up. (This is in the Customer Care⇨Assist Services area of the WebEx site.)

Going back to school: WebEx University

If you want the full treatment, try exploring WebEx University at http://university.webex.com/training/student/index.jsp. Here you can take advantage of self-paced training and instructor-led training. You have to be a registered user of WebEx to attend. Check with your site administrator to see if your company has access to WebEx University based on the package you've purchased.

To sign up for a course

- ✔ Click the Self-Paced Training tab, choose a course, and click the Begin Training button; or

- ✔ Click the Live Instructor Training tab. Click the button in the Select Day/ Time column for the course you want to take and you'll be asked to log in with your WebEx username and password. Then proceed to choose a day and time and fill out the registration form for the course.

There's also a How Do I? function you can use to learn about any single feature. From the WebEx University page, under the Self-Paced Training click the link labeled "How Do I...?" A How Do I...? page appears organized with tabs for the various centers such as Training Center and Meeting Center. Click on a tab to display a center, click on a topic, and a self-paced training module launches.

Generally speaking, WebEx University offers courses on how to actually use WebEx services and tools; whereas public seminars provide ideas and information about more general topics, such as how to get the most out of online training or what makes a good online presentation. Check out the online catalog for the university (see Figure 3-11) for current courses. You'll find a link for the catalog on the Training page of Webex.com.

Figure 3-11: The WebEx University catalog, available in Adobe Acrobat format by clicking the catalog link on the university page.

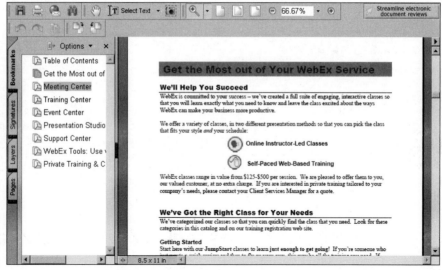

If you will be the one training others in your organization on how to run meetings, consider taking the Train the Trainer session. If you're the IT person supporting users, try the Technical Support/IT Program.

Part II
Always Be Prepared

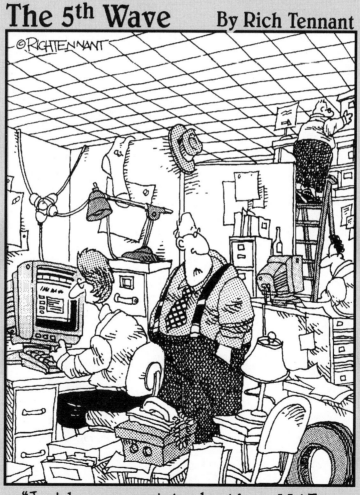

The 5th Wave   By Rich Tennant

"Just how accurately should my WebEx
Meeting Center reflect my place of business?"

In this part . . .

Somebody said look before you leap, right? So, heeding those words from the wise, you can't just leap into your first online meeting. First, you have to discover the ins and outs of scheduling an online meeting. Here's where you tap into advice for customizing your meeting settings, inviting attendees, and assigning attendee privileges. This is also the part where you explore the possibilities of working with remote computers to support, share, or inform your employees or customers. Finally, here you learn the best way to prepare for marketing events.

Chapter 4

Setting Up Your Very First Meeting

- -

In This Chapter

▶ Scheduling a meeting

▶ Establishing the date and time

▶ Inviting attendees

▶ Setting up registration

▶ Choosing meeting options

▶ Setting attendee privileges

▶ Reviewing your settings

- -

Meetings happen when people come together with some common purpose. (I know, sometimes you have to work a while to find that common purpose, but it's there!) Meetings are where we communicate, commiserate, come up with solutions, and collectively brainstorm. WebEx is first and foremost about meetings.

But you can't host a meeting until you schedule a meeting. With WebEx meetings, that could be as simple as filling in a meeting name and password; or it could involve designing a custom registration form, setting up attendee privileges and meeting options, and sending out a slew of reminder e-mails. The process of scheduling a WebEx meeting is flexible according to your meeting needs. There are even shortcuts to get meetings going: Instant meetings and one-click meetings.

In this chapter, I explain all about setting up a meeting by using the various options that WebEx makes available to you in Meeting Center.

Scheduling a Meeting

Before you can hold that staff meeting in Conference Room D, you might have to make sure you have enough chairs, set up the flip chart, order donuts — well, you get the idea. For an online meeting, you do have to set some things up, but the process is (thankfully) way less painful than organizing an offline conference.

When you set up a WebEx meeting, you simply have to fill out a series of forms. They are easy to complete, probably taking you only about five minutes. I walk you through filling them out so you know what to expect.

Let the scheduling begin!

You start scheduling a meeting by clicking the Host a Meeting menu on the Meeting Center page and then clicking the Schedule a Meeting link. The first page that appears offers the following nine sections on which you can enter information to schedule a meeting: Required Information, Date & Time, Teleconference, Invite Attendees, Registration, Agenda & Welcome, Meeting Options, Attendee Privileges, and Review.

Here's a shortcut: You can also start scheduling a meeting by clicking the Host a Meeting link on the WebEx Welcome page, which appears by default every time you go to your WebEx site.

At a minimum, you have to enter the Required Information (see Figure 4-1). After you enter that information, you can either go on to the other sections and fill them in or click the Start button at any time to begin the meeting.

Figure 4-1:
The Required Information for starting a meeting

On the Required Information page, enter the following information:

✔ Enter a topic in the Meeting Topic field. (This is a required field.)

✔ Select the Listed on Calendar check box if you want to list the meeting on your calendar of meetings at your WebEx site.

✔ If you want to erase the meeting from your My Meetings page when the meeting is done, select the Delete from My Meetings When Completed check box.

✔ Enter and confirm a meeting password that attendees must use to enter the meeting (these might be required fields, depending on how your site administrator has set you up) and click Next.

You might see additional fields, such as Tracking Codes, Schedule For, and Meeting Type, again depending on what settings your WebEx site administrator has made. See Chapter 13 for more about these settings.

What date, what time?

Your next stop is the Date & Time page, as shown in Figure 4-2. Here's where you indicate the temporal parameters for your virtual meeting (beam me up, Scotty!).

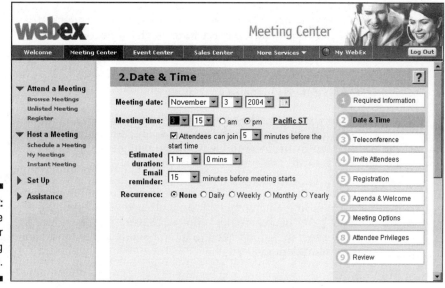

Figure 4-2:
Set the date for your meeting here.

Use the various fields in this section to specify the following:

- ✔ **Meeting Date:** You can choose this from the month, date, and year drop-down lists, or click the Calendar icon and choose a date in a calendar format.

- ✔ **Meeting Time:** If you want to change the time zone for the scheduled meeting, click the time zone link (which shows your site's default time zone) to open a list of available time zones. Note that you can use the settings in this area to allow attendees to join the meeting a set number of minutes before the actual meeting time. You can then start a Universal Communications Format (UCF) presentation before the meeting is officially started if you wish, which will play when early birds show up.

- ✔ **Estimated Duration:** You set this in two fields: hours and minutes.

- ✔ **E-mail Reminder:** This sends out automatic reminders at a certain interval of time before the meeting. The default is 15 minutes. I recommend you determine how much time your attendees need to join the meeting and modify the default if necessary.

- ✔ **Recurrence:** This is the recurring interval for the meeting (if any). If you choose to schedule a meeting to occur weekly, for example, additional settings appear, such as the day of the week for the meeting, and the end date.

When you finish adjusting these settings, click Next.

After you fill in the required information, you can click any of the section buttons to jump to another section of the form in any sequence that you like instead of clicking Next to proceed through the sections in order.

Shall I call you?

Although you might take a plane, car, or taxi to get to a land-bound meeting, you use your Internet connection and some form of voice connection through a phone line or the Internet to attend an online meeting. This part of the form lets you give attendees voice-access to your meeting.

People who attend your meeting can use an Internet Phone connection, the WebEx teleconferencing service, or another teleconferencing service to connect. But participants are not required to use a phone connection at all; this makes sense if they don't need to interact with you but just want to view your presentation online.

When you go to the Teleconference Settings page, as shown in Figure 4-3, you can configure the following settings:

- ✔ Whether to use an Internet Phone connection. This is VoIP (Voice over Internet Protocol) technology that lets you make phone calls from your computer over a broadband Internet connection with no phone line present.

- ✔ Which (if any) teleconference service to use — WebEx's own or a third party's. If you choose a third party, you have to enter various access numbers, pass codes, and other instructions to connect.

- ✔ If using WebEx's teleconference service, whether to allow international call-in numbers.

- ✔ If using WebEx's teleconference service, whether attendees should call in or receive a call back

Note that you can offer both VoIP and teleconference options for your meeting — they aren't mutually exclusive. Customize these settings to your liking and then click Next to proceed to the next section.

It might interest your accounting department to know that VoIP can save you lots of money because you don't incur standard phone line long distance charges. When you won't much interaction between attendees and presenter, consider using VoIP as your connection method of choice.

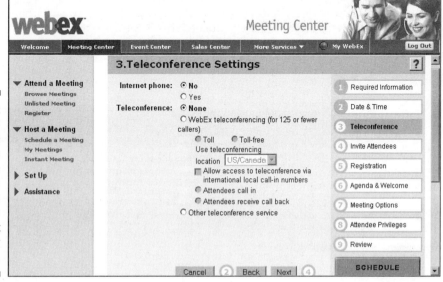

Figure 4-3:
The Tele-conference Settings page is where you establish how to connect with your meeting.

You're invited!

To invite people, you can select their names from an address book or enter them as new contacts. Note that the company Address Book is typically created and maintained by your Site Administrator, as I describe in Chapter 13.

People whom you invite to meetings receive an e-mail notification that contains a link that they click to join the meeting. The notification also advises them to download the Meeting Manager client software before the meeting and also tells them how to go about doing that.

Note that you don't actually have to invite anybody to a meeting to schedule it. Instead, you can start the meeting and send out invitations to folks from within the meeting itself. Of course, this assumes that you've told these folks that an invitation is in the offing, to wait for it at their computers, and to join the meeting promptly when they receive the invitation.

To add invitees to your meeting, in the Invite Attendees page shown in Figure 4-4, do the following:

1. **Click the Select Attendees button.**

   The Select Attendees page appears (see Figure 4-5).

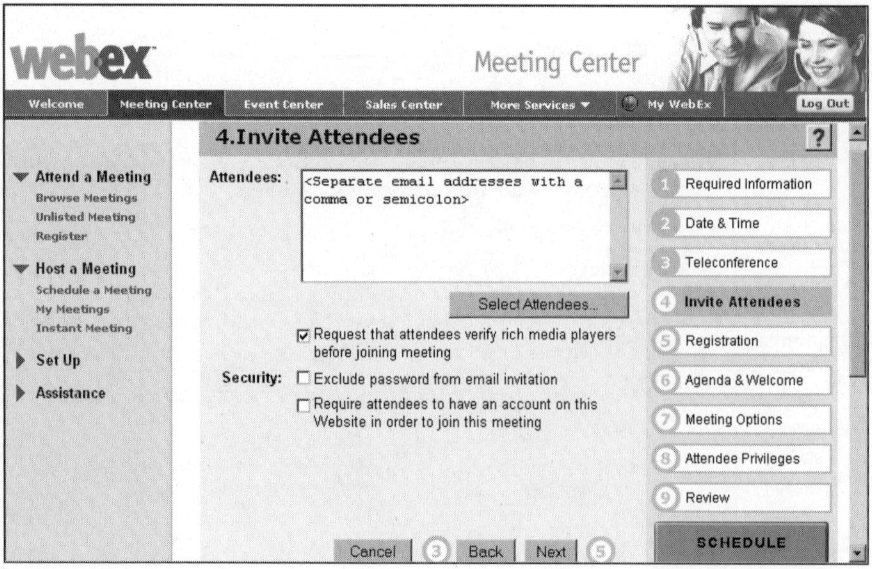

Figure 4-4:
The Invite
Attendees
page.

2. **Click the arrow on the Address Book field and choose a different address book, if you wish.**

3. **Select names from the list in the left-hand box and then click the Attendee button to invite folks to the meeting.**

   The invited attendees are listed in the right-hand box.

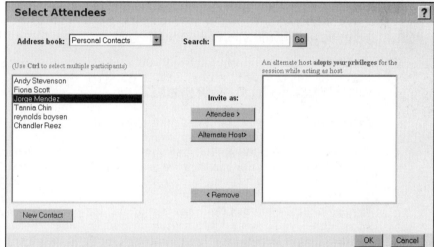

Figure 4-5:
The Select
Attendees
page.

4. **After you select all the invitees, click OK to close the Select Attendees window.**

5. **On the Invite Attendees pages, select any of the three check boxes to designate the following:**

   • If a request to verify that invitees have the appropriate rich media players to view your presentation (as required if you're using any UCF objects) should be included in the invitation. Meetings go much more smoothly when everybody is set up with these players ahead of time.

   • Whether to include or exclude the password information in the e-mail invitation.

   • Whether attendees must have their own account on your business' WebEx account to attend.

Note that the last two items in the list above are a great way to enhance your meeting's security. Also, if you don't include password information in the e-mail invitation and you're using a password, you have to contact all the attendees yourself to provide the password.

Once again (say it with me now!), click Next to go to the next page.

If you want to invite somebody as an alternate host, instead of clicking the Attendee button in Step 3, click the Alternate Host button. An alternate host takes on all host privileges. You might do this if somebody joins the meeting who you want to run a portion of the meeting.

Getting folks registered

In some cases, you want to have people register for your meeting. It's a case of knowledge being power: Registration not only helps you get a handle on how many folks will attend, but it also provides you with certain information about the attendees that might prove useful in planning your meeting and following up after it's over.

If you leave the default of None selected on the Registration page, as shown in Figure 4-6, you choose not to register anyone. From here, you might as well move on to the next page of the scheduling form. If, on the other hand, you want folks to register, here are the steps to customize your registration form:

1. Select the Require Attendee Registration radio button.

Figure 4-6:
The page where you select what information to include in your registration form.

To register or not to register . . .

When would you *not* accept a registration to a meeting? Perhaps you are inviting people from an industry association list but you don't want people from a competing company to attend because you're discussing a new product line. Or perhaps it's not appropriate to have people from a certain locale attend because their site won't be involved in the project under discussion. When excluding attendees this way, be sure to include the necessary information in the registration form, such as Company Name or State, that rules out your excluded attendees.

Keep in mind that if you specify that registration requests are automatically approved and you've set up a password, you just undermined your own security. That's because after registrants are approved, they don't have to enter a password to join the meeting after it's started.

2. **Select the various check boxes in the columns labeled Obtain Detailed Attendee Information to choose what items will be included in your registration form.**

3. **If you want to have the right to authorize registration, skip to Step 4; if you want to allow anybody who registers to attend, select the Automatically Accept All Registration Requests check box.**

4. **Click Next to proceed.**

Welcome. Our agenda today . . .

When you move to the Agenda & Customizable Welcome page (see Figure 4-7), you can enter agenda items in the Agenda field. What you enter here appears on the Info page displayed in the meeting. Those invited to the meeting can review the agenda by clicking the meeting topic on the Browse meeting page. At that point, they will be asked for the meeting password — if the meeting is password-protected.

In addition to entering an agenda, you can configure the following settings on the Agenda & Customizable Welcome page:

✔ By using the Browse button in the Automatically Share Presentation or Document Once a Participant Joins the Meeting item and selecting a file, you can play the file automatically when a person joins the meeting. The file must be stored in your personal My Files folder on your WebEx site, and be a UCF file. By using the Browse button here, you can pick a file that you've already stored in My Files or upload one to that folder and convert it at this time. You can also control the automatic playback by choosing either the Start Automatically or Continuous Play box. You can also choose the interval of time before your presentation advances or allow participants to control the playback themselves.

✔ Specify whether you want Meeting Center to display a Quick Start page for the host and any presenters. This is a page that helps people making presentations quickly access common commands such as sharing a document.

Figure 4-7:
The Agenda & Customiz-able Welcome page.

Note that when you use the Browse button to specify a file to display, you can select a file that you already uploaded to the My Files area of your WebEx site, or you can upload one from another source. However, remember that any file you choose must be in the WebEx Universal Communication Format (UCF) format.

After you finish entering your agenda and adjusting settings for what appears when somebody joins the meeting, click Next.

We've always got options

Not every meeting requires the same bells and whistles. For example, you might not want to make the chat feature available if you're giving a one-way presentation and don't want to deal with a lot of questions. Or, you might not want your presenter to be able to record the meeting. The Meeting Options page is where you make those choices.

The first category that you deal with on this page is the Meeting Options (see Figure 4-8). Here's a rundown of the options that you can choose:

- ✔ **Chat:** Allows people to use the text-messaging feature to communicate during the meeting. Attendees can chat with the presenter and other attendees.

- ✔ **Video:** Controls use of either a single-point or multi-point video stream, which appears on the Video panel. Single-point allows only the presenter to send live video. Multi-point allows the presenter and up to three other participants to send live video during the meeting. Multi-point is an option that your company might or might not have bought into, so check with your system administrator.

- ✔ **Notes:** Lets a single person or all attendees take notes in the Notes panel. You can control this and switch between the two options during the meeting itself. Notes can be printed out at the end of the meeting (use the Meeting menu, Options command) and could form the basis of meeting minutes.

- ✔ **Enable Closed Captioning:** Allows one participant to enter closed captioning comments during the meeting. Closed captions are then published to all participants each time that the transcriber presses Enter.

- ✔ **File Transfer:** Specifies that the presenter can publish files that attendees can then download during the meeting.

- ✔ **Recording:** Makes recording features available during the meeting. The host and presenter can record the meeting, and participants can use the recording feature if they have recording privileges (set by your trusty site administrator).

- ✔ **Send Feedback Form to Host Email:** Just what it says. When the meeting ends, a feedback form appears on which attendees can tell you about their meeting experience. This setting directs those forms to the host's e-mail address.

- ✔ **Enable UCF Rich Media for Attendees:** Allows attendees to share rich media files in the WebEx UCF format (if they have the Share Documents privilege).

Note the two additional settings on this page:

- ✔ **Entry and Exit Tone:** Choose from this drop-down list whether you wish a signal — a beep or an announcement of the person's name — to sound when somebody joins the meeting. This is sounded through the phone line only if you use the WebEx integrated teleconferencing option. You also can choose None, which means that you won't hear a thing when somebody joins your meeting. Note that the new attendee's name appears on the participants' list, so you'll know when somebody's joined.

✔ **Mirror Options:** If you want to let attendees explore the meeting environment, displaying different panels (such as chat or video) as they wish, select the second option: Attendees Can Independently Control Panels and Views. If you want to force attendees to follow along with you and see what you choose to display, remove their free will by selecting the first option, All Attendees Mirror the Presenter's Panels and View.

Click Next when you're done with these settings.

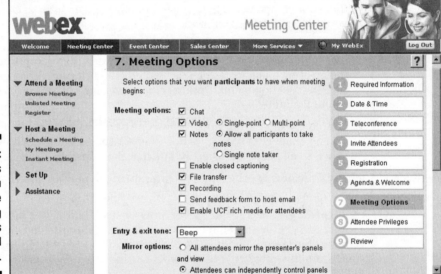

Figure 4-8:
Here's where you set what the meeting participants can and can't do.

It's a privilege

On the Attendee Privileges page that appears, as shown in Figure 4-9, you have a whole bunch of check boxes to choose from. These endow certain privileges on attendees, such as whether they can print, annotate, or save documents that you share in meetings; whether they can control shared applications or Web browsers; and whether they can participate in chat.

Some of these are selected by default; others aren't. Click the ones that are preselected that you want to deselect, and mark the ones that aren't selected if you want to select them.

Those are all the choices available to you, but note that you can change privileges after the meeting gets underway. Choose the Participant menu and then the Assign Privileges command to do so.

Now it's time to make sure you got things right, and to get the meeting going. Click Next. . . .

Figure 4-9:
Here's
where you
control your
attendees'
privileges.

Reviewing Your Settings and Starting the Meeting

The final page in the meeting scheduling sequence is the Review page. This shows you all the choices you just made (see Figure 4-10). If you see that something's amiss, just click one of the numbered items on the right and go back and make changes.

When you're happy with your meeting settings, you have three options:

✔ If you didn't specify a date and time, click the Start button to start the meeting immediately.

✔ If you specified a date and time for the meeting, click the Schedule button. A page appears, as shown in Figure 4-11, confirming that you have successfully scheduled your meeting. Click the MyWebEx link here. Or, when you are ready to meet, just go back to the Meeting Center area of WebEx, locate the meeting through the Attend a Meeting menu, and click the meeting link. When the meeting overview appears, click the Start Now button.

✔ Click the link in the confirming e-mail that WebEx sends you to go to the page in Figure 4-12, where you can click the Start Now button.

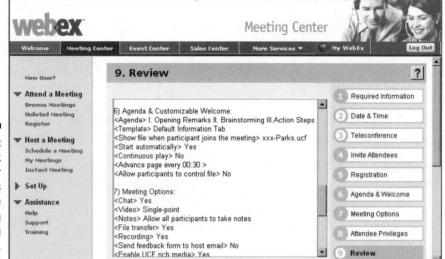

Figure 4-10:
Take a look at all your choices before scheduling or starting the meeting.

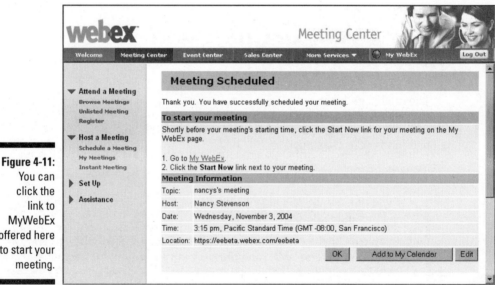

Figure 4-11:
You can click the link to MyWebEx offered here to start your meeting.

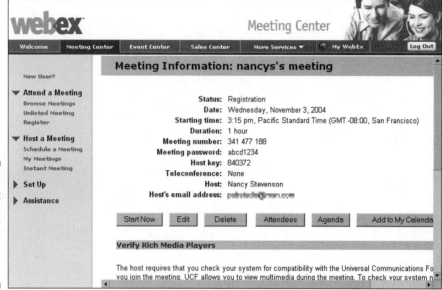

Figure 4-12:
Click Start
Now to
begin your
meeting
from this
page.

Instant Gratification

There are two options for getting your meeting going right away.

From My WebEx, under the Host a Meeting menu, you can click the Instant Meeting link. A dialog box appears in which you fill in the meeting topic, password, and choose teleconferencing options. Then click the Start button and your meeting begins. You can then invite attendees using the Participants menu in the meeting itself.

You can click on the One-Click Meeting tab in the My WebEx My Meetings page and complete a few simple options to download a one-click button to your desktop. Click it, and complete a few short screens of settings, including one to place a shortcut on your desktop. Then any time you want to start a meeting, just click the button on your desktop and a meeting begins.

You can also download a one-click feature to Outlook so you can begin meetings from there with one click. Go to the Support section of Assistance on the Meeting Center page to find the Integration to Outlook link to download the feature.

Chapter 5

Taking Advantage of Remote Computers

In This Chapter

▶ Downloading and setting up Access Anywhere

▶ Connecting to a remote computer

▶ Working remotely

▶ Disconnecting when you're done

*Y*ou can choose to take advantage of a WebEx feature called Access Anywhere.™ This is an apt name because this program allows you to access any computer, from anywhere. You install and set up Access Anywhere on one computer (the *remote computer*), and then you can access that computer from any other computer (the *local computer*, the one you're working on when you access the remote computer).

This simple process makes amazing things possible. For instance

▶ You can access your PC remotely. If, say, you're at a customer site in New York and you forgot a very important file that is stored on your computer at your home office in San Francisco, this comes in pretty handy. (And no one has to know. You can turn the remote computer's screen blank so no one can see the data you are accessing if they walk by your cube.)

▶ You can show an application or transfer any document stored on your computer back at the office while you're on the road.

In this chapter, I explain how to download and set up Access Anywhere so you're all ready to go. Then I get into the mechanics of running a computer remotely outside of/during a meeting or session.

Setting Up a Remote Computer

You scheduled your meeting and prepared attendees. There's one more thing that you might need to do before the meeting starts: Set up access to a remote computer.

Imagine you're in Tallahassee for a convention, and you have to run a project team meeting. You'd like the team to see something in your project management application, which is saved on the desktop of your computer back at the office. No problem. If you want other people attending a meeting to view applications or a desktop located on a remote computer, you can. All you need is the WebEx Access Anywhere Agent installed on the remote computer.

Your minimum requirements

Before you go to the trouble of downloading Access Anywhere, you should verify that both your computer and the computer that you want to hook up to meet the minimum requirements for using it. Here they are:

- ✔ Microsoft Windows 95, 98, Millennium Edition (Me), XP, NT, or 2000
- ✔ Intel Pentium 166 MHz or faster processor
- ✔ 32MB (64MB recommended) of RAM
- ✔ Microsoft Internet Explorer 4.x or later, Netscape Navigator 4.x or later, or AOL 5.0 or later
- ✔ JavaScript and cookies enabled on the Web browser, and ActiveX enabled if you are using Internet Explorer
- ✔ A dedicated broadband Internet connection, such as digital subscriber line (DSL), cable modem, Integrated Services Digital Network (ISDN), or a T1 connection

If you want to install Access Anywhere on a computer running Windows NT or 2000, you must have administrator privileges on the computer/network.

Downloading Access Anywhere

Follow these steps to download the Access Anywhere Agent:

1. **Click the My Computer link on the left side of the My WebEx screen.**

2. **Click the Set Up Computer button.**

   The Setting Up WebEx Access Anywhere window displays a progress bar as Access Anywhere downloads to your computer. (This could take as long as 10 minutes.)

Setting up Access Anywhere

After the download in the previous section is complete, a WebEx Access Anywhere Setup Wizard window appears. Click Next to begin the wizard, and then follow these steps to set up Access Anywhere:

1. **Enter a name for the computer, as well as WebEx account information including the URL for your WebEx account, User Name, and Password in the form shown in Figure 5-1. Then click Next.**

Figure 5-1:
Enter information about you and your WebEx account in the Access Anywhere Setup Wizard.

> **WebEx Access Anywhere Setup Wizard**
>
> **Account Information**
>
> Please enter a nickname for this computer.
>
> Computer name: Nancy
>
> Please provide your WebEx account information.
> Note: An email message containing your account information was automatically sent to you once you downloaded Access Anywhere to this computer.
>
> WebEx account information
> URL: ee1.webex.com
> User name: lisav
> Password: *****
>
> Please provide the URL for your WebEx service.
>
> < Back   Next >   Cancel

2. **Select the various check boxes to adjust the settings for your remote session (especially the settings for how the remote computer will perform when it is being accessed) on the Options page that appears, as shown in Figure 5-2, and then click Next.**

   You can also make changes to these options while running an Access Anywhere session.

   I strongly recommend that you leave the Disable This Computer's Keyboard and Mouse option selected in the Session Options. This ensures that nobody at the remote computer can start to play around with it while you're in control. It's also a good idea to enable the Disable Pop-up Messages option because if a pop-up appears while you're working, you can't control it (that is, close it) from a distance.

3. **In the Applications window that appears, select the radio button for either the Entire Desktop or for Specific Applications. Then click Next.**

   If you choose Specific Applications, click the Add button, and choose the application that you want to be able to access from the list that appears. Then click Select to place it on the list before clicking Next.

Figure 5-2:
Choose
options for
viewing the
remote
computer.

4. **In the Authentication window, choose the authentication method: Access Code or Phone.**

• If you choose Phone, the settings shown in Figure 5-3 appear. Making this choice causes the remote computer to call you whenever you try to access it remotely.

• Choosing Access Code displays the settings shown in Figure 5-4, in which you can enter an Access Code that you supply whenever you want to access the computer remotely.

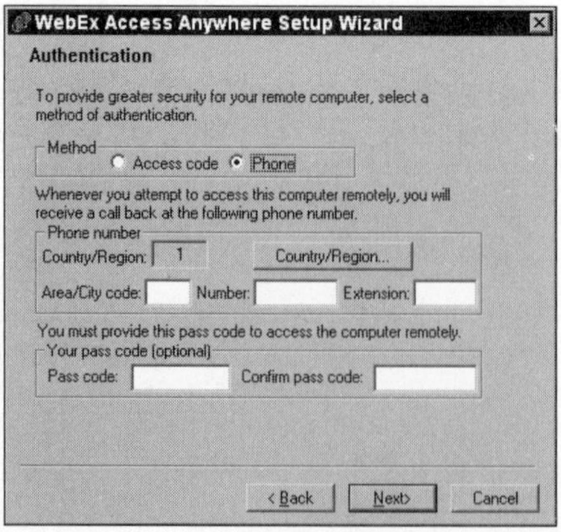

Figure 5-3:
Choices for
authentica-
tion by
phone.

5. **Set your phone number and pass code or your access code and then click Next.**

The final dialog box appears confirming that the computer has been set up for remote access.

6. Click Finish.

A progress box appears indicating that Access Anywhere is being set up on the computer.

Now when you click the My Computers item on the My WebEx Navigation bar, the computer that you just set up is listed (see Figure 5-5). In addition, a WebEx Access Anywhere icon appears on your computer taskbar.

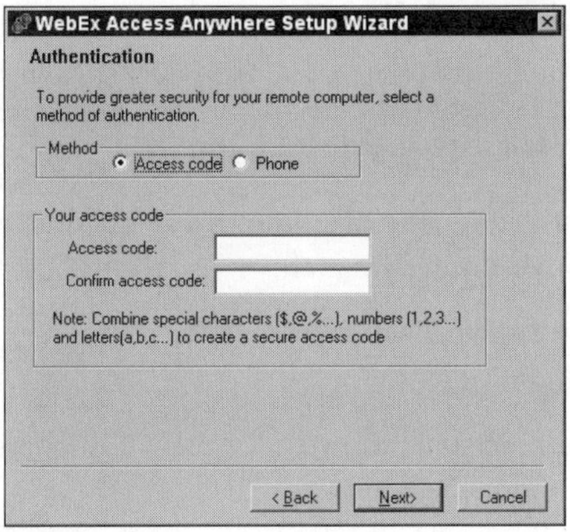

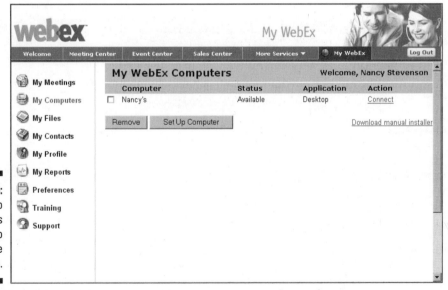

Figure 5-4:
Settings for
authentica-
tion by
access
code.

Figure 5-5:
My desktop
computer is
now set up
for remote
access.

Working Remotely

After you install Access Anywhere on the remote computer, you're ready to tap into it from across town or around the world through the magic of the Internet. This section shows you how.

Making the connection

To remotely access the computer that you set up with Access Anywhere, it must be connected to the Internet, and the Access Anywhere Agent has to be running. (Ask the department assistant to do it for you while you're in Florida.)

First, here's how to connect to a remote computer if you're not in a WebEx session or meeting:

1. **Display the My WebEx page on your WebEx site.**

2. **Click the My Computers link.**

   The My WebEx Computers list, as shown in Figure 5-6, appears.

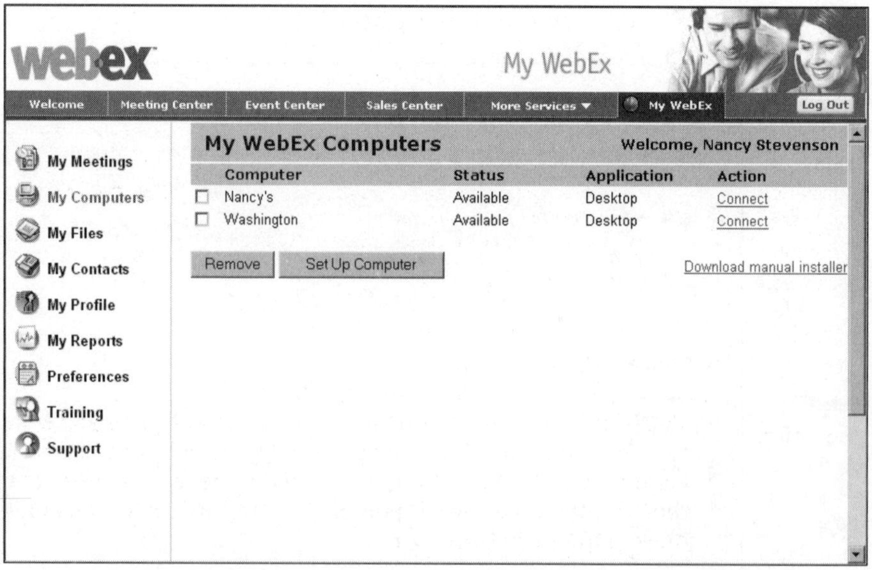

Figure 5-6:
The remote computer(s) you have set up with Access Anywhere.

3. **Click the Connect link for the computer that you wish to connect to.**

   If you choose Applications when you set up Access Anywhere, a list of applications appears. Click the Connect button for the one that you want to use. If you chose the Entire Desktop option, you won't see this list.

If you chose phone authentication, the remote computer calls you. Provide your pass code, following the voice instructions that you hear.

If you are accessing a computer that runs Windows NT or 2000, a window appears for you to log in as administrator.

The Access Anywhere in Progress page appears in a window. Leave this window open, or you'll end your connection. Finally, the Access Anywhere window opens, revealing either the application that you selected or the remote computer's desktop.

You can connect to a remote computer while running a meeting, and all meeting members can view the remote desktop. You do this by choosing Share⇨ Remote Computer from the Meeting window. Note that the commands available on the Access Anywhere menu differ somewhat when you share a remote computer during a meeting.

Remotely working

After you connect to a remote computer, you can work with it almost as if you were sitting in front of it. In addition to working on the computer, you have some Access Anywhere commands to help you out. Notice the little Access Anywhere button in the upper-right corner. Click this button to display a menu of choices (see Figure 5-7).

Figure 5-7:
The Access
Anywhere
menu
options.

The items on this menu are

- ✔ **Transfer File:** This option allows you to send files to and from the remote computer. This command opens the File Transfer window (see Figure 5-8). Browse to find the file that you want on either computer, and then use the right- or left-pointing arrow buttons to transfer files from one computer to the other.

- ✔ **View:** This opens a submenu with various settings for zooming in or out of the remote screen at various settings (such as 75% or 200%).

- ✔ **Remote Computer:** This option includes a submenu of commands:

  - • Make Screen Blank

  - • Disable Keyboard and Mouse

• Reduce Screen Resolution to Match This Computer

• Send Ctrl+Alt+Del

The first three of these commands are settings that you chose when you set up the remote computer; choosing one of them from this menu changes that setting for this one session but not for the computer connection as a whole. So, for example, if you did not choose to disable the keyboard and mouse when setting up the computer but you choose to disable them here, the next time you connect, they will be enabled according to the overall remote computer settings.

The last command allows you to initiate a Ctrl+Alt+Del action on any Windows NT or 2000 computer.

✔ **End Access Anywhere Session:** Choose this command to end this session and disconnect from the remote computer.

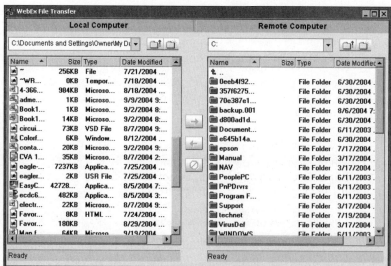

Figure 5-8:
Easily transfer files between the remote and local computer via this window.

If you're accessing a remote computer application, the Remote Computer menu includes the command Bring Shared Application to Front. This is a shortcut to restore a shared application that you minimized or to bring it to the front of other application windows that you might have opened.

If you disable the remote computer's keyboard and mouse, when you end the Access Anywhere session, they are automatically enabled again.

Chapter 6

Preparing for a Dynamic Marketing Event

*I*n the previous chapters of this book, I introduce you to WebEx Meeting Center and help you with the ins and outs of scheduling your first meeting. But before I let you loose in an actual meeting, I have a few things to say about preparing for a successful presentation.

Most of the advice in this chapter deals with preparing for a big time marketing event through Event Center. Many organizations derive a substantial percentage of their sales leads from informative online events. But don't think for a minute that this advice applies only to splashy marketing launches. Except for the most compulsory staff meeting, to get people into your company meeting, training session, product announcement, or sales event, you have to give them a compelling reason to come. Then, it's up to you to be prepared by creating an exciting presentation, practicing it, and planning all the technical details so there are no glitches.

Pushing the Marketing Envelope

Many companies spend hundreds of thousands of dollars on advertising agencies and product launch event consultants, but neglect to put all but the most basic planning efforts into online events. Why? Maybe it's because they are relatively inexpensive to produce. Who knows? But before you produce your first big online event, I want to give you some sound marketing advice, WebEx style.

Event strategy

Strategy begins at the top, where you target your highest-level goal. Ask yourself specific questions about your event, such as

- Who do you want to reach?

- What response do you want from them at the end of the event?

- How many responses are you expecting?

- Do you have a specific budget number to work with, or do you have to request your budget after you've assessed your needs and likely return on investment (ROI)?

- What topic is relevant and interesting to your target audience?

Picking just the right date

Picking the right date for an important event is something of an art. Some guidelines seem obvious, such as avoiding holidays, and the days immediately preceding them. Other maxims of veteran date pickers are less obvious. For example, consider that

- Mondays and Fridays average lower attendance than Tuesdays, Wednesdays, and Thursdays.

- You should avoid times when your target audience is generally unavailable (for example, at the end of month for Finance, or in August for academic types).

- Events held in the last two weeks of your quarter typically receive less sales support, because those folks are usually busy closing business rather than prospecting.

- Events held early in the quarter have a better chance of raising sales in that quarter.

- Event times between 10:00 a.m. and 1:00 p.m. Pacific Time generally get the best national attendance.

How many people is enough?

Should you hold an intimate event with just your most golden prospects or clients? Would a huge meeting with global presence make more of a splash? And even if you decide that a mere 100 people would be the perfect number for your event, how do you guarantee that you'll get 100 people to attend? (Remember that party you threw in high school when you invited 35 people and 5 came? I still shudder at the thought of all that leftover Cheez Whiz and punch).

The bottom line for planning attendance is to calculate how many invitations to send and determine how targeted your invitation list is. There are some common assumptions about response rates, enrollment rates, attendance rates and lead ratios you want to consider when deciding how many invitations to send to reach a certain audience size goal. Your response rate will vary depending on a variety of factors including the

- ✔ Richness of your purchased or owned e-mail list
- ✔ Use of unsolicited lists versus known leads
- ✔ Resonance of your event title and description to your target audience
- ✔ Quality of your invitation copy
- ✔ Ability of your invitation to get past spam filters
- ✔ Appeal of your brand and any guest speakers
- ✔ Amount of advance notice you provide your invitees
- ✔ Time and day of the week your event is scheduled for
- ✔ Ease of the registration process

The rule of thumb is that you get a better response rate from lists of people who already know your organization than from "cold" lists you buy or rent from some third party. But for the sake of argument, take a look at the numbers when using a relatively cold invitation list.

If you do a pretty good job of planning and promoting your event, on average you can assume you need to send 100 invitations for each enrollee. Typically 40–60 percent of enrollees will attend. These statistics, of course, change dramatically for the better if you are holding an event for employees who are required to attend or with whom you have an existing relationship, such as your customer base.

E-mail campaigns are frequently used to promote Web seminars, which makes sense because those who communicate online often are probably more comfortable learning online.

Strategizing for sales

If your event is meant to generate sales, you should be aware before you start your meeting what you can expect to gain from it.

Here's how online events typically relate to follow-on sales:

- Typically 5–15 percent of attendees will qualify as "A" (likely to buy soon) leads.
- A similar fraction will also qualify as "B" (interested but with a less urgent need) leads.
- A lesser percentage of those who enroll but do not attend are likely to qualify as "A" and "B" leads, as well.

Your sales conversion rate is highly dependent on what you have to offer; even the snappiest online meeting can't sell bad merchandise or out-of-date materials. That said, 15 percent is a common sales conversion rate. A gross assumption suggests you'll close 1–5 sales per 10,000 e-mail invitations.

You are also likely to benefit if you get prospects who are already in the sales pipeline to come to your event. Even if they don't attend because they are familiar with your offering, they may refer others to it.

Planning the numbers

So what's all this going to cost? WebEx offers a calculator to help you estimate the cost and likely ROI for your event, and your account rep will be happy to make suggestions about how to enhance your ROI. The key is to increase your total effect (gain) and efficiently manage your expenses (costs), thereby improving your ROI.

Here are some items to consider when creating an event budget:

- Determine your target audience, the desired response you want from attendees, and the number of attendees you hope to reach.
- Decide on the most interesting and relevant topic and speaker(s) to attract enrollment and get attendees to give you the desired response.
- Design an event promotion campaign to reach your ideal target audience.
- Determine the amount of time you'll need to define, promote, design, and prepare the event (six weeks is a good start with larger events).
- Select the best event date.
- Calculate the promotion, content creation, Web seminar, and telephony costs, as well as the cost of inducements and follow-ups.

Don't neglect techniques for leveraging other programs' budgets. If you have an ad campaign under way, request a mention, a bullet, an extra insert, or anything else that provides exposure for your event at little or no extra cost. If your company is involved in PR activities, make sure it also touts this event. If you are co-presenting with a partner or industry expert, consider what promotional activities and mailing lists that person can contribute.

Are there public interest groups, online forums, or professional associations that might be willing to mention your event, if it's related to a topic its membership would find interesting?

If you are sending invitations using rented or purchased unsolicited lists, you'll face some challenges in getting your money's worth. List brokers are adding restrictions because of new liability laws that may affect the terms and conditions of your purchase. Also, be aware that spam filters increasingly block e-mails, including those with a lot of HTML, a lot of text, and key words such as *free, promotion, special offer,* and *sale.* Always test your invitation using several spam filters to see if your message is getting through. (On the bright side, some lists are coming down in price and may offer more value).

Letters, direct mail, brochures, and other related marcom (marketing communications) pieces should all make note of the event. If they don't, consider paying for a sticker to add to existing materials. A sticker is typically cheaper than a whole new promotional piece, after all, and you can piggyback on in-place postage or distribution budgets.

Don't forget to let your employees and sales force know what's going on. They should be promoting the session in every appropriate interaction.

Asking attendees all the right questions

The registration process is your first point of contact with enrollees, and you can use it to strategize about who will join your meeting and whether they will pay off in future sales or repeat business.

When you design your enrollment form, consider the objective of the event: Several of your qualifying questions could be very important in establishing the quality of each lead.

You have the option of assigning a score to each possible enrollment answer at the time you create your enrollment page. These scores can then be automatically tallied and ranked in reports to help you quickly route the hottest leads to your Sales team.

Think about how you want to use the description page. From a marketing point of view, you want the prospective attendee to be intrigued with the content and have a compelling reason to attend. Include either a logo or a photo of the presenter to post together with your written description. Consider adding eye-catching fonts and active HTML links within the body of the description itself (see Figure 6-1). Don't forget that you have the ability to send your enrollee to a URL of your choice when the enrollment form is submitted. Use this feature to reinforce your message and branding.

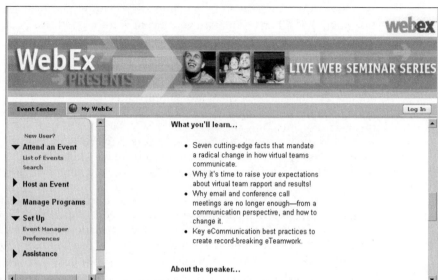

Figure 6-1:
A catchy
description.

You can set up the enrollment to allow for either instant approval or a pre-approval review. WebEx Event Center lets you establish criteria for automatic approval (for example all those for whom Plan to Buy = "In the next 30 days") or automatic rejection (when an e-mail address contains @competitor.com, give them the boot, for example). This automated feature can reduce your labor and turn-around time on approvals.

Don't forget: Reminders

It's essential to map out a reminder campaign to keep the event foremost in the attendees' minds and get them into your event.

When you schedule an event, you can customize any of the e-mail messages that Event Center sends to event invitees, enrollees, and attendees.

Follow these steps to set up reminders:

1. **On the Schedule an Event page, in the E-mail Options section (see Figure 6-2), select the check box for the e-mail messages that you want to send to confirm enrollment or send updates on the event:**

   • Enrollment Pending

   • Enrollment Accepted

   • Enrollment Rejected

   • Event Updated

Figure 6-2:
Here you set
various
e-mail
options.

2. **Select checkboxes in the following two categories:**

   • **Reminder:** You can send up to two reminders and choose the date and time to send them.

   • **Follow-up:** You can send a thank you to attendees after the event, and a follow-up message to those who enrolled but did not attend. Again, you choose the date and time for delivery of these messages.

3. **Click the link for any e-mail message to open the Edit Email Message window; click Save to save any changes.**

   When you customize the content of an e-mail message, you can use several variables that Event Center automatically replaces with information about the event when sending the message. For example, you can use the variable %Topic%, which Event Center automatically replaces with the event name specified on the Schedule an Event page. You can also restore an e-mail template by clicking the Restore to Default button.

4. **Click the Schedule button to save all the event schedule settings.**

   The Event Information is displayed.

5. **In the Emails Messages section of this form, select checkboxes to choose those you wish to e-mail an invitation: Host, Panelists, Participants, or Vendors.**

6. **Click the Send Emails button at the bottom of the Event Information form.**

   Your invitation e-mails are sent, and all reminder e-mails you scheduled on the previous form will be sent when you scheduled them to be.

Here are some things you can do in the WebEx Event Center that can help you drive such reminders:

✔ Design and post the event description and information on your Web site to get visitors excited.

✔ Generate enrollment reports so you can map your progress.

✔ Use host-controlled, automated, customizable e-mails to provide connection information and reminders to attendees.

✔ Use something called *viral marketing tools* (for example, automated links in attendee e-mails that they can use to forward invitations to others) to encourage attendees to spread the word (like a virus, hence the term *viral*) and invite other interested friends to the event. Invitees can submit names of interested parties or forward information to them.

✔ Add visually appealing elements to your Event Center site including graphics, text, and enrollment information.

✔ Come up with a compelling event title and description.

✔ Consider creating a program of related events to promote at the same time. (This can provide additional perceived value, increased mindshare, and cost savings.)

✔ Review reports leading up to the session to be prepared for the probable number of attendees (remember, typically 40–60 percent of enrollees attend).

✔ Schedule and draft automated thank-you-for-attending messages, and sorry-you-couldn't-make-it e-mails (see Figure 6-3).

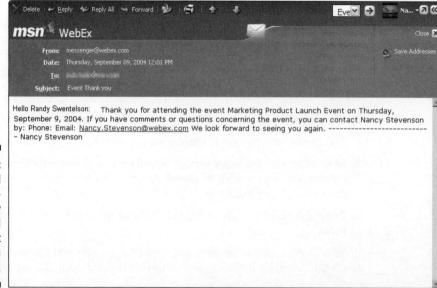

Figure 6-3:
A typical automatically generated event thank-you message.

Statistically, sending two reminders e-mailed 24 hours and 1 hour in advance of the event, has the greatest benefit.

For some event topics and audiences, it may make financial sense to leave telephone reminders a day or two in advance of the event. Yes, this involves extra cost and time; the benefit is that this contact often adds an extra psychological dimension, which can cause a noticeable increase in attendance rates.

An offer they can't refuse

Don't you just love special offers? Today only . . . 15 percent off . . . buy one, get one free! If the purpose of your Web event is to gather qualified leads and increase sales, be sure to plan a little something special for attendees. Your offer can be discounted products or services, a free demo or consultation, or simply an incentive to speak with a sales rep. Mention your special offer at the beginning and end of your event, as well as during the presentation, if appropriate.

One great way to make responding to an offer instantaneous is to use a *Web push*. This WebEx feature enables you to deliver a Web page to attendees' computer screens that they can control and navigate. This really cool tool allows your attendees to register an incentive offer, provide information, and offer feedback about the event on the spot. Ask your system administrator about how to go about this for your service.

You can also set up a drop-off URL that displays a Web page when each attendee leaves the event or when the event ends. Use this feature to send your attendees to a special offer form. Then pass those forms on to your sales folks.

Promote, promote, promote

Old-time carnivals had quick-talking folks called *barkers* standing outside tents, convincing people to step inside and see the show. You have to become a 21st-century virtual barker for your event. Luckily, technology puts a lot more promotion tools at your disposal than our sideshow friends had.

Leave no stone unturned in your efforts to spread the word about your Web event and drive prospects and customers to your enrollment page. Some of the media successfully used to promote Web events include

- ✔ E-mail
- ✔ Direct Mail
- ✔ Newsletters

- ✔ Advertising on your Web site
- ✔ Online advertising at sites where potential attendees visit
- ✔ Links to your event from related sites
- ✔ Telephone
- ✔ Home page placements
- ✔ Banner ads
- ✔ Personal sales rep invitations
- ✔ Public relations
- ✔ Ad tie-ins
- ✔ Viral marketing

Invite your prospect base, customers, and partners using the medium that most effectively gets to your audience. For example, many companies advertise Web seminars in a customer newsletter, which is sent to each new customer. Always be careful about respecting those who want to opt-out and make sure that your e-mails include the necessary opt-out links and company information.

In your e-mail, newsletter items, and direct mail, make the Web seminar your main call to action and the focus of the creation/design. Emphasize the title, date, and time and make sure that any URL you provide easily directs visitors to the enrollment page.

You can use your internal mailing lists or purchase lists. Be sure you advertise the event on your Web site, customer/partner information sites, and industry portals.

Look for third-party sponsors that will send an e-mail to its mailing list for a fee or in exchange for being listed as a sponsor in your promotional materials. E-mails and newsletters sent by a third party to its opt-in lists can generate more interest if the third party is a key player in the industry or is a trusted association or name. This approach also avoids the list rental process.

Making the announcement

If you send out your event announcement the day before the event, I guarantee you'll be disappointed with the attendance. They say timing is everything, so time your promotional messages appropriately. Promotion should begin three to four weeks before the scheduled date. Send out reminders and announcements for both prospects and enrollees one week, one day, and one hour before the event. Also include "tell a friend" links so that your target audience can invite others who might be interested. If you've got the people power, call enrollees the day before to personally remind them of the event.

Specify lead-source tracking ID's on your promotional materials to measure which sources are getting people to follow through and enroll. You may double your efforts with the winning sources even before the event to boost attendance. As you continue to market to this target audience for future events, this information can be invaluable for fine-tuning your promotional strategy.

When you're in a hurry

When is the last time you had more than enough time? It's inevitable: There will be times when you need to plan and set up a large event in less than the optimum six weeks.

In general, the more experienced you are at conducting online events, the faster you can determine your strategy, set up your event, and promote it. But even if you're new to online events, here are some short cuts and exceptions to help you out:

✔ If you are repeating an event you have conducted before, you can essentially skip many of the planning steps and jump to designing your promotion and initiating your promotional campaign. This can reduce lead-time to about three weeks.

✔ If you are promoting an event to a "friendly" audience (for example, customers, partners, association members who know you, and so on), you may get by on less than three weeks promotion time. Keep in mind though, that most people book their calendars one or more weeks ahead, so the less lead-time you give them, the less chance that they'll be available.

✔ If you are planning a series of related events as a single program, those events can share a single strategy phase, design, setup, and event promotion phase. The events themselves can be days or even hours apart.

✔ Use promotional media where you have more control over how soon your message is delivered. For example, don't send an announcement by regular mail — the speed at which regular mail arrives at its destination varies according to the how far it has to travel and the time of year it is sent. Instead, use media such as newspaper ads with a specific insertion dates, or e-mailed announcements that will arrive at most inboxes within 24 hours. This minimizes lag time between creating the event and promoting it.

✔ Be realistic about your resources. If you don't have the time or resources to optimize every part of the event process, focus on your areas of greatest strength that will get you the highest attendance.

✔ If you can recruit creative or logistical talent from any group in your organization that stands to gain from a successful event, you may be able to divvy up the workload and race through the strategy and setup phases more quickly.

✔ If all else fails, consider bringing in a hired gun. WebEx Production Services may be able to help you out on a short lead-time and ensure a smoother experience for your speakers and attendees.

Follow up

Promotion doesn't end with your event. Here are some things to consider after the meeting ends:

- ✔ Schedule a calling campaign by your sales force for one to three days after the event to qualified attendees and enrollees.

- ✔ Create a PDF version of the final presentation and send it out to attendees.

- ✔ Assemble event-specific sales scripts for follow-up calls and sales collateral materials, such as informational press kits that you can mail out to assist sales reps in converting attendees into purchasers.

- ✔ Schedule a marketing special-offer e-mail one week after the event.

- ✔ Organize event attendee data and quickly distribute it to appropriate people for action.

Being Prepared

You wouldn't want to plan a terrific promotional campaign for your event and then lay an egg, would you? Make sure your event presentation delivers on your promotional promise by planning the content and logistics carefully.

Planning your presentation to work online

Chances are, you've stood up before a group of people before spouting words of wisdom you clicked through a bullet point presentation. You used gestures, facial expressions, and your powers of observation to pick up on how your audience was reacting to you. With an online presentation, you may have quite a large group of people, but they will only hear your voice and see your slide presentation. This means that in an online event, your slides become even more important than in an in-person presentation.

You may already know these presentation guidelines:

- ✔ Use no more than four to six bullet points per slide

- ✔ Use clean, simple fonts and not too many colors

- ✔ Include transitions and animation to drive home points and emphasize key messages.

But online presentations have their own set of rules, including:

- ✔ Keep slides moving briskly because they're all the audience has to look at (except a Minesweeper game they can bring up on screen if your presentation gets dull); allow about one minute per slide.

- ✔ People are used to getting up-to-the-minute information online: The information you present should be timely and target what your audience needs today. The best online seminars are about new trends or current changes in the relevant industry.

- ✔ Be sure to include relevant examples and case studies; bring in customer success stories and experts from your organization to add value. This might be information you would normally include in your patter, but with an online presentation, consider preparing a video of a customer testimonial or sharing an application or Web site to give a product demonstration.

- ✔ Consider how polling and chat will blend into the flow of the meeting. Also, think about Q & A: Will questions be interspersed or come all at the end (at the end is easier)?

- ✔ Storyboard the presentation using all these elements to ensure a tight Webinar (a "Web seminar") that keeps the audience's attention.

Making your event engaging

Businesspeople today are exposed to a lot of presentations, from those they encounter in their own company meetings to training sessions and industry conferences (not to mention the in-mirror TV screen in the airport bathroom). They can be pretty jaded about what makes for an interesting presentation, so you have your work cut out for you.

One way to grab attention is to design your theme as a question, for which the logical answer is your call to action. The call to action is the next step you want attendees to take, to walk down the path towards making a purchase, putting a new job skill to work, or using a service. You are alerting your audience to a problem or opportunity. Think of it this way: If you inspire them to want to act on this information, what is the obvious action you would take if you were a member of the audience?

Sample calls to action are

- ✔ Request a one-to-one consultation with one of our experts today!

- ✔ Contact an account rep to see how others in your industry have succeeded with our product or service!

> ✔ Use our online cost-savings calculator to see how much you can save!
>
> ✔ Order by the end of the month and save 30 percent!
>
> ✔ Call today for a free trial/demo/sample!

Right at the outset, you should outline the valuable, interesting, and compelling benefits of sitting through the entire seminar to the audience. Include some tempting nuggets and some specific examples of the valuable information they will gain to establish that your seminar is worthwhile. Remember, these folks can "walk out" of your meeting at any time if they don't see the value in staying.

Conduct polls early and intermittently. A popular technique is to poll the audience after the second or third slide to find out what area is of the greatest interest. This has many benefits. It hints at the multiple ways that the presentation is of value. It lets audience members see what others are interested in. Most importantly, it prompts them to interact and lets you assure them that you will tailor your comments to their needs. This can be a very powerful way to engage them through an online medium. Additional polls throughout the session continue to keep them engaged and add value by making the live audience part of the show.

Real-world examples are particularly valuable for helping audience members absorb and assimilate abstract concepts. The more credible and concrete you can make your case, the fewer audience members will duck out the back during your presentation.

In general, a 30- to 35-minute presentation is your best bet for marketing seminars. If the seminar is too short, attendees may not feel they've received substantial value. If the presentation is too long, a lot of the audience won't hang around for your call to action at the end. Or, the audience may be so saturated and fatigued that they feel less vigorous about responding to your call to action. It's also a good idea to leave at least ten minutes for Q&A after the presentation.

Use more than one speaker if possible. A male and a female speaker subconsciously attract extra attention so if, like Noah, you have one of each available, pick them as your speaker duo.

Making enrolling easy and rewarding

Admit it: If you didn't absolutely have to file your taxes every year, you'd take one look at that 1040 form and skip the whole thing, right? A bad form can stop a potential attendee in his or her tracks in the same way. Conversely, a simple enrollment form can maximize registrations for your event.

When you schedule an event, you can save yourself a little time by using the Copy From link next to the Event name field in the Schedule an Event form. This copies any customized enrollment form you've used in other events, saving you the effort necessary to recustomize it every time.

Designing the form

In the Schedule an Event form there's a section for Enrollment. In this section you can set requirements for enrollment ID and password requirements, and designate whether approval of the enrollment form is required before someone can attend. There's also a Customize Enrollment Form button. To make your form just the way you want it, click that button, and then follow these steps:

1. **Use the first column of checkboxes next to the items lists (such First Name, Last Name, Address, and so on) to include or exclude those fields from the form (see Figure 6-4).**

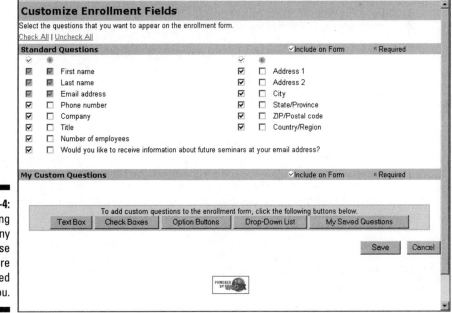

Figure 6-4: Customizing fields. Many of these items are preselected for you.

2. **Use the second column of checkboxes (the one labeled with an "R" at the top) to indicate the items that are required to complete the form.**

3. **Depending on what you'd like to add, click on any of these five buttons at the bottom of the form: Text Box, Check Boxes, Option Buttons, Drop-Down List.**

In the form that appears fill out the appropriate information. For a checkbox, for example, enter a label for the set of checkboxes, and labels for each individual box. If you like, add a score to each item; you can use this score to automatically approve or reject an enrollment. For a drop-down list, you enter the label for the list, and a label for each item that appears in the list.

4. **When you've finished entering labels, click the Save button.**

5. **To add questions you've created for other events, click the My Saved Questions button, click on the checkbox for the question(s) you want to include, and then click the Add button.**

6. **When you've finished adding questions to the form, click the Save button.**

Providing a clear, to-the-point overview

When creating an enrollment form, you get a chance to enter an event description. This is your hook to get people to want to attend, to want to fill out the enrollment form and submit it.

Consider these pointers about writing a dynamic description:

✔ Stress the value for those who attend, not the sales pitch.

✔ Include bullet points for easy scanning.

✔ Include speaker bios so attendees get to know the expert(s)/speaker(s).

✔ Make the topic and goal of the session clear.

✔ Point out anything that will go beyond an online bullet point presentation, such as sharing of documents, applications, or Web content; video; or interaction.

Showing them an event face

Online events can often have a faceless quality (making people feel they have to talk to the technology, so to speak). Try to make the event seem more personal by branding the enrollment form with company logos and including pictures of the people who will be presenting.

Making it easy for them

Your enrollment form is a place for enrollees to do a last check that this is the right event for them before they sign up. List fees, if any, technical requirements, or a link to an FAQ where questions can be answered.

Your enrollment page is also an excellent place to qualify attendees, but don't bombard them with questions. A few questions — no more than 15 — help you better understand your audience and you can actually shape your presentation to match their needs (see Figure 6-5).

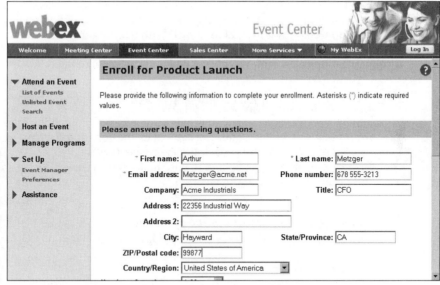

Figure 6-5:
A typical
enrollment
page with
a few
targeted
questions

Using an auto-populated registration form, which pre-populates the answer
fields on the enrollment form, makes the registration process for your customers and prospects a snap!

Practice, practice, practice

You know the old joke about how to get to Carnegie Hall: Practice, practice,
practice! The same is true for online meetings. At least one week before the
Web event

✔ All speakers should meet online to do a complete "dry run."

✔ Review slides, practice transitions, test any rich media being used, and
practice using the online tools and features.

✔ It's important to use the same computer equipment you'll be using in
the actual event and to make sure that the speakers know how and when
they need to join the actual event.

✔ Make sure speakers actually go through their spoken presentations,
including the use of their slides. Participating in an online event is a
unique experience, and practice makes perfect.

✔ Practice verbal transitions if there are multiple speakers (you can't look at
each other to get visual cues). The host/moderator should be prepared to
pass Presenter control from one speaker to another when needed.

The most common feedback from first-time online presenters, including those who have a lot of public speaking experience, is how difficult it is to speak to a computer. With no visual or audio feedback from the audience, even a seasoned public speaker can become uneasy. But with a little practice, even the novice presenter can become an effective online speaker.

Schedule another dry run the day before the event just to make sure everything will run smoothly when you go live.

Start your Web event 30 minutes ahead of the scheduled start time to give attendees a chance to sign on and the presenters a chance to get prepared. Plan to keep attendees occupied with a video or details about a special offer until the actual start of the meeting.

Avoiding technical glitches

When was the last time you made a live presentation and didn't have a technical glitch? The technical requirements for holding a Web event are minimal, but they are important, so don't neglect them.

Be prepared by checking well in advance that you have the right equipment and make sure it's adjusted correctly by using the following checklist:

- ✔ **Check your computer.** You need a PC with a minimum of 128MB RAM, a Pentium III or better, and a sound card if you are using VoIP or any rich media with audio.

- ✔ **Check your Internet connection.** All presenters should have DSL or T1 connections so they can share media at an acceptable speed.

- ✔ **Check your headsets.** Hand-free headsets offer better audio quality than handsets or speakerphones.

- ✔ **Check your location.** Broadcast your Web event from a quiet office location (not the one next door to the fire station) and use your phone's mute feature when you're not speaking.

- ✔ **Check audio quality.** Make sure all speakers are at the same volume level. Many folks underestimate the importance of having very high quality audio. In an online presentation, you can't lip-read (as most of us unconsciously do with a live speaker), so make sure it's clear and crisp.

- ✔ **Check the recording setup.** Do a test recording before the event begins to make sure the audio is actually being recorded.

If you need to use a lower screen resolution, let your attendees know that they can scale a presentation to fit their event windows by using Zoom tools and the Full Screen view. If you're sharing an application, they can also scale the view of the application window.

Enough Preparation Already!

Perhaps there is such a thing as being too prepared. At some point, you have to jump in and run a meeting or host an event. The next part of this book is where you get going running meetings with Meeting Center, which will make you hands-on types happy!

Part III
Let the Meetings Begin

The 5th Wave   By Rich Tennant

"Well, that's typical. Ever since I started meeting online with my parents, my mother keeps looking for a toolbar function that brushes the hair off my forehead."

In this part . . .

You have watched a demo and scheduled your first meeting. You're finally ready to run your first meeting and discover all the tools and features that WebEx makes available to you. Here's where you begin to share documents, applications, Web content, and even your very own desktop. You take a poll of attendees, show folks a video of your own smiling face, and brainstorm like crazy using the whiteboard feature.

The flip side of the coin is always interesting, too, so in this part I talk about what it's like to attend a meeting: how you dial in, get the presenter's attention, and save various items from your meeting.

Chapter 7

Hosting a Meeting

*W*hether it was a book report in third grade or a sales report to a hundred executives, were you sweaty-palmed the very first time you gave a presentation? Running your first WebEx meeting in front of all those attendees might seem intimidating to some, but trust me, it's a piece of cake. The meeting environment and tools that WebEx provides are very easy to use. You don't even have to worry about plugging in the LCD or getting somebody to turn off the lights when you're ready to run a slide show.

But even the simplest task can seem daunting the first time you do it — especially with lots of other people watching what you do. This chapter provides all the steps for starting, running, and ending that first meeting. By the time you've read this chapter, you'll feel like an old pro.

Starting Your Scheduled Meeting

First things first: Get your meeting started. If you already have a meeting scheduled (see Chapter 4 for all the details of scheduling one, if you haven't), you can access it via your WebEx Meeting Service Web site. Here's how:

1. **Go to your WebEx Meeting site.**

   Enter your WebEx URL in your browser. When your WebEx meeting site appears, click the Log In button and sign in with your user ID and password.

2. **Click the My WebEx tab.**

3. **In the list of meetings that appears, click the Start link under the Status column, as shown in Figure 7-1.**

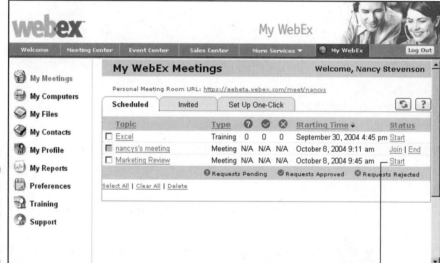

Figure 7-1:
I'm about to start my scheduled meeting.

Click here to start the meeting.

Starting an Instant Meeting

The Web server just crashed, and customers can't get into their accounts to check their balances. A quick, high-level meeting is definitely called for, but you don't have time to fill out a scheduling form and have people register. You need a meeting, and you need it now! If this is your situation, don't worry. Just use WebEx's Instant Meeting feature.

The following steps show you how to start a One-Click Meeting:

1. **On the Meeting Center tab, click the Instant Meeting link under the Host a Meeting menu.**

   The Instant Meeting page, as shown in Figure 7-2, appears.

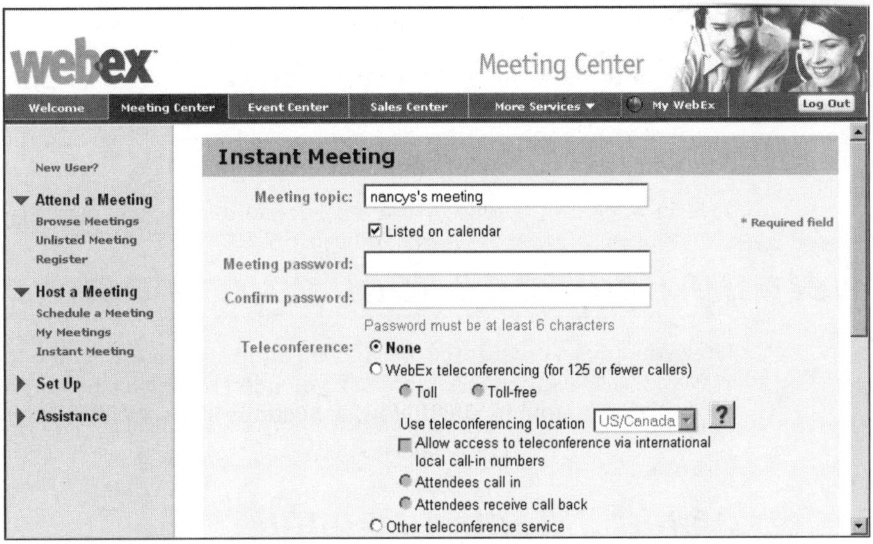

Figure 7-2:
The Instant
Meeting
page.

2. **Enter the meeting topic, password, password confirmation, and tele-conferencing options that you prefer.**

3. **Click the Start button.**

   A dialog box appears telling you that Meeting Manager is being prepared; when that's done, your meeting opens.

Making sure your attendees are ready to go

In order to participate in a WebEx meeting, all participants must have installed *WebEx Meeting Manager* (the plug-in that makes WebEx work). I also recommend asking attendees to take part in a 20-minute WebEx tutorial to ensure two things:

✔ **Basic training.** Attendees find out how WebEx works and are ready to use the annotation, mute, and other basic features that the demo discusses. Even ten minutes of wandering around the demo meeting will get them comfortable with these features if they're short on time.

✔ **Meeting Manager is installed.** In order to participate in the live demo, attendees need to quickly install the Meeting Manager plug-in. By having them participate in the live demo prior to their meeting with you, you can be sure that everyone is ready to jump into the meeting right away.

Keep in mind that Meeting Manager has some options that you can specify as the meeting host. Check out the Meeting Center Help pages at `http://webex.com/customercare/downloads-webex.html` for more on these options.

After you start your instant meeting, you can invite attendees by choosing Participant⇨Invite and then choosing a delivery method (by E-mail, by Phone, or by Messenger). Each invited attendee receives an invitation that includes information about the meeting and either a link that the attendee can click to join the meeting or a phone call to hook them into the meeting, depending on what invitation method you choose.

Getting People to Join Your Meeting

After you have a great topic for your meeting and you schedule the meeting in WebEx (as I explain in Chapter 4), you need to publicize that meeting and allow people to join in. The following sections show you how.

Sending a link in e-mail

When you schedule a meeting, anyone whose e-mail address you include in the list of attendees receives an e-mail with the meeting details and a link to the meeting. Figure 7-3 shows an example of an e-mail invitation to a scheduled meeting.

Figure 7-3: WebEx automatically generates an e-mail invitation from the attendee list.

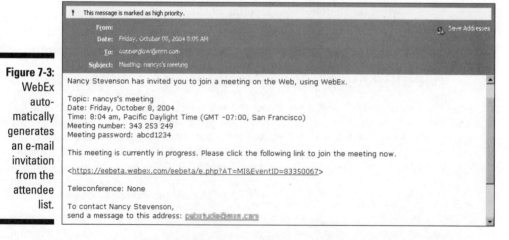

When the attendee clicks the link, she gets a dialog box asking for a password. After that is entered, she goes directly to the Meeting Information page in a Web browser, as shown in Figure 7-4.

Figure 7-4:
The meeting
information
page (from
the
attendees'
view).

Sending people to your personal WebEx site

As Virginia Wolff said, there's nothing like a room of one's own. That could be why WebEx provides an online meeting room called your *Personal Meeting Room,* a customizable space from which you control all your meeting activities. One simple way to get people to join your meetings is to send them a link to your Personal Meeting Room site, which shows information about all the upcoming meetings that you're hosting. Your site can even include files that you want to share with people who attend your meetings.

To customize your Personal Meeting Room, click the My Profile link at My WebEx and make changes in the Personal Meeting Room section, uploading an image and a welcome message to display.

You can customize your Personal Meeting Room page. Figure 7-5 shows one example.

To get someone to join a meeting via your Personal Meeting Room site, follow these steps:

1. **In your normal e-mail program, start a new e-mail message addressed to all the people whom you want to participate in your meeting.**

2. **In the body of the e-mail, paste a link to your Personal Meeting Room site.**

   When attendees arrive, the list of scheduled meetings that you are hosting appears.

3. **Instruct everyone to click the Join Now link in the Status column, as shown in Figure 7-5, to join a specific meeting.**

Figure 7-5:
A Personal
Meeting
Room of
your own.

 As the host, you can turn on the "join before host" feature when scheduling a meeting to allow your attendees to join up to 15 minutes in advance. This feature is very useful if your attendees arrive to the meeting early.

As I explain in Chapter 4, you can create a custom welcome message for your meetings in the Agenda and Customizable Welcome window that appears as you go through the steps of scheduling your meeting. If you plan to send people to your WebEx site to have them join your meetings, you might want to include a special welcome message that lets them know that the meeting will start very soon — and to sit tight until it does.

Let Me Share This with You

Your parents taught you all about the value of sharing, right? With WebEx, you can share any document or application on your computer. Whether you share a word processing document, a Web site, or a proprietary application, all your attendees can see it just as if they were sitting at your computer. You can even share applications, your desktop, a Web browser, or Web content.

Attendees can also view any animation and transition effects on shared Microsoft PowerPoint slides. Media files (such as movies or audio) embedded in a PowerPoint presentation require conversion, so WebEx enables you to easily convert such files with something called UCF (Universal Communications Format). See Chapter 4 to read more about UCF files and how to create them.

Let the sharing begin!

Sharing a presentation or a document

Okay, so just what kinds of things can you share? Sharable documents and presentations include

 ✔ Documents created by a word processor

 ✔ Presentations (for example, those created in PowerPoint)

 ✔ Graphics and videos

As soon as your meeting is underway, you can open a document or presentation to share it. Here are the steps for sharing a document or presentation:

1. **In the Meeting window, click the Share Document button. You can also choose Share⇨Presentation or Document instead.**

   The Share Presentation or Document dialog box appears, as shown in Figure 7-6.

2. **Use the Look in field to locate the folder and file for the presentation or document, select it, and click the Open button.**

   Meeting Manager first opens the document or presentation in your content viewer. Attendees can then view the document or presentation in their content viewers.

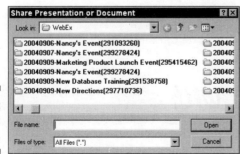

Figure 7-6: Locating a file to share.

3. **To display the next page or slide, click the Next button. If you want to display the previous page or slide, click the Previous button (see Figure 7-7).**

4. **If you are sharing Microsoft PowerPoint slides that include animations, do the following to display different slides and their animations:**

   - To display the next slide or animation, press the right arrow on your computer's keyboard.

   - To display the previous slide or animation, press the left arrow on your computer's keyboard.

If you open another document or presentation, Meeting Manager adds another tab to the top of the content viewer. You can display different documents or presentations by clicking the tabs.

To stop sharing a PowerPoint presentation or other document, click the X in the presentation or document tab in the content viewer.

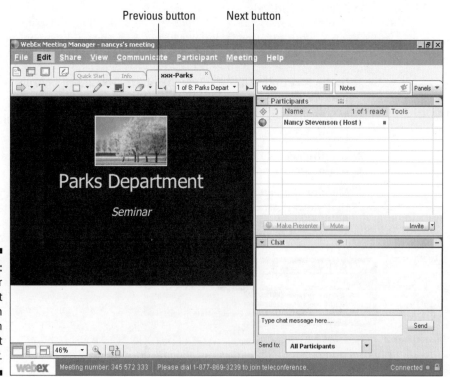

Figure 7-7:
A Power
Point
presentation
displayed in
the content
viewer.

You can use various annotation tools that appear on each document panel in the content viewer to mark up documents or presentations during a meeting. These are the same annotation tools that appear on the WebEx Whiteboard view. The use of each of these tools is explained in the upcoming section, "Working with the whiteboard."

Sharing an application

Sharing an application gives control of that application to an attendee. An attendee can request to control an application, and a host can hand over that control. Sharing a document within the application sharing mode allows meeting attendees to both see the document and annotate it by using the WebEx annotation tools.

You can also simply share a document without sharing an application. See the preceding section, "Sharing a presentation or a document," for more about that.

This method of sharing can be "quicker to the punch" in a training setting. While a student is trying a procedure, you can jump in and control an attendee's application remotely to show him or her what to do, which can really save time: Rather than describe a process, you just demonstrate it while students watch, and then you're on to other topics.

Sharing an application also enables you to show software that an attendee doesn't have or might not understand how to use. For example, if you are a software manufacturer and you want to demonstrate a proprietary application, you can share the application and show it off to potential customers.

Starting application sharing

Here's how you go about sharing an application:

1. **In the Meeting window, choose Share⇨Application.**

   The Share Application dialog box appears showing a list of all applications currently running on your computer.

   Any running applications appear in the Share Application dialog box. Although you can share applications that are not yet running (by clicking New Application), I suggest starting the application before your meeting begins and then minimizing it. That way, you don't need to keep your meeting attendees waiting while you start the software.

2. **In the list of applications, select the application that you want to share.**

3. Click Share.

The Meeting window minimizes on your computer. If the application is not already running, it starts automatically.

Your application appears in a sharing window on attendees' screens.

Taking sharing further

The application-sharing feature of WebEx is very flexible. If necessary, you can return to the meeting window, causing all attendees to return to the meeting window as well. You can also

✔ Share additional applications.

✔ Make the shared application appear full-screen on attendees' screens.

✔ Temporarily pause application sharing at any time to freeze attendees' views of the shared application.

When you share an application, a small green button labeled Sharing appears on the application window (see Figure 7-8). Click this button, and a menu appears with the following choices:

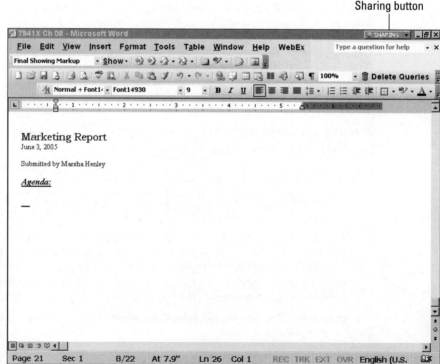

Sharing button

Figure 7-8:
A shared application displaying the Sharing button.

✔ **Select Application:** This takes you back to the Share Application dialog box so you can choose a different or additional application to share.

✔ **Share:** This choice switches you to Document Sharing; from this window you can select a document or presentation to share).

✔ **Allow to Annotate and Allow to Control Remotely:** These are commands that a presenter can use to control what attendees can do in the shared application.

✔ **Start Annotation:** This choice displays a set of annotation tools (see Figure 7-9) that you can use to annotate what's displayed in the shared application.

✔ **View:** This choice allows you to view the shared application full screen or reduced in size.

✔ **Pause Sharing and Stop Sharing Application:** These are used to freeze the application or to close it, respectively.

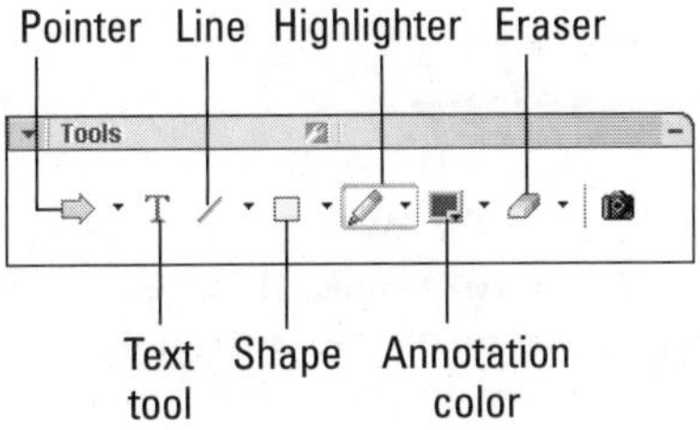

Pointer   Line   Highlighter   Eraser

Figure 7-9:
Annotation
tools.

Text   Shape   Annotation
tool   color

A set of tools called a *Floating Icon tray* displays when you share an application (see Figure 7-10) that includes the following features (from left to right):

✔ **Move tray:** Click this and hold down your mouse button to drag the tray of tools around your screen.

✔ **Return to Main Window:** Use this to go back to the meeting environment.

✔ **Participant Panel, Chat Panel, Video Panel, Notes Panel, Polling Panel:** Each of these choices displays a floating version of the appropriate panel.

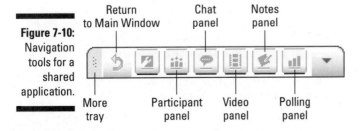

Return
to Main Window   Chat   Notes
                    panel   panel

Figure 7-10:
Navigation
tools for a
shared
application.

More   Participant   Video   Polling
tray   panel   panel   panel

Stopping application sharing

When you want to stop sharing an application, you can use either of the following series of steps:

1. **In the Meeting window, choose Share➪Application.**

2. **In the list of applications, highlight the application that you no longer want to share.**

3. **Click Stop Sharing.**

Or

1. **Click the Sharing button in the title bar of the application that you are sharing.**

   The Sharing menu appears.

2. **Click Exit Application Sharing.**

Touring the Web together

Today, it seems like the whole world is on the Web. Sometimes, all you need to share is a Web site to get your point across. With this type of sharing, you can display your company Web site, your corporate intranet, or a special Web site that you built just for the meeting, for example. You do this kind of sharing in one of two ways: by sharing your Web browser or by sharing Web content.

When you share your Web browser, you call the shots. Any page or file that you browse is displayed on attendees' screens, including HTML pages stored on your computer or pages in your corporate intranet. You can annotate these Web pages or let attendees annotate them. Any links that you follow are displayed on attendees' screens as well. Note that when you share a Web browser, attendees might not see all animations or other multimedia content (such as movies) or hear streaming audio. They also can't wander off to other pages or sites unless you take them there.

Comparatively, when you share *Web content,* you basically take attendees' browsers to the URL of your choice. Sharing Web content is a good idea if you want attendees to fully experience a Web site — Flash animations and any other multimedia content (like the ever-popular Hamster Dance) are fully available, and attendees can interact independently with the Web site.

You can also grant attendees control of your Web browser by choosing Share➪Web Browser from within your meeting.

Sharing a Web browser

When you share your Web browser, attendees can essentially come along for the ride as you surf around the Web.

To share your Web browser with others, follow these steps:

1. **In the Meeting window, choose Share⇨Web Browser.**

   The Meeting window minimizes on your computer and your default Web browser opens, as shown in Figure 7-11.

   Your Web browser (and any content that it's displaying) appears in a sharing window on attendees' screens.

2. **Browse to any Web page or HTML file that you want to display on your Web browser.**

   The file then is also displayed to attendees.

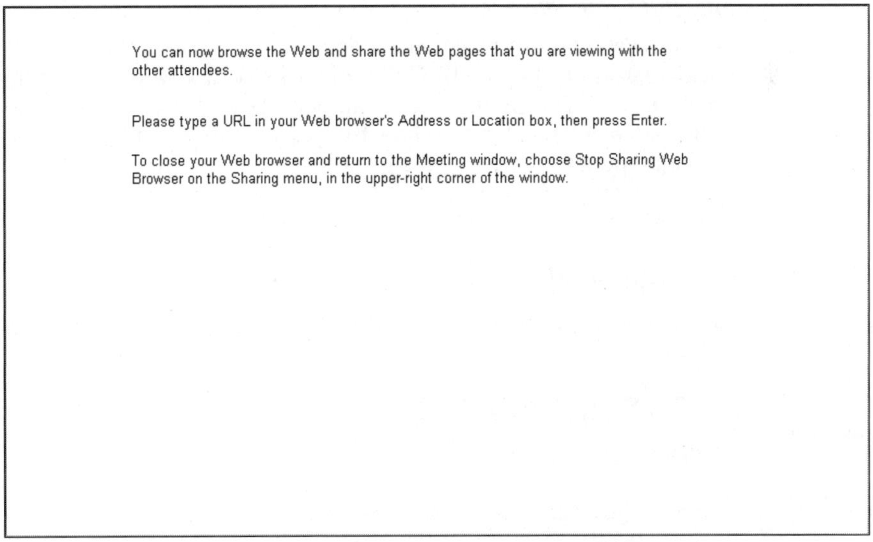

You can now browse the Web and share the Web pages that you are viewing with the other attendees.

Please type a URL in your Web browser's Address or Location box, then press Enter.

To close your Web browser and return to the Meeting window, choose Stop Sharing Web Browser on the Sharing menu, in the upper-right corner of the window.

Figure 7-11:
Sharing a
Web
browser.

When you want to quit sharing your Web browser, do the following:

1. **On the title bar of the Web browser that you are currently sharing, click the Sharing button.**

2. **On the menu that appears, choose Exit Web Browser Sharing.**

Special effects for Web browser sharing

While sharing a Web browser in a WebEx meeting, keep the following factors in mind:

✔ You can return to the Meeting window, causing all attendees to return to their Meeting windows, by choosing click the Return to Main Window icon on the floating icon tray.

✔ Attendees can view any new Web browser windows that you open. Thus, attendees can view several Web pages simultaneously.

✔ You can display your Web browser in a full-screen view on attendees' screens.

✔ You can temporarily pause Web browser sharing at any time to freeze attendees' views of the shared Web browser.

Use the tools on the Sharing menu to control your shared Web browser.

Sharing Web content

Sharing Web content provides some advantages over sharing a Web browser because users can enjoy the full functionality of a Web page, including animations. However, sharing content can be a mixed blessing because you can't fully control what attendees see; they can act independently on the sites that you take them to.

The following steps explain how to share Web content:

1. In the Meeting window, choose Share⇨Web Content.

The Share Web Contents dialog box appears (see Figure 7-12).

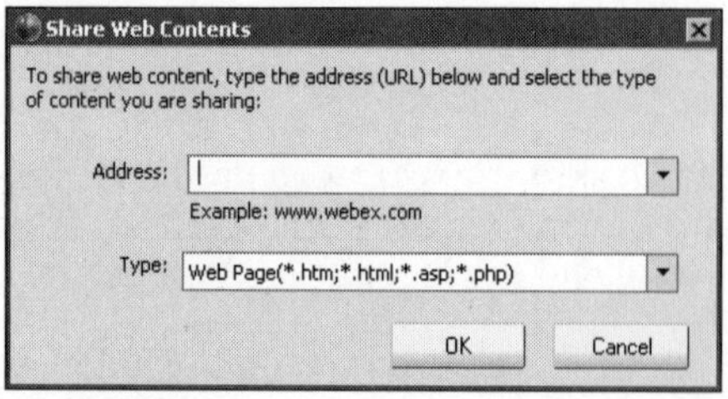

Figure 7-12:
The Share
Web
Contents
dialog box.

2. In the Address box, specify the Web address (URL) of the content that you want to display.

You can copy a URL from any source — such as another browser window — and then paste it in the Address box, if you prefer.

3. **Click OK.**

The Web page opens on each participant's screen within the content viewer.

Participants can navigate to other Web pages within the content viewer in the Meeting window. Attendees can navigate to other pages by clicking links on the shared page.

Sharing your desktop

Don't worry if your desktop is a clutter of paper, pens, and old donuts. I wouldn't ask you to invite anybody to browse around *that* desk. However, you can share your Windows desktop, and it comes in handy for several uses. Desktop sharing is great for showing how you switch among applications or use other operating system features, or for sharing multiple applications when you don't want to share them all individually. When you share your desktop, attendees can see everything on your desktop and everything you do on your desktop, including any applications that you run. Here's how to share your desktop:

1. **In the Meeting window, choose Share⇨Desktop.**

2. **Click OK.**

The Meeting window minimizes on your computer, and your entire desktop appears in a full-screen view on attendees' screens.

When you want to stop sharing your desktop, follow these steps:

1. **On the title bar of any window that is open on your computer's desktop, click the Sharing button.**

2. **On the menu that appears, choose Exit Desktop Sharing.**

If you click the Close and Exit Desktop Sharing icon on the Floating Icon tray, you stop desktop sharing and return to the meeting window — but you can't switch between desktop sharing and the Meeting window as you can with other types of sharing.

Managing a Meeting

When you are in charge of a WebEx meeting, you have a whole rainbow of features to pick from to help you communicate, instruct, inform, and otherwise connect to the attendees. You can also let attendees take over now and then by allowing them to annotate information you present on a virtual whiteboard, or by passing them the WebEx ball and letting them run things for a while.

Using chat

If you've used chat features on other Web sites, you know just how this works. Participants can type in a question and send it to the person running the meeting, a presenter, or to everybody in attendance. The person who receives the chat comment or question can then type in a reply, and send that reply to the sender, or others in the meeting.

Figure 7-13 shows a chat in progress. The area where the messages appear after they're sent is the *chat panel.* Enter a message in the area just below the chat panel, and then choose who should receive your message from the Send To drop-down list. Click the Send button next to it to send your message, which then appears in the chat panel.

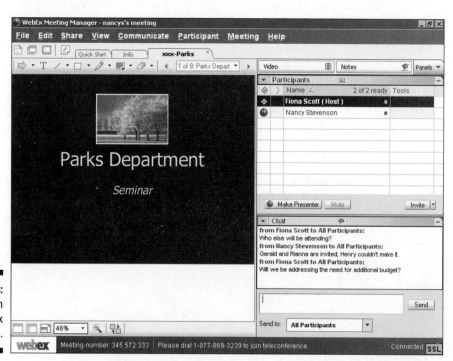

Figure 7-13:
Chatting in
a WebEx
meeting.

Taking a poll

Political polls might not be much fun, but polls in a WebEx meeting can be a great way to learn about your attendees, gauge how well they're grasping the information you're presenting, and keep them involved in the meeting.

It's ideal in the typical meeting to run a poll shortly after the meeting starts, one around midway, and one near the end, but don't overdo it: No more than five polls an hour, please!

Here are the steps involved in running a poll:

1. **With a meeting open, if the Polling panel isn't displayed, display it by clicking the Panels button and choosing Polling (see Figure 7-14).**

2. **Select a question type: Short Answer or Multiple Choice.**

3. **Click the New button.**

   Your cursor becomes active in the Polling viewer area.

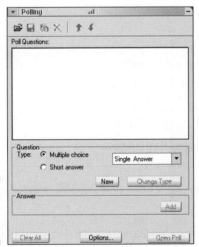

Figure 7-14:
The Polling panel.

4. Type your poll question and press Enter.

Your cursor moves to the next line. If you chose Multiple Choice, when you enter a choice and press Enter, it is formatted with a radio button and labeled alphabetically, as in Figure 7-15. If you chose Short Answer, a small text box in which attendees can enter an answer appears.

Figure 7-15:
A couple of
questions
entered
in a poll.

5. Create as many questions as you wish by repeating Steps 2–4.

6. To start the poll, click the Open Poll button.

You will see the posted questions and Polling status information, letting you know how many people have completed the poll.

7. To end the poll, click the Close Poll button.

The results are shown to you.

8. To share results with others, select the Poll Results check box and then the Apply button.

The Options button on the Polling panel allows you to display a timer that alerts people to the amount of time they have left to finish the poll. You can change the amount of time to allow for the poll in the Options dialog box that appears when you click the Options button.

Taking notes

The *Notes feature* is a window in which meeting participants can enter notes about the meeting and save them. This is a good place to write down ideas that you want to communicate so they don't get lost, as shown in Figure 7-16.

To designate a single note taker for the meeting while it's in progress, choose Meeting➪Options and change the setting from Allow all participants to take notes to Single notes taker.

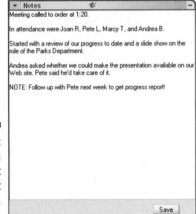

Figure 7-16: Taking important notes about the meeting.

You can select one person to be a note taker and publish notes for everyone in the meeting, or you can allow participants to each take their own notes and save them. You cannot have all the participants take notes and have them visible to everyone in the meeting.

Working with the whiteboard

One of the old standbys of great brainstorming sessions is the low-tech whiteboard (also know as a blackboard or flipchart). In a WebEx meeting, the old whiteboard has gone high-tech, with tools for entering and annotating information. Everybody can grab a virtual pen and start adding their ideas, thoughts, and scribbles to the mix.

You display the whiteboard by choosing Share➪Whiteboard. Here's a run-down of whiteboard features (see Figure 7-17):

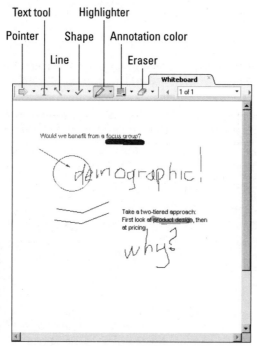

Text tool
Highlighter
Pointer | Shape | Annotation color
Line | Eraser

Figure 7-17:
The WebEx
whiteboard
in action.

✔ The **Pointer tool** is used to display an arrow with the user's name in it. Move this arrow around the whiteboard to point out something, and everybody will know who is doing the pointing.

✔ The **Text tool** is the one you use to type on the whiteboard. Click the Text Tool, click anywhere on the whiteboard, and then begin typing.

✔ The **Line and Rectangle tools** actually offer more tools than you can see in Figure 7-17. Click the arrow on either tool, and additional shapes are displayed. When you choose one of those shapes, the tool name changes to that shape (for example, Check Mark or Double-Headed Arrow). Choose one of these tools, and then click and drag on the whiteboard to draw the shape.

✔ The **Highlighter tool** also changes its name if you click the arrow and choose the Pencil tool. These two tools are used to emphasize or annotate information or to draw on the whiteboard area.

✔ The **Annotation Color tool** displays a color palette for the virtual ink that is used by the highlighter tool.

✔ We all make mistakes! That's why there's an **Eraser tool.** You can either click the arrow on this tool and choose different items to clear; or click the tool and then with the little eraser cursor that appears, click individual shapes, annotations, or text to clear items one by one.

The Edit menu has several useful commands for whiteboarders:

- ✔ Choose Edit➪Add Page to create a new, blank whiteboard page.

- ✔ Choose Edit➪Annotate On and choose either light background or dark background to change the whiteboard to a whiteboard with a dark background.

- ✔ Choose Edit➪Clear and choose My Pointers, All Pointers, or All Annotations to wipe out what's been done and start again.

- ✔ Choose Edit➪Font to display a Font dialog box that allows you to format the text that you enter on the whiteboard and use different fonts and font styles.

You can also copy and paste text and objects onto the whiteboard. When you are sharing a whiteboard, you choose Edit➪Paste as New Page command to paste the contents of the Windows Clipboard to the current whiteboard.

Passing the ball

The little WebEx globe icon that appears next to one name in the list of participants in a WebEx meeting indicates the individual who has the floor: This is the head honcho, the designated presenter.

As nice as it is to be the star player, there are times when you'll want to pass the ball to let somebody else take it to the hoop. Here's how you do that:

1. **Right-click a person's name in the Participant panel.**

2. **Choose Participant➪Change Role To➪Presenter.**

   The little globe icon jumps to the left of that person's name.

3. **When the person wants to hand back the reins to you (or you want to ask them to hand them back), he can click your name and choose Participant➪Change Role To➪Presenter.**

Using the same Change Role To menu, you can also change a person's role to Host (the host has control of various aspects of the meeting, which I outline in more detail in Chapter 2), Note Taker (the only person allowed to enter notes), or Close Captionist (someone who can type in commentary and then display it as a close caption for all participants, which is useful for meetings using audio where some folks either don't have speakers or are hearing impaired).

Keeping attendees' attention

Just as sports announcers use snappy patter to keep you planted on your couch and following the action, you can use these tips to avoid viewer burnout:

✔ **Start a chat session.** Chat isn't just for the socially dysfunctional anymore. You can use it to keep meeting participants involved in your meeting by conducting ongoing chat sessions. Chat is a great way to conduct brainstorming exercises within a meeting or to voice opinions on key decisions.

✔ **Take a poll.** WebEx's polling feature is a quick way to take the temperature of a group of meeting participants on a particular issue. For example, how many prefer Coke to Pepsi? You can also use a poll to quickly find out who is snoozing.

✔ **Share a whiteboard and use annotation.** If you are sharing a document and you're not sure people are paying attention, ask people to point out the part they most like or dislike and then see who starts scribbling on the whiteboard.

✔ **Pass the ball.** Pass presentation rights ("the ball") to the person you suspect of dozing off. If nothing happens, you'll have your answer.

✔ **Throw out some non sequiturs.** If participants seem like they're not listening, say something really strange. Nothing gets people's attention like, "In order to boost third quarter profits, we will be asking employees to contribute a month's salary."

✔ **Push an unexpected Web page.** With WebEx's push feature, you can send out any Web page you want. I can think of several that would get people's attention, and several more that could cost you your job. (So be careful how you use this idea!)

✔ **Run a short mid-meeting contest.** At one place where I worked, we used to add short trivia contests to the middle of agendas. Usually, the prize was very small, but the trivia questions could be pretty good. This technique woke people up again in the middle of the meeting. It was a way to take a break, exercise the mind, and yet quickly return to the task at hand.

✔ **If all else fails, eject.** Remember that you have the power of the Expel feature. If you are faced with meeting participants who are not paying attention, you can always eject them. After all, they might not even notice!

Ejecting the unruly

The Expel feature of your WebEx meeting is to be used cautiously. It abruptly and completely disconnects the person from your meeting. If you're sure that's what you want to do — because the person doesn't belong in your meeting or is acting inappropriately — go for it. Here's how:

1. **Click the person's name in the Participant's panel.**

2. **Choose Participant➪Expel.**

   A dialog box appears, confirming that you want to cut this person off.

3. Click Yes.

Bye-bye, participant!

Wrapping Up

Even if you often spend the last minutes of a meeting checking your watch and thinking about that candy bar in your desk drawer, you know deep in your heart that a good wrap-up is important to any meeting.

To get some closure for your meeting, you should do the following things:

✔ Document what was discussed at the meeting (for example, meeting minutes).

✔ Identify action items for participants.

✔ List documents that need to be exchanged.

✔ Set a date, time, and initial agenda for the next meeting.

WebEx enables you to wrap up a meeting and perform all these tasks practically on autopilot. Many WebEx features enable exactly these kinds of wrap-up activities in ways that are sometimes more efficient than the standard face-to-face meeting. WebEx can document chat and create a transcript on the fly, and then you can easily distribute this transcript to all the meeting participants.

Transferring files

You can transfer files, such as spreadsheets, word processing documents, drawings, and so on while you meet. I especially like this feature because file exchange is taken care of on the spot, not put off until after the meeting ("I'll e-mail those files to you as soon as I get back to my desk. I promise!") and then forgotten.

Starting file transfer

Here's how to start a file transfer:

1. Choose File⇨Transfer.

The File Transfer window appears, as shown in Figure 7-18.

2. Click Share File.

A standard Open File dialog box appears.

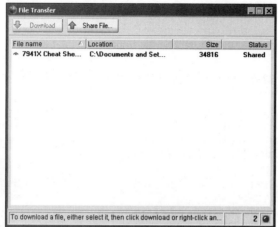

Figure 7-18:
The handy
File Transfer
window.

3. **Select the file that you want to share.**

4. **Click Open.**

The File Transfer window automatically appears in each attendee's Meeting window.

The number of attendee Meeting windows in which the File Transfer window is open, including your own, appears in the lower-right corner of the File Transfer window.

When you want to stop file transfer, just close the File Transfer window by clicking the X button as you would to close any other window.

Saving the transferred file

After you transfer a file to meeting participants, each participant must save the file to his or her hard drive, as follows:

1. **From the File Transfer window, select the file to save.**

2. **Click Save to save the file.**

Saving stuff

One of the great things about WebEx is that it constantly keeps track of your chat and notes during your meetings. All you need to do to have a permanent record of your meeting is to save a transcript of those communications. The following sections explain how.

Saving notes

After you have a really full notes window from a productive meeting, you probably should save them, right? Here's how:

1. **Click the Save button in the Notes area or choose File⇨Save in the Meeting window.**

   The Save Notes As window appears, as shown in Figure 7-19.

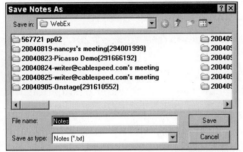

Figure 7-19: Saving notes to your hard drive.

2. **Browse to a location where you want to save your notes.**

3. **Type a name for your notes file in the File Name text box.**

4. **Click Save.**

   Meeting Manager saves the file as a text file (.txt). You can open it in any word processing program.

You can now use the File Transfer feature to distribute the notes to other participants, or you can use the Send Transcript feature and include the notes in an e-mail attachment. To do so, follow the steps in the section, "Transferring files," and select the notes file you just saved as the file to transfer.

Saving chat

Chat can sometimes be meaningless chatter, but sometimes it's the place where the neatest ideas of your whole meeting surface. In that case, you'd better save it for posterity. To save a new chat, follow these steps:

1. **In the Meeting window, choose File⇨Save.**

2. **In the menu that appears, choose Chat.**

   The Save Chat As dialog box appears.

3. **Choose a location where you want to save the file.**

   4. **Type a name for the file in the File Name text box.**

   5. **Click Save.**

   Meeting Manager saves the file as a text file (.txt) at the location you chose. You can open the file in any word processing program.

Saving everything

If you have generated chat, polling results, notes, and so on, you might find it easier to just save the whole shebang at once. To do so, follow these steps:

   1. **In the Meeting window, choose File⇨Save All.**

   2. **In the dialog box that appears (see Figure 7-20), select the options that you want to save.**

   When you choose Save All, a folder name is provided for you, but you can browse to find or enter a different folder destination. Notes and chat are saved in .txt format.

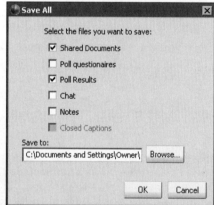

Figure 7-20:
Selecting
what to
save.

   3. **Accept the suggested folder or choose a location where you want to save the file.**

   4. **Type a name for the file.**

   5. **Click OK.**

   Meeting Manager saves everything you specify as a text file (.txt) at the location you designate. You can open the file in any word processing program.

Sending a Meeting Transcript to Participants

Sometimes people get lost in a meeting, or join late and need to be brought up to speed. One great way to accomplish this is to publish a transcript. A *transcript* is an e-mail message that contains the following information:

- ✔ Meeting topic

- ✔ Meeting number

- ✔ Meeting starting and ending times

- ✔ The URL for the Meeting Information page on your meeting service Web site

- ✔ The list of all participants

- ✔ The meeting agenda

You can also attach any of the following files to the transcript if you saved them during the meeting:

- ✔ Shared documents

- ✔ Poll questionnaire

- ✔ Poll results

- ✔ Chat

- ✔ Public notes or closed captions that you took or that the note taker or closed captionist published during the meeting

If you want to send a meeting transcript to participants, follow these steps:

1. **In the Meeting window, choose File⇨Send Transcript.**

   If you have saved any files during the meeting, the Send Transcript dialog box appears, allowing you to attach the files to the transcript e-mail message.

   If you have not saved any files during the meeting, a transcript e-mail message opens.

2. **If the Send Transcript dialog box appears, select the check box for each file that you want to attach to the transcript, and then click OK.**

   The transcript e-mail message opens.

3. **Review the e-mail message and make any changes that you want.**

4. **Send the e-mail message.**

You should keep several important things in mind when you send a transcript:

- You have to save notes, polling, and chat in order to include them in your transcript.

- The transcript is sent to all participants who provided their e-mail addresses when joining the meeting, regardless of whether they are still attending the meeting.

- Participants who receive a transcript e-mail message cannot see the other participants' e-mail addresses.

The transcript contains notes only if you are the meeting host, the public note taker, or the closed-captionist, and you have saved the notes to a file. The notes that are sent in the transcript are the latest version of notes that you saved, so if new notes are in the notes window since the last time you saved them, they will not be included unless you save the notes again.

Recording and Playing Back Meetings

It's often useful to make a recording of a meeting. You can record everything that goes on screen including chat, whiteboard annotations, and sound. Such a recording can act as a self-paced tutorial or let those who couldn't make the meeting know what went on. Recording and playing back meetings is simple to do.

Recording for posterity

If you've used any of the common media players such as Windows Media Player, a lot of the features used to record, pause, and playback your meeting recording will be a piece of cake for you. If you've never used a media player — well, it's still a piece of cake.

Note that to capture all audio in your teleconference you need to set up a phone recording adapter. If you don't set this up, the only audio the Recorder captures is through your computer's microphone, if one is attached.

Follow these steps to record a meeting:

1. **Choose Meeting⇨Start Recording.**

   The Save Recorded Meeting As dialog box, as shown in Figure 7-21, appears.

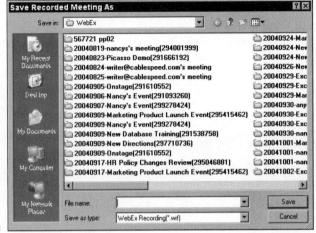

Figure 7-21:
A familiar
Save As
dialog box
auto-
matically
sets your
file type
to .wrf.

2. **Enter a name for your recording in the File Name text box, and click Save.**

   The Recorder Panel shown in Figure 7-22 appears.

Figure 7-22:
Control your
recording
activity with
these tools.

3. **Click the Record button (a bright red circle).**

   The recording begins. You can now use the Pause, Stop, Insert Marker (this divides what preceded from what follows as separate segments), or Annotation buttons to control the recording.

4. **When you're done recording, click the Stop button.**

If you want to control your audio settings, choose Meeting⇨Recorder Settings⇨Audio Panel. In the dialog box that appears, you can control the compression scheme and sampling rate. The *compression scheme* deals with the method used to handle how the recording is streamed across the Internet. The sampling rate controls the audio quality: Higher numbers here give better quality because more tiny bits of sound are recorded, but a high sampling setting makes for a larger recording file as well.

Watching meeting reruns

Playing a recorded file is simplicity itself. Just locate the file on your computer and double-click it. It opens and begins playing, and the WebEx Player shown in Figure 7-23 appears.

Figure 7-23:
The tools used to playback a recorded session.

The tools allow you to (from left to right) Open, Play, Pause, Stop, Go to the Previous Segment, Rewind, Fast Forward, and Go to the Next Segment. The last tool button on the right toggles you to and from a Full Screen display. You can also use the two sliders to adjust audio volume and jump to any point in the playback, respectively.

You can also use the File and Controls menus to initiate these actions. The Controls menu also offers both a Loop and Mute command to allow you to keep the recording playing back again and again *(looping)* or to mute the audio.

You can play back a recorded meeting on your own desktop, play it back from within a WebEx meeting by sharing the file or your own desktop, or allow people to access it on your Web site.

To stop the playback, click the Close button in the top-right corner of the WebEx Player.

(Finally) Ending the Meeting

No matter how great your meeting was, I know this is the moment you've been waiting for — The End of the Meeting!

To end a meeting, follow these steps:

1. **In the Meeting window, choose File⇨End Meeting.**

   A confirmation message appears, in which you verify that you want to end the meeting, as shown in Figure 7-24.

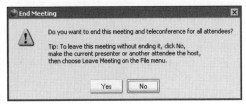

Figure 7-24:
Ending the
meeting.

2. **Click Yes.**

   The Meeting window closes, and you are free!

When you end a meeting as the host, the Meeting window closes for all attendees. If the meeting includes an integrated voice teleconference, the conference also ends.

If you're the host and want to leave the meeting but not end it, first choose Participant⇨Change Role To⇨Host to designate a presenter or attendee as the host. Now you can head off to your next meeting!

If there is any meeting information that you have not yet saved (such as shared documents, chat, a poll questionnaire, poll results, or notes), Meeting Manager asks you whether you want to save them before ending the meeting. If you choose to save a file, Meeting Manager uses the default filename for the file. So, if you have already saved the file under another name, Meeting Manager does not overwrite that file. Meeting Manager also automatically prompts you to send a transcript when you end a meeting.

Chapter 8

Attending Meetings

A great portion of this book is written from the perspective of somebody who holds the reins, so to speak. That is, some chapters address you as the person who will make the choice to purchase a WebEx solution for your company. Others put you in the role of a meeting host who has to set up and run a meeting or other online event. One chapter even puts the hat of the site administrator squarely on your head to show you some of the tasks involved in administering a WebEx site. But this chapter is a little different.

Here's where you get the perspective of somebody attending a WebEx meeting. Somebody else is in charge; somebody else is making the decisions. All you have to do is appreciate how incredibly easy it is to interact with folks as an attendee in an online meeting.

So sit back and relax: I'll run this meeting. You just have to show up!

You're Invited!

You know that you're invited to a WebEx meeting when you get an e-mail invitation that looks a lot like the one shown in Figure 8-1. When you get such an invitation, there are a few things you might do to get ready for the meeting (but you might not have to do anything!). The possibilities are

✔ Register for the meeting (sometimes this is mandatory, sometimes you don't have to register at all).

✔ Download software (the Meeting Manager or rich media players).

✔ Add the meeting to your calendar.

I give you the steps for each of these options in this section.

Registering for a meeting

When a host sets up a meeting, he or she may require folks to register for the meeting. If that's the case, the e-mail invitation you receive includes a link you can follow to see a summary of information about the meeting and register. Just click this link and you go to the WebEx site, where you see a summary of meeting information such as the date, time, duration, agenda, and so on.

At the bottom of this summary is a Register button. Click it and you see a form resembling the one shown in Figure 8-2.

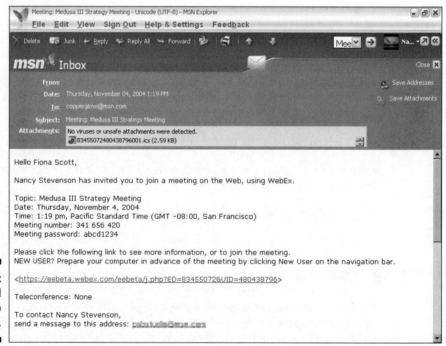

Figure 8-1:
Your e-mail
invitation to
a meeting.

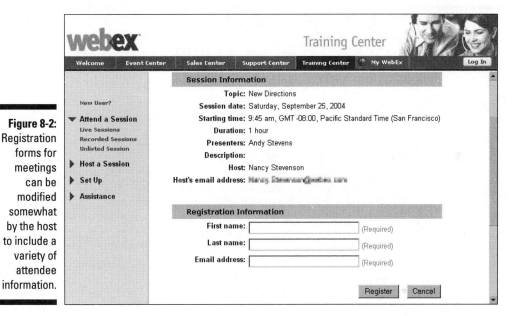

Figure 8-2:
Registration
forms for
meetings
can be
modified
somewhat
by the host
to include a
variety of
attendee
information.

Fill out the form and click the Register button. That's all you have to do!

In some cases, a host has the ability to approve registration; this means your registration may or may not be accepted. In either case, you will receive an e-mail verifying that you are registered or that you have not been accepted to attend the event.

Getting ready to attend

You can do a couple of things as an attendee to prepare to deal with the technology involved in an online meeting:

- ✔ You can download the Meeting Manager software client ahead of time. Although this software is downloaded automatically when you join a meeting, it can take a few minutes. Downloading ahead of time helps you get to the meeting on time.

- ✔ The e-mail invitation you receive may include a link that you use to verify that you have the versions of rich media players (Flash and Windows Media Player) that you need to view presentations in online meetings. Better to get these all installed ahead of time to save you the embarrassment of missing half the presentation.

Getting Meeting Manager software ahead of the curve

Though WebEx is an online service, you must install one piece of technology on your computer to interact with it. Meeting Manager is a small software program that allows you to attend WebEx events. It takes only minutes to download.

To download the Meeting Manager client, follow these steps:

1. **Click the link in your e-mail invitation that takes you to the WebEx site for more information.**

2. **Click the New User link on the Navigation bar.**

   The Setup for New Users page appears (see Figure 8-3).

3. **Click the Setup button.**

   A dialog box appears, telling you to wait while the file is set up.

4. **Wait a minute or so. A window appears, telling you that the download is complete. Click OK.**

   That's really all you have to do.

You may also notice Meeting Manager downloads occurring from time to time even after you've installed the software. These are just small automatic updates WebEx makes to your software.

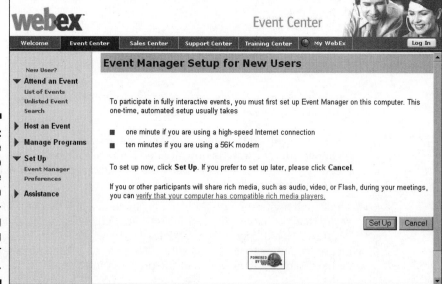

Figure 8-3: Click the Setup button here to begin downloading Meeting Manager software.

Downloading rich media players

When the meeting host schedules the meeting, he or she can indicate that attendees should verify rich media players. If that's the case, your e-mail invitation contains a link for determining which rich media players you already possess and whether they are compatible with WebEx's Universal Communications Format.

Click the link and you speed over to the page shown in Figure 8-4. Here you can simply click the Check Now links (there's one for Flash and one for Windows Media Player) to verify your software.

When you click one of these links, a window appears and an animation (for Flash) or video (for Windows Media Player) should play, as shown in Figure 8-5. If it doesn't, click the link provided to update your player. If the media files do play, just click the Close button — your system passed the test.

Depending on your computer, it can take a few moments for these presentations to play. Use the time to water your desktop plant — it will thank you for it.

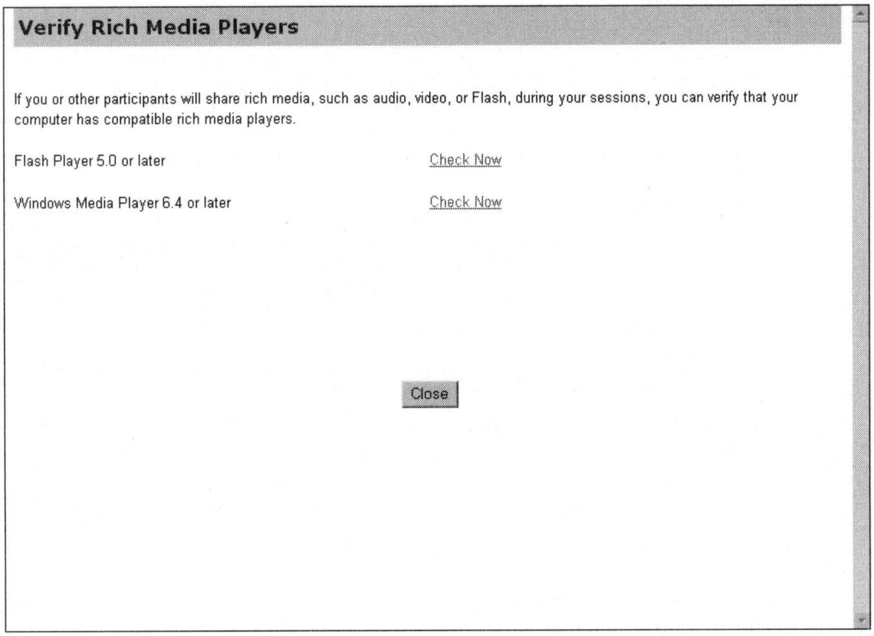

Verify Rich Media Players

If you or other participants will share rich media, such as audio, video, or Flash, during your sessions, you can verify that your computer has compatible rich media players.

Flash Player 5.0 or later   Check Now

Windows Media Player 6.4 or later   Check Now

[Close]

Figure 8-4:
Choose which player to check.

Figure 8-5:
Watch the
little Flash
animation to
verify that
you have
the latest
version.

Adding a meeting to your calendar

If a meeting occurs but it's not on your calendar, is it real? Of course not! WebEx provides a couple of mechanisms for adding meetings to your calendar program (such as Outlook or Lotus Notes).

The easiest way to do this is one click away: Just click the link provided in your e-mail invitation to see meeting information (you may be required to enter a password to complete the link); when you see the meeting information, click the Add to My Calendar button to add the meeting to Microsoft Outlook. When you click this link, you see the dialog box shown in Figure 8-6. Just select the Open This File with Microsoft Office Outlook option and then click OK.

The e-mail also includes instructions for adding the meeting to Lotus Notes. Here's how you do that:

1. **Right-click the iCalendar format (*.ics) file that is attached to the e-mail invitation and then choose View.**

2. **Click Import All.**

   A new broadcast e-mail message is added to your Lotus Notes Inbox.

3. **Open the new message.**

4. **Click the Respond button.**

   A menu appears.

5. **Click Accept.**

Joining a Meeting

It's meeting time! Grab your pad, a pen, your cup of coffee, and dash off to — nowhere. You can sit tight right at your desk, or lean back on the couch in your hotel room with your laptop on the coffee table. That's the beauty of a WebEx meeting.

After you're all cozy, read the next few sections to see how you join a meeting.

Follow the links

The e-mail invitation you receive provides a link that you click to get more information or to join the meeting. Click that link and you go to a page in WebEx showing you the meeting information.

Click the Join Now button to join the meeting. You may be required to enter your name, e-mail address, and a password that has been provided to you. After you've entered this information, click the OK button.

Depending on whether you've already downloaded Meeting Manager, you may have to wait a few minutes while WebEx sets you up. After that, Meeting Center, which looks something like Figure 8-7, appears on your computer screen.

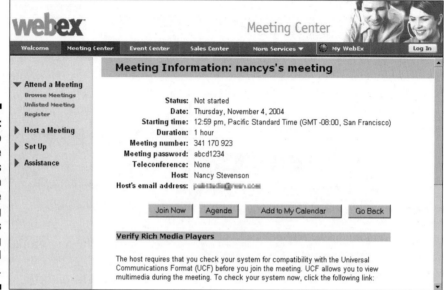

Figure 8-7:
The Info
page
provides
information
about the
meeting
such as
meeting
number and
password.

The message that appears on-screen when you're waiting to join the meeting says it eloquently, but I'll repeat it here for you: Do not refresh your browser, or navigate away by clicking the Back arrow in your browser, or you could get disconnected. If you are disconnected, you can always join again, but why bother with the hassle? If you absolutely have to go to your e-mail or some other site while the meeting is being set up, just open another browser window so that your meeting will stay intact.

Dialing in

Is this the quietest meeting you've ever been to, or what? Well, that's because at this point you're hooked up only to the visual portion — not the audio portion — of your meeting. You can connect to the audio portion by making a phone call or by using Internet Phone with Voice over Internet Protocol (VoIP) technology.

If your host has set up the meeting to use teleconferencing, the dialog box in Figure 8-8 appears shortly after you enter the meeting environment. It tells you what number to call to connect to the meeting, and what meeting number to enter when you make the call.

The host may have set things up so that you get a call rather than *make* a call to join the audio portion of the meeting. If this is the case, you see the Join Teleconference dialog box shown in Figure 8-9. Just enter your phone number and, in the blink of an eye (honestly, your phone rings almost immediately — it's spooky!), you get called in.

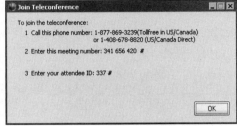

Figure 8-8:
Call this number and provide the secret word (that is, meeting number) to get in.

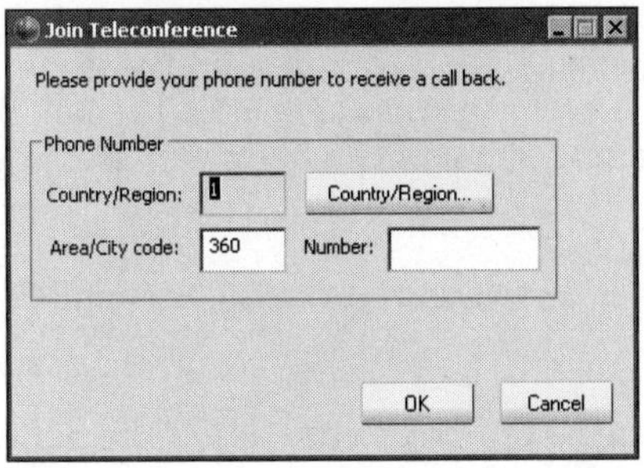

Figure 8-9:
We'll call you; just enter your phone number.

When is the Internet a phone?

VoIP isn't a new kind of robot kit. VoIP (Voice over Internet Protocol) is a technology that enables you to make phone calls over the Internet. VoIP turns analog voice signals into little digital packets of information that get sent over the Internet, sort of like sending a file of data. Based on something called the Internet Protocol (IP), you can hold two-way conversations using VoIP. And believe me, that's all the techie stuff you need to know (and more) to use Internet Phone.

Here is how to get on board with an Internet Phone meeting. Be sure you have speakers and a microphone hooked up to your computer. Then, join the meeting. After you join, you should see a pop-up window asking you to partic-ipate in the Internet Phone conference. At this point you can click the Yes button. Or, if you wait a minute or so and the pop-up window doesn't appear, choose Tools⇨Internet Phone⇨Join Conference.

Getting Heard

Are you sitting at your desk, connected to a WebEx meeting, but haven't a clue how to jump in and participate? No wonder. This is a brand new world.

There are buttons and panels here you've never used. You don't know which panels you control and which are controlled by others.

So, in this section, I go over the ways attendees can interact in WebEx Meeting Center.

You should be aware that what you're able to do will vary based on what privileges the host of the meeting has granted to attendees. See Chapter 4 for a rundown of the various privileges that a host can dole out.

Chatting away

Call it chat. Call it instant messaging. It's essentially a pretty straightforward way for participants in an online event to communicate by typing their comments to each other. The comments appear in a chat panel, and you can scroll up and down to review the conversation.

The Chat panel in Meeting Center, shown in Figure 8-10, is simplicity itself. Here's how it works:

1. **Enter a message by clicking in the box to the left of the Send button and typing your words of wisdom.**

2. **Choose the person to whom you want to send your comment by clicking the arrow on the Send To field and choosing your recipient: Host, Presenter, Host & Presenter, All Participants (which includes host, presenters, and attendees), or All Attendees (only those who are neither hosts nor presenters).**

   Note that your host controls with whom you can communicate when he or she sets up the meeting, so you might not see all these options.

3. **Click Send to send your message.**

4. **View your message and any replies in the main chat window.**

Sharing your thoughts on the whiteboard

You are obviously a creative person. (I just have a sense about these things.) You love to brainstorm and add your two cents to anything from a snappy company slogan to a clever product logo. The WebEx whiteboard was meant for you.

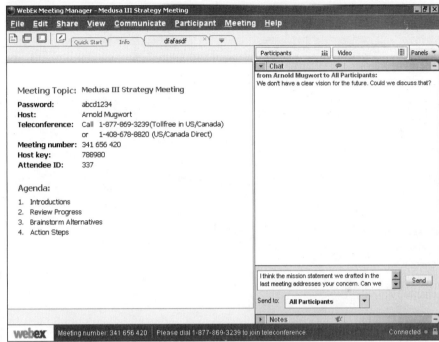

Meeting number 341 656 420 | Please dial 1-877-869-3239 to join teleconference

Figure 8-10:
Chatting
away!

WebEx's whiteboard is much like any whiteboard in a typical conference room, in which a person can get up in turn, grab the marker (try shaking it if it's running dry — they're always running dry!), and add a word, phrase, or drawing to the current brainstorming session. But with an online whiteboard, nobody has to worry about whether the markers are going dry, if you're running out of paper, or where the masking tape that you use to stick the darn things on the wall went to. You just click the annotation tool, choose pencil or highlighter (see Figure 8-11), and have at it.

The host must grant you annotation privileges, either when setting up the meeting or during the meeting, or you can't annotate on the whiteboard. Sorry!

Being part of a poll

Remember the last time you were in the shopping mall and a guy with a clipboard and a tie spotted with gravy stains asked you to fill out a poll about your favorite flavor of frozen yogurt? Well, an online poll is similar, but much faster and less painful. The presenter designs some questions and posts them, and you respond. The results from all attendees are compiled quickly, and the next thing you know, you're moving on to the next item of business.

Annotation tool

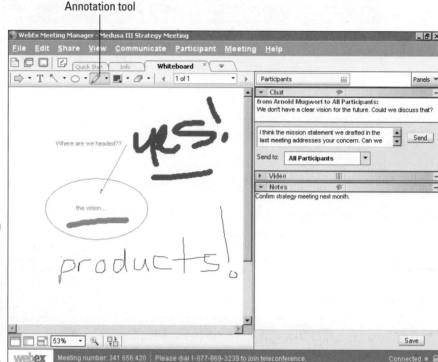

Figure 8-11:
Annotating
on the
whiteboard
can be a
brain-
stormer's
dream!

If a presenter in your meeting runs a poll, it's a piece of cake to participate. The question, which may be in the form of a multiple choice or short answer question, appears in the Polling panel. Select your choice or enter your answer and click the Submit button. The results appear only on the screen of the person running the poll, and he or she chooses whether to share the results with everybody.

Changing the view

Once again, depending on what settings the host made when scheduling the meeting, you may or may not have control over your view. One option the host may choose is to have you constantly follow whatever it is he or she is showing you on screen. But another choice gives you free will: You can display whatever panels and views you wish while the meeting is going on.

Panels are displayed along the right side of the Meeting Center window (see Figure 8-12).

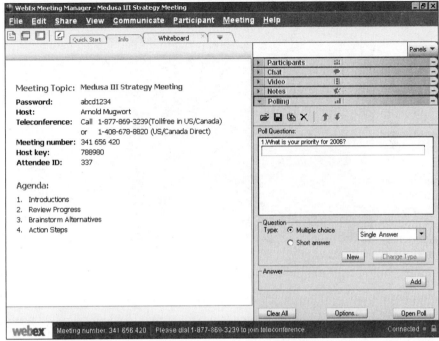

Figure 8-12:
You can
display
several
panels at
once in the
Panel area.

Here are the ways you can control panels (assuming you have been granted control):

✔ Click the arrow on the Panels button at the top right of the panel area to choose which panels to display from a drop-down menu.

✔ Click the Minimize button in the top-right corner of any individual panel to close it.

✔ Click the arrow to the left of the panel name; if the panel is expanded, this is the Collapse Panel button and does just that; if the panel is collapsed, this is labeled the Expand Panel button and . . . well, you get the idea.

✔ Place your mouse near the bottom of a panel and the cursor becomes two lines with arrows pointing up and down. Click and drag to change the size of the panel.

✔ If you close a panel, it appears as a button in the Panels title bar. Just click that button to display the panel.

In addition to panels, you may see some tabs in the Meeting Center. The Info tab will always be there. Depending on what the presenter has opened, these may also be tabs labeled Whiteboard or with the name of a document being presented to all attendees (see Figure 8-13). Click one of these tabs to view its contents.

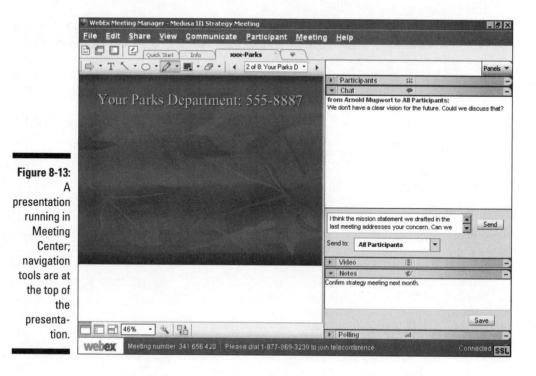

Figure 8-13:
A presentation running in Meeting Center; navigation tools are at the top of the presentation.

Saving Things and Wrapping It Up

After you've had your fun and chatted, drawn annotations on the whiteboard, and generally interacted in a productive way, your meeting will, eventually, come to an end. When it does, your host has the ability to send a meeting transcript to everybody. If he or she does, you'll receive the transcript via e-mail.

You have some ability to save things from your meeting yourself (again, if the host has allowed you the privilege of saving). You can save shared documents, polls, or the contents of chat or closed captioning.

Leaving a meeting and saving it all

Gotta move on to that *next* meeting? You can leave a meeting at any time by choosing File⇨Leave Meeting. A dialog box appears, asking you to confirm that you want to leave the meeting. Click Yes. The Save Meeting Files dialog box shown in Figure 8-14 appears.

Figure 8-14:
Depending
on your
privileges,
you can
save
elements of
your
meeting.

Your host will have set various privileges for the meeting, so what you can save will differ, but the options may include

- ✔ Shared Documents
- ✔ Poll Questionnaires
- ✔ Poll Results
- ✔ Chat
- ✔ Closed Captions

Select the items you want to save; if you like, you can click the Browse button and choose another location to save your file to. When you've made your selections, click Yes.

Don't forget to thank the host!

When you leave a meeting, a feedback form appears (see Figure 8-15) asking about your meeting experience. It's a polite gesture to fill in the form to let the host know what you thought of the meeting. This feedback helps the host and the host company to discover how to provide more effective online meeting experiences. When you've filled out the feedback form, click the Submit button to send in the form.

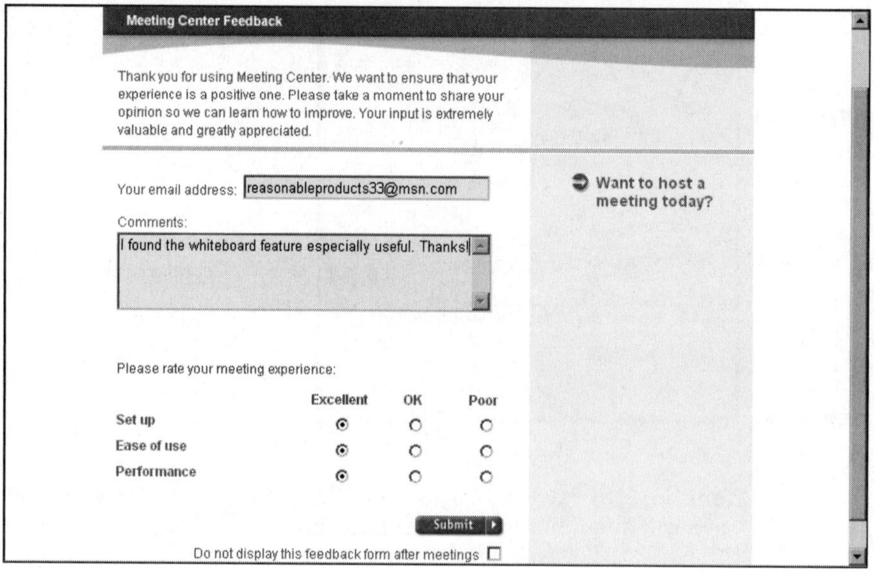

Figure 8-15:
Provide your
feedback to
help your
host make
future
meetings
better.

Part IV
Selling, Supporting, and Training with WebEx

The 5th Wave   By Rich Tennant

"I have to say, I am really impressed with the interactivity of this soap manufacturer's WebEx conference."

In this part . . .

WebEx is more than meetings and large-scale events. Through Support Center, Training Center, and Sales Center, you can take the power of online communication and commerce even further.

First, discover how to get the deal closed through Sales Center in Chapter 9. Set up an online support program all your own through Support Center in Chapter 10. And in Chapter 11, explore how to use the power of a virtual class-room to deliver information and training economically with Training Center.

Chapter 9

Closing More Deals Faster with Sales Center

....

In This Chapter

▶ Understanding roles in sales meetings/calls

▶ Setting up and using customer portals

▶ Scheduling sales meetings/calls

▶ Inviting sales team members and subject matter experts

▶ Monitoring sales meetings/calls

▶ Using the Sales Manager Report

▶ Pushing the presentation envelope with Presentation STUDIO

....

*R*emember the last time you set up a sales meeting with a customer? You had to catch a plane from Indianapolis to Detroit (routed through Salt Lake City), grab a cab to the customer's office, sign in, get a little plastic badge with your name misspelled on it, and sit for twenty minutes, only to have your customer's assistant come down to the lobby and tell you that her boss had to rush off that morning to the plant in Des Moines to fix a huge problem on the production line and that she sends her regrets. . . .

Sales meetings can be the lifeblood of your organization. They can help you land a new client, close a sale, or keep a current customer happy. But meeting in person can be costly and time-consuming, and meeting by phone is clumsy and doesn't allow you to share the information and documents that help you make your point. That's where a Sales Center online sales call comes in. In this intimate online meeting room, you can sit and chat with your customer, share applications on your desktop, get personal by showing yourself on video, and invite sales teams members, subject matter experts and prospects to join in on the fly. You can display presentations or even browse the Web together to demonstrate how you compare with the competition.

In this chapter, you discover the unique features of a sales meeting, how to set one up, and how to generate a sales meeting report when the meeting is over.

Understanding Roles in Sales Meetings

In WebEx Sales Center, the roles are slightly different than they are in WebEx Meeting Center. Here's the rundown on who's who:

- ✔ **Host:** Just as in Meeting Center, Sales Center meetings have a host who has a WebEx Sales Center user account. The host is normally the sales representative or the admin for the sales representative who schedules, starts, and controls the meeting. The host is also the person who assigns roles to others. At the outset, the host is the presenter, but the role of presenter can be handed to any other sales team member during the course of the meeting.

- ✔ **Presenter:** There's only one presenter at any given time; this is the person who holds the meeting floor, so to speak. The presenter shares and annotates presentations, documents, and the whiteboard. This person can also share software, and allow participants to take control of shared software applications. Presenters also can turn meeting options on and off, run polls, transfer files, and control live video feeds. The WebEx globe icon appears next to the current presenter's name in the Participants window in a sales meeting (see Figure 9-1).

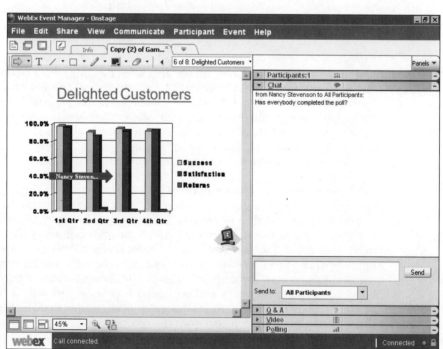

Figure 9-1:
A sales
meeting in
progress.

✔ **Sales Team Member:** This is a two-pronged type of role. A sales team member can be a sales manager, sales team colleague or a subject matter expert. By default, the host and the presenter are Sales team members. Invited sales team members typically observe the meeting rather than make presentations, although a subject matter expert may be called on to chip in his or her two cents. A sales team member may also take on the task of taking notes.

✔ **Expert:** The meeting host can invite an expert to join any meeting in progress by choosing Participant⇨Invite as Expert. The Participants List will designate anyone invited as an expert, and list his or her area of expertise. This is a quick way to get somebody "in the know" in the loop.

✔ **Prospect:** Ah, the golden prospect, the potential customer. Prospects can listen, chat, and share a desktop or document. This person can also share information if the current presenter hands over the reins, and he or she can also transfer files using the File Transfer feature. Sales Center provides a simpler, easy to use interface for the prospects that there is no learning needed to attend and experience the sales calls.

Setting Up and Using Portals

A communications portal is essentially a uniquely branded place on the Web where your prospects go to access documents, missed sales calls recordings, videos, or links to documents on the Website related to their account and even join the next sales call. You can post materials on the portal, and your prospects can direct others to the portal to view information about your company, in effect helping to sell your product or service for you. You can also include information about you, the sales rep and your sales team in the portal, such as your phone numbers or e-mail addresses.

Each portal is built around a specific account and *opportunity*. An opportunity is simply a word or phrase you designate that describes what kind of sales interaction you might have with this account; for example, if you are introducing a new product line to a large customer the opportunity might be *New Product Line*. When you create a portal, you can choose an existing account or create a new one, and specify an opportunity, either from those you've created in the past (such as a consulting opportunity or product sales opportunity), or by creating a new opportunity. Figure 9-2 shows a portal for my company. Notice that you can even personalize the portal with an image or logo.

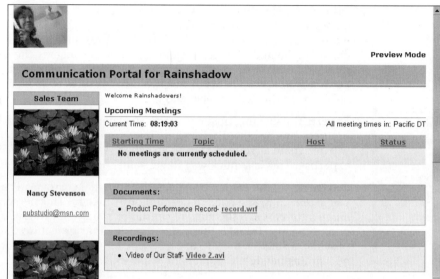

Figure 9-2:
A portal
shows
upcoming
meetings
associated
with this
account, as
well as
stored
documents.

To set up a portal, follow these steps:

1. **On the Sales Center page, click the Create Portal link in the Portals menu.**

   The Create Prospect Portal page shown in Figure 9-3 appears.

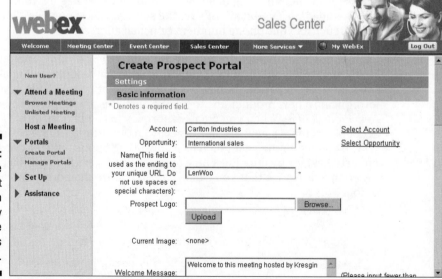

Figure 9-3:
Designate
an account
and an
opportunity
or create
new ones
here.

2. **Click the Select Account link.**

   The Select Account dialog box shown in Figure 9-4 appears.

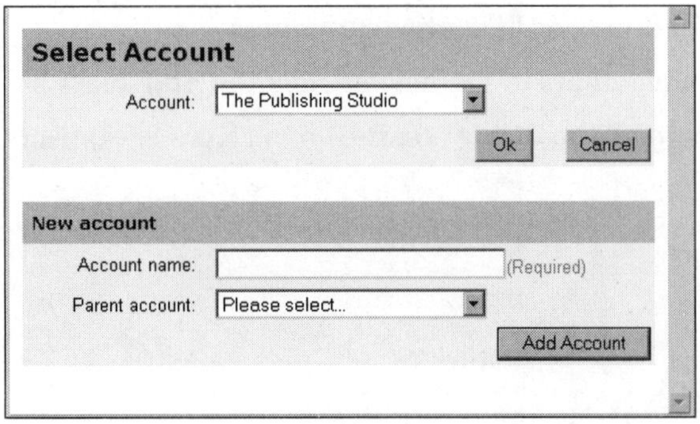

Figure 9-4:
Create a
new
account or
choose
an existing
one here.

Figure 9-4:
Create a
new
account or
choose
an existing
one here.

3. **To select an existing account, choose it from the Account drop-down list. To create a new account, enter a name in the Account Name text box; if the account has a parent account — for example, if it's a division or subsidiary of an existing account — select that account from the Parent Account drop-down list.**

4. **Click Add Account.**

   The account you just selected or created appears in the Account field.

5. **Click OK to specify the account.**

   You return to the Create Prospect Portal page.

6. **Click the Select Opportunity link.**

   The Select Opportunity dialog box appears.

7. **To select an existing opportunity, choose it from the Opportunity drop-down list. To create a new opportunity, enter a name in the Opportunity Name text box.**

8. **Click Add Opportunity.**

   The opportunity you just selected or created appears in the Account field.

9. **Click OK to specify the opportunity.**

   You return to the Create Prospect Portal page.

10. **To upload a logo or other image, click the Browse button; in the Choose File dialog box that appears, locate the file and click the Open button. Click the Upload button to upload the image file.**

11. **Enter your welcome message for the portal in the Welcome Message text box.**

12. **If you want to allow your prospect to invite others into the portal, select the Prospect Can Invite Others check box.**

13. **In the Options section of the page, select various check boxes to add elements of your and your team's profiles to the page, such as e-mail addresses, photos, or office phone numbers.**

14. **To add team members to the portal, click the Add Team button.**

    The Select Sales Team dialog box shown in Figure 9-5 appears.

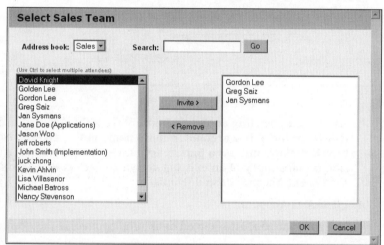

Figure 9-5:
Folks in your
address
book will
automatic-
ally be listed
here.

15. **Select a team member's name and then click Invite. Repeat this for each team member you want to add to the portal and then click OK.**

16. **To add a recording, URL link, or document to the portal, click the appropriate button, and then locate and upload the file.**

17. **In the Invite section of the page, click the Add Users button to display the Select Prospects dialog box shown in Figure 9-6. Invite any users you want and then click OK.**

18. **Click Submit to finish creating the portal.**

    The Portal Management page appears (see Figure 9-7), showing all your portals. To open a portal, click the link under the Portal column.

You can display the Portal Management page at any time by clicking the Manage Portal link in the Portals menu of Sales Center. To make changes to the portal, simply click the Edit icon in the Action column on the Portal Management page.

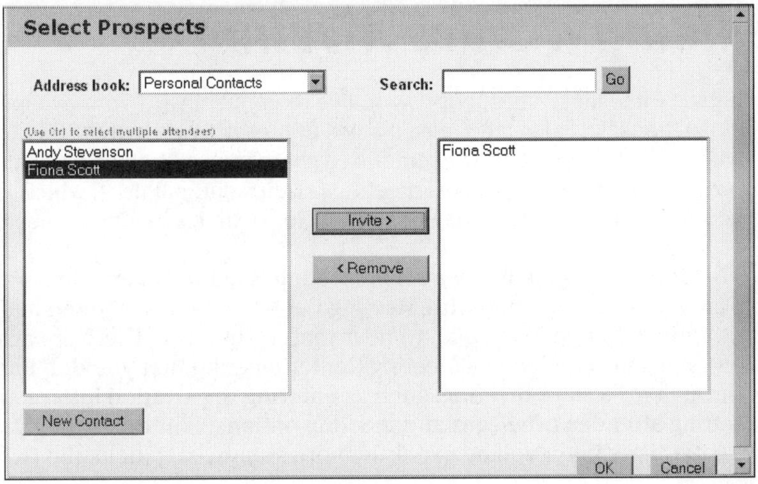

Figure 9-6:
Choose an existing user from your personal or other address book.

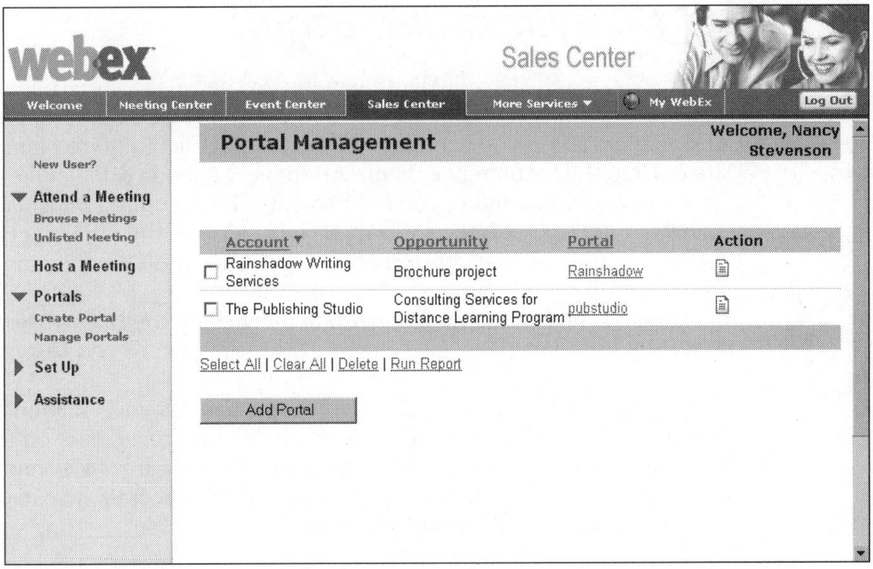

Figure 9-7:
All your portals are listed on the Portal Management page.

Each of the folks you invite to your portal will receive an e-mail with a link to the portal and a link to your e-mail address to contact you with any questions. Just to close the e-mail loop, you will also receive an e-mail confirming that those you invited have been sent their e-mails.

Scheduling a Sales Meeting

If you're like most salespeople, you live to connect with your prospects and close that sale. Sales meetings in Sales Center provide a great way to hook up with prospects or existing accounts to share information or presentations. The process of scheduling a sales meeting is quick and painless, which is lucky for you because you're too busy to spend a lot of time scheduling meetings.

The process of scheduling a sales meeting is actually very similar to that of scheduling a meeting with Meeting Center, which is covered in detail in Chapter 4. But you'll be glad to hear that it's quicker: There are actually a few steps in scheduling a Meeting Center meeting that you don't have to go through for a sales meeting, such as entering registration information and setting attendee privileges and meeting options. I hit the highlights for Sales Center here, but if you need a little more step-by-step help, flip to Chapter 4.

Let the scheduling begin!

Start by clicking the Host a Meeting menu on the Sales Center page. As you can see in the first page that appears, shown in Figure 9-8, there are seven sections of information you can enter to start a meeting: Required Information, Date & Time, Teleconference, Invite Attendees, Agenda & Welcome, Emails, and Review. At a minimum, you have to enter the Required Information. After you have entered that information, you can go on to the other sections and fill them in, or click the Start button at any time and begin the meeting.

You can also start scheduling a meeting by clicking the Host a Meeting link on the WebEx Welcome page.

On the Required Information page, you can use the Select Account and Select Opportunity links to choose these items from drop-down lists on the pages that appear. The Select Account page is shown in Figure 9-4. If you haven't created any accounts or opportunities by creating portals, you can create one now within this dialog box. (See the earlier section, "Setting Up and Using Portals," for instructions on how to do this.)

After you return to the Required Information page, enter and confirm a meeting password (note that this may or may not be mandatory, depending on how your site administrator has set things up) and click Next. The Date & Time page shown in Figure 9-9 appears. Use the various fields to specify the date, time, duration, e-mail reminders you'd like to send, and recurrence for the meeting (if any). Click Next.

You can also click the button for each of the sections to go to them in any sequence you like, rather than clicking Next.

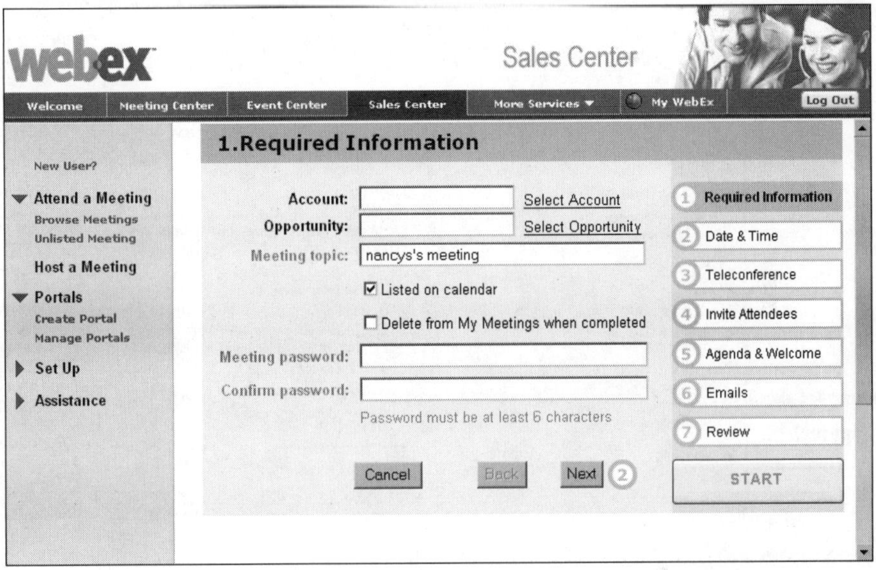

Figure 9-8:
The
Required
Information
for starting
a sales
meeting.

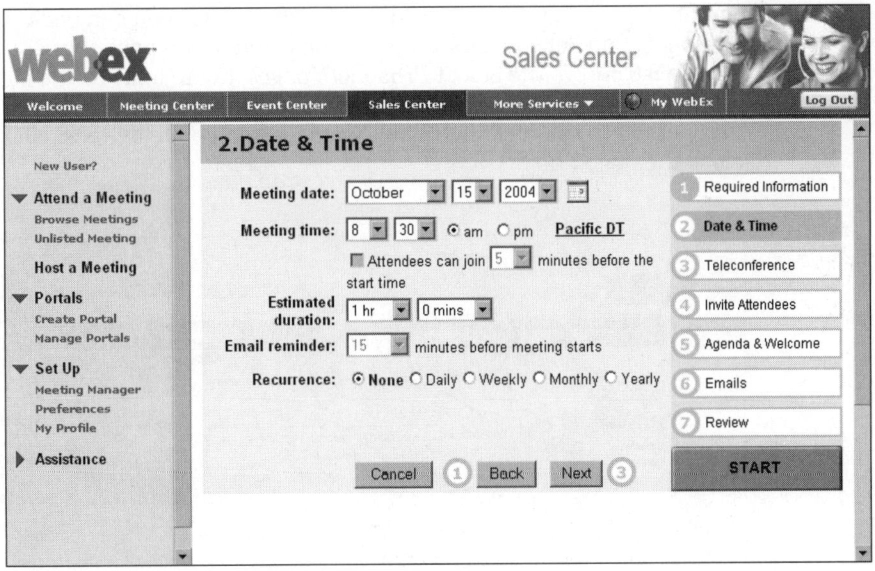

Figure 9-9:
Set the date
for your
meeting
here.

The Teleconference page shown in Figure 9-10 appears. On this page, you set up which (if any) teleconference service to use (WebEx's own or a third party's). If you use WebEx's teleconferencing service, you can also designate whether attendees should call in or receive a call back; and what sound (if any) is heard when somebody enters or exits the meeting. Adjust these settings and then click Next.

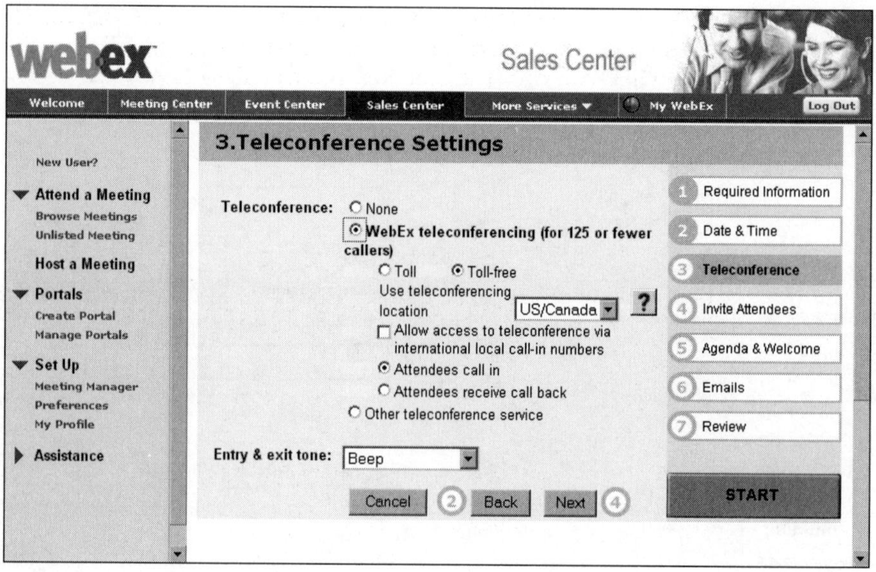

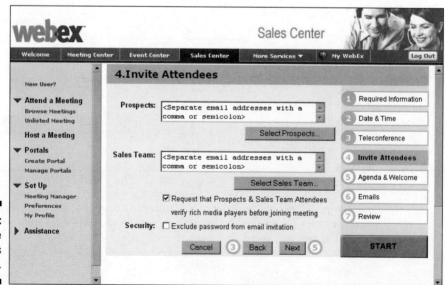

Figure 9-10:
The Tele-
conference
page.

On the Invite Attendees page shown in Figure 9-11, you can click the Select Prospects and Select Sales Team buttons, and in the page that appears (Figure 9-6 shows the Select Prospects page), invite folks to the meeting. When a dialog box opens, select a name and click the Invite button to invite that person to the meeting. When you've selected all invitees, click OK to close the dialog box.

Figure 9-11:
The Invite
Attendees
page.

When you click Next to move to the Agenda & Welcome page (see Figure 9-12), you can enter agenda items in the Agenda field and upload a file that will appear when you start the meeting. You can also control playback by choosing either the Start Automatically or Continuous Play button. Click Next when you finish.

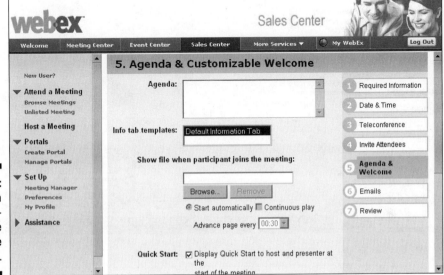

Figure 9-12:
The Agenda & Customizable Welcome page.

On the Emails page shown in Figure 9-13, you can leave the default messages or enter personalized messages for both prospects and your sales team.

Those are all the choices available to you. Now it's time to make sure you got things right and get the meeting going. Click Next.

Reviewing your settings and starting the meeting

The final page in the sales meeting scheduling sequence is the Review page (see Figure 9-16). This shows you all the choices you just made (see Figure 9-14). If you see that something's amiss, just click one of the numbered items to the right and go back and make corrections.

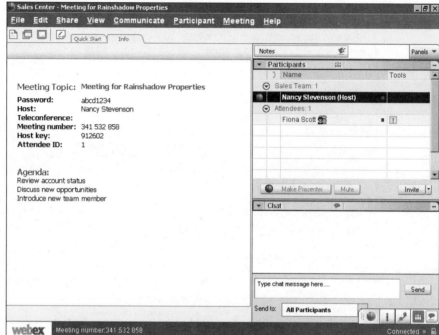

Figure 9-13:
Here's
where you
control
e-mail
messages
about the
meeting.

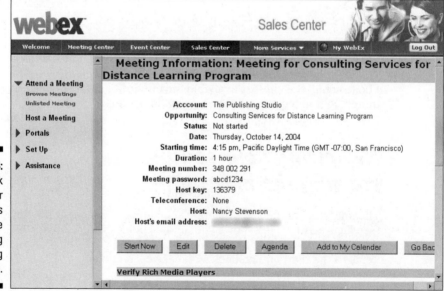

Figure 9-14:
Take a look
at all your
choices
before
scheduling
or starting
the meeting.

When you're happy with your meeting settings, you have three options:

- ✔ If you have not specified a date and time, click the Start button to start the meeting immediately.

- ✔ If you specified a date and time for the meeting, click the Schedule button. A page appears giving you the option of starting the meeting immediately. If you're not ready to start right now, that's fine; when you are ready to meet, just go to the Sales Center area of WebEx, locate the meeting on the Attend a Meeting menu, and click the meeting link. When the meeting overview shown in Figure 9-14 appears, click the Start Now button.

- ✔ Click the link in the confirmation e-mail. WebEx sends you to the page shown in Figure 9-14. Click the Start Now button.

Though there's no Instant Meeting option on the Sales Center page, you can set up an Instant Meeting for Sales Center by following these steps:

1. **Go to My WebEx.**

2. **Select My WebEx Meetings.**

3. **Click the One-Click Meeting tab.**

4. **Under Service Type, select Sales Center Sales Session to set up a Sales Center meeting.**

Seeing and Monitoring Sales Meetings from Different Perspectives

If you're the sales manager, you can make use of a unique feature that allows you to observe your sales reps in action with accounts. Because nobody will know you're attending, this is called *silent monitoring*. Using this feature helps you to coach your sales reps. This ability is usually restricted to managers by your site administrator.

Another handy feature allows a meeting host to see your meeting from your prospect's perspective. Being able to see the meeting from the participant's perspective helps you get another look at your own presentation so that you can fine-tune it. During a meeting, the host opens another browser window and goes to My Meeting on his or her WebEx site. Click the Prospect View link there, and you'll join the meeting, seeing what the participants see.

Finally, there's another monitoring feature called the Participant Attention indicator. This icon tells you a couple of things about the prospect's desktop that allows you to know whether he or she is paying attention or playing Minesweeper: The indicator appears next to a name in the Participant's panel if that participant has either minimized the meeting client window or opened another window on top of the meeting client window.

If your prospect joined the meeting as a group huddled around a single PC and they entered the name of each person in the group, you'll only see a group icon in the Participants List (see Figure 9-15). Click the group icon to see a list of all the folks attending.

What do you do if you find your meeting looks dull from the participant's perspective, or if she keeps opening other windows on her desktop? Time to spice things up. Ask some interesting questions in chat, or have the current presenter ask the prospect to share a document or application with others in the meeting.

Another great way to know how your prospects experience your meeting is to encourage them to fill out the feedback form that appears automatically when the meeting ends.

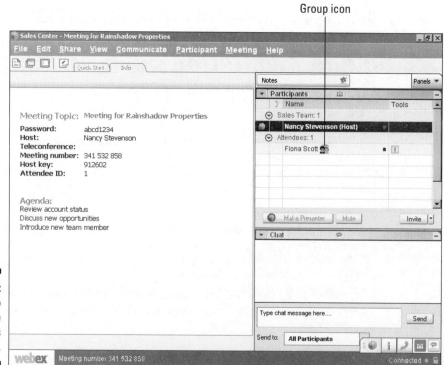

Group icon

Figure 9-15:
The Group icon in the Participants Panel.

Using the Sales Meeting Report

The Sales Meeting Report provides usage information about Sales Center meetings for a specified time period. If you're the manager of a group of salespeople, you can use this report to keep track of your group's communications with customers and prospects. If you are a salesperson with lots of accounts to juggle, review your own sales meeting activity to spot accounts or prospects that haven't had a meeting in a while so you can set one up.

To generate a Sales Meeting Report, follow these steps:

1. **Go to the My WebEx page and click My Reports.**

2. **Click the Sales Center Reports link.**

3. **On the Sales Center Reports page that appears, click the Sales Meeting Report link.**

   The Sales Meeting Report page shown in Figure 9-16 appears.

Figure 9-16: Specify the range of dates the report should cover.

4. **Select dates from the drop-down lists in the From and To fields to specify the starting and ending dates of the range you want the report to cover.**

5. **If you want to see information for every meeting, leave the All Meetings radio button selected; if you want to see reports for only certain accounts, click the Select Accounts radio button and then select any accounts you want to include from the list that appears (hold down the Ctrl key to select more than one account).**

6. **Choose an option in the Sort Results By drop-down list.**

7. **Click the Display Report button.**

   The report appears, looking a lot like the example shown in Figure 9-17.

Figure 9-17: A sample Sales Meeting Report.

The report shows activity on all accounts you selected in Step 5. If you want more detail about a particular item, click the link in the Topic column for that session and it is displayed (see Figure 9-18), including the start and end time of the meeting, and the prospects and sales team members who attended. Note that you can click the Export Report button in this detailed report to save it in Excel's comma-separated-value format.

Sales Managers can also generate reports that provide an overview of the sales meetings hosted by those who report to them. Choose the Sales Manager Report from the My Reports area to generate this report.

Want to quickly review all administrative activity on a WebEx account? Click the Manage Portals link in the Portals menu in Sales Center, select the check box for an account, and then click the Run Report link. You'll see a record of all kinds of activities, from creating a portal to adding documents. (See Figure 9-19.)

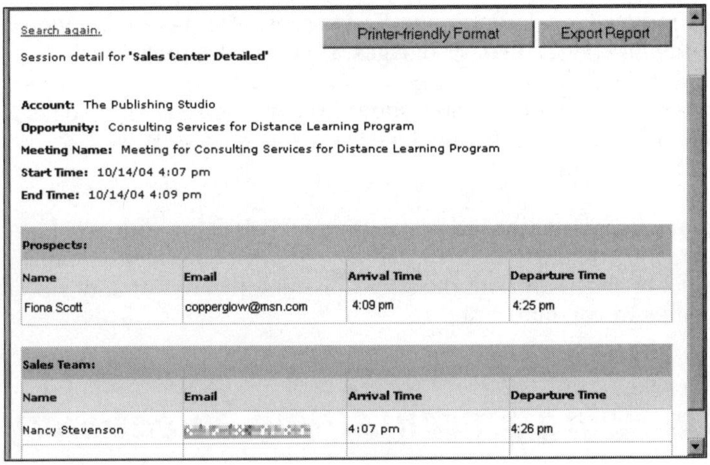

Figure 9-18:
Details about a particular sales meeting.

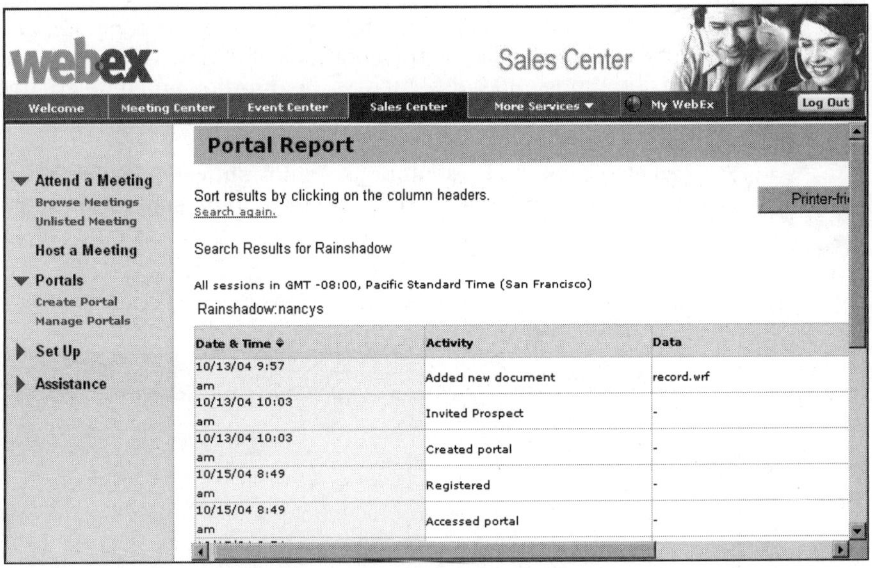

Search again.

Session detail for **'Sales Center Detailed'**

Account: The Publishing Studio
Opportunity: Consulting Services for Distance Learning Program
Meeting Name: Meeting for Consulting Services for Distance Learning Program
Start Time: 10/14/04 4:07 pm
End Time: 10/14/04 4:09 pm

Printer-friendly Format   **Export Report**

Prospects:

Name	Email	Arrival Time	Departure Time
Fiona Scott	copperglow@msn.com	4:09 pm	4:25 pm

Sales Team:

Name	Email	Arrival Time	Departure Time
Nancy Stevenson		4:07 pm	4:26 pm

Figure 9-19:
The Portal Report.

webex   Sales Center

Welcome   Meeting Center   Event Center   Sales Center   More Services ▾   My WebEx   Log Out

Portal Report

▾ **Attend a Meeting**
  Browse Meetings
  Unlisted Meeting
  Host a Meeting
▾ **Portals**
  Create Portal
  Manage Portals
▶ **Set Up**
▶ **Assistance**

Sort results by clicking on the column headers.
Search again.

Search Results for Rainshadow

All sessions in GMT -08:00, Pacific Standard Time (San Francisco)

Rainshadow:nancys

Date & Time ⬍	Activity	Data
10/13/04 9:57 am	Added new document	record.wrf
10/13/04 10:03 am	Invited Prospect	-
10/13/04 10:03 am	Created portal	-
10/15/04 8:49 am	Registered	-
10/15/04 8:49 am	Accessed portal	-

Printer-fri

Managing Presentations with Presentation STUDIO™

Being able to run sales sessions is one thing, but bringing dynamic presentation content to each session is another. Presentation STUDIO is an add-on product you can purchase from WebEx that allows you to play, manage, and deliver dynamic presentations. These presentations can include PowerPoint slides, narration, video, Web pages, surveys, and quizzes.

Many WebEx customers rave about Presentation STUDIO, so it's worth a quick overview here. If it intrigues you, talk to your WebEx account manager about purchasing it.

You must have purchased Presentation STUDIO for your WebEx account to use it, and you must log in to use the STUDIO. Your site administrator will designate which areas of the site each person can visit and use, so features available to you may differ.

Managing presentations by category

With Presentation STUDIO you get an easy-to-use interface (see Figure 9-20) where all your presentations are listed by category. Use the Search feature on this page to enter a keyword to find your presentation, or simply click on a category to display a list of presentations within it. This list shows you information about presentations, such as the duration and date created, and to playback presentations on demand (see Figure 9-21).

You can also click the Presentations All link shown in Figure 9-20 to display all presentations for your account rather than presentation categories.

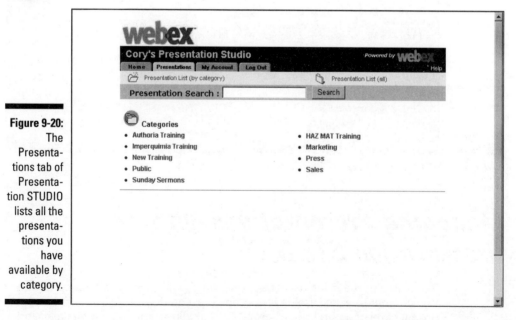

Figure 9-20:
The Presentations tab of Presentation STUDIO lists all the presentations you have available by category.

When you click on the More Options link for any presentation in the list shown in Figure 9-21, you get tools to manage playback settings and to down-load the file to your computer or PocketPC.

Playing back presentations

In the More Options window for any presentation, you can click the Audio/ Slides Playback or Slides Only Playback icons and use the media player that appears (see Figure 9-22) to review your presentation. You can click the Change the Player Setting button (it looks like a little bulleted list) to set which media player you want to use from those you have installed on your computer.

Use the Search tab in the media player to look for a particular slide, and the Notes tab to enter notes about the presentation.

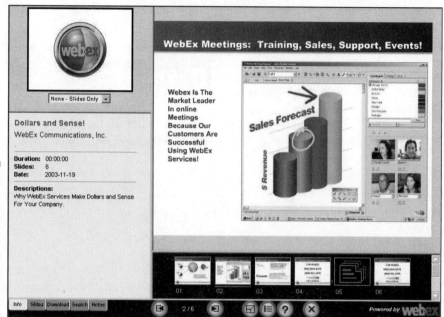

Figure 9-22:
Jump
around your
slides and
download
the
presentation
from here if
you wish.

Chapter 10

Delivering Virtual Support
with Support Center

You used an online support service yourself when you contacted that major software manufacturer last year to find out why the four-hundred-dollar piece of software you just installed crashed your computer. Little did you suspect that someday you might have to create your own means of online support for your customers.

WebEx's Support Center is a like a virtual cubicle that you and your supportee (whether a customer or an employee) can slide into to chat about problems, walk through a process on a shared application or desktop, and generally discover solutions.

In this chapter, I explore the time- and money-saving possibilities of supporting your customers or employees online.

Understanding How Support Center Works

If you're in a technical business that provides computer or software solutions to customers, you might find that WebEx's Support Center is an off-the-shelf solution that works right from the get-go. It's economical and easy to use — and best of all, you don't have to install or maintain a thing.

A word about SMARTtech

SMARTtech is a Web-based technology that enables you to create a remote-access and remote-management network of computers. If you're in the IT department, using SMARTtech allows you to resolve support issues without ever stepping foot out of the information technology (IT) department. (This should appeal to shy IT types.)

With SMARTtech, you can securely access any systems on your network from a Web browser, even if you're on the road to Morocco. You can also work with other experts to resolve problems live online. If your company gets set up with a WebEx site, have your site administrator check out all the advantages of SMARTtech with your WebEx account manager.

It's tech support . . .

Support Center provides a virtual meeting place where you can provide one-on-one support. The ideal application of Support Center is troubleshooting technical problems that occur within a software application, operating system, or network environment. In this scenario, your support staff can

- ✔ Take a look at what is going on with the customer's or employee's system by sharing the application or desktop.
- ✔ Use the System Info feature to see key system information instantly.
- ✔ Transfer necessary patches and log files to and from a customer's or an employee's computer.
- ✔ Take remote control of your user's system or give him control of yours.

Here's a technical word to the wise: WebEx's Support Center is easy to implement because it works through virtually all firewalls. It's secure, but you don't run into barriers every time you try to connect to your customers.

. . . but it's more than tech support

What if you sell grapefruit online instead of computer software? Maybe you simply want an environment where you can meet with your Web site's customers to discuss issues related to your products or services. You might also consider Support Center as a place to go to share files, chat, demonstrate processes or procedures), or transfer documents.

Support Center can be a useful tool for your business because it

✔ Provides instant support sessions to solve trouble on the spot.

✔ Allows support staff to add a face and a voice to the interaction with video and chat.

✔ Gives you a place to share documentation or demos.

✔ Offers access from virtually anyplace in the world that has a Web connection.

Starting Up: Getting a Support Session Going

Starting a support session is about as easy as falling off a log (and a lot less painful). Simply go to your WebEx site; on the Welcome page, click the Start Session link under Support Center. (You can also go to the Support Center page and click the Start link located there; see Figure 10-1.)

You can also set up One Click Meeting so that you can start sessions from your desktop, browser, or even Microsoft Office applications. See Chapter 6 for more about how to do this.

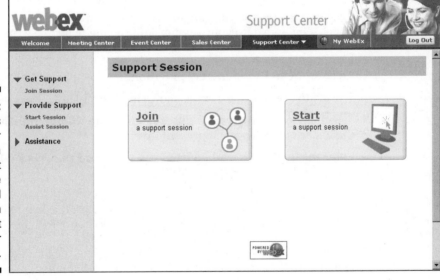

Figure 10-1: The choices to Start or Join a support session are front and center on the Support Center page.

When you start a session, WebEx takes a few moments to prepare the session and download or update Support Manager. Then you see your support window page, looking just like the one shown in Figure 10-2 (except that you don't have any customer in the session — yet!).

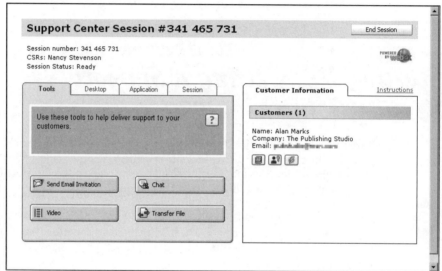

Figure 10-2:
A support session in action.

When you start a session, you can do darn little until a customer joins. So, it's time to get somebody into your session. You can invite people to your session by following these steps:

1. **Click the Send E-mail Invitation button.**

   The Invite Users dialog box, as shown in Figure 10-3, appears.

2. **Select one of the two radio buttons to indicate whether the invitee is a Customer or a Support Representative.**

3. **Enter the invitee's e-mail address and name and then click OK.**

   The invitation is on its way.

Your customer can also go to your WebEx site and click the Join button on the Support Center or Welcome page to join the session.

If for some reason you don't want to invite people over the Internet, you can always invite them over sneakernet. Simply note the Support Session Number of your session, walk over to the person whom you want to invite (or phone her up), let her know about the session, and give her the Support Session Number.

Now just sit tight until your customer joins in.

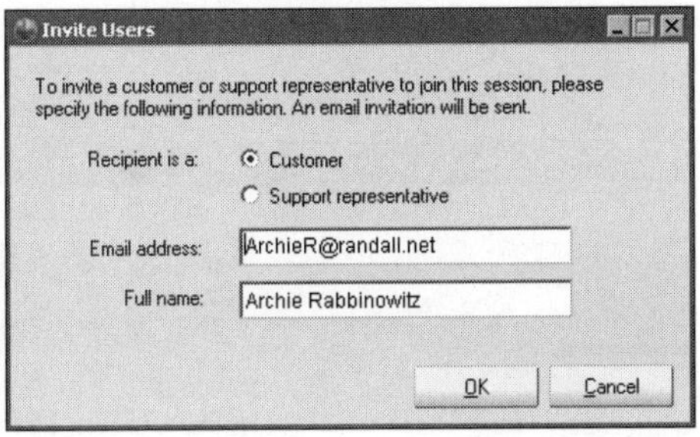

Figure 10-3:
The Invite
Users dialog
box.

Jumping on the Support Bandwagon

Anybody with access to a WebEx site that includes the Support Center feature can start a support session and have others join. The person who starts a session is called the *support technician*.

Whoever started the thing, if somebody else starts the session and you want to get in on it, you can do so by joining or by assisting in a session.

Joining a session

When you're invited to a support session, you can get into the session in a couple of ways:

- ✔ If you receive an e-mail invitation, just click the link in the e-mail.
- ✔ If you're invited in some other fashion (by phone, or on-the-fly in the hallway, for example), you can join through your WebEx site. Go to the Welcome page and click the Join link for Support Center or go to the Support Center page and click the Join link there.

Either of these methods takes you to the Pre-Session form, as shown in Figure 10-4. If you didn't follow an e-mail link, you must enter the Support Session Number, which you have to get from the person who is running the session. Enter your first name, last name, e-mail address, and company name, and then click Submit.

After you click Submit, the screen shown in Figure 10-5 appears. Here you can either click the Chat button to initiate a chat or click the Leave Session button to exit (but hey, you just got here!). Note the Video button, which you can read about more about in the later section, "Using video."

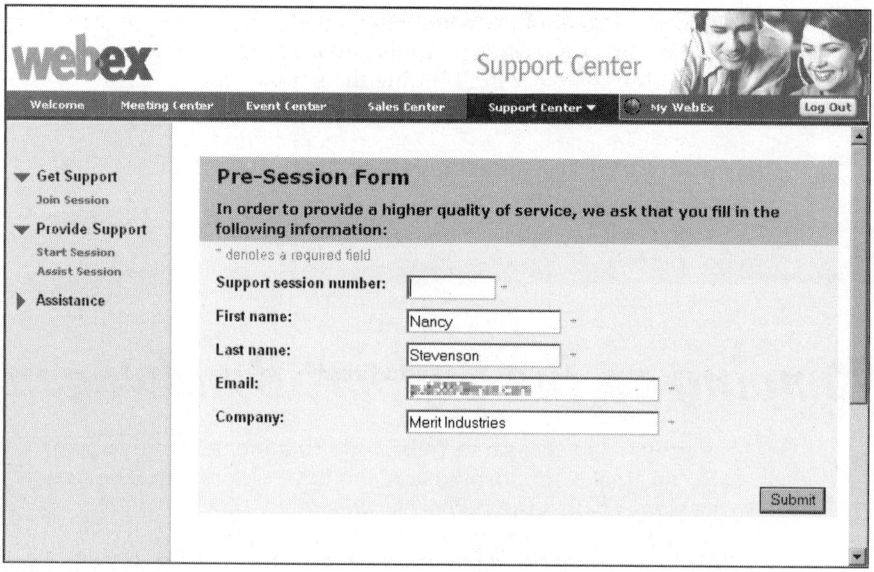

Figure 10-4:
The Pre-Session signup form.

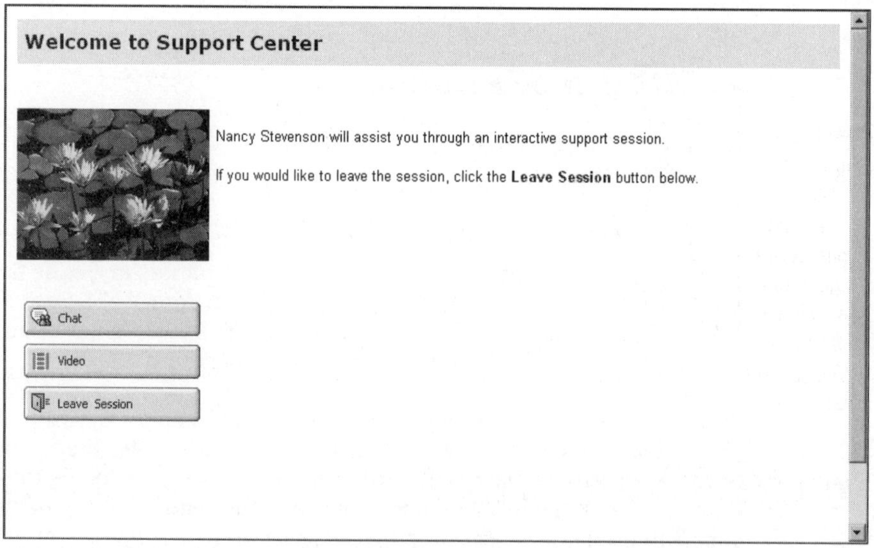

Figure 10-5:
When you join a session somebody else started, this is what you see.

Assisting the support effort

Sometimes you want somebody who isn't a customer or a support representative to join a support. For example, wouldn't it be nice to have an engineer join in a support session to review the problem the customer is having with the latest and greatest version of your product? That involves joining through the Assist Session link. When you join a support session in an assisting capacity, you see the same tools and options the session initiator sees (see Figure 10-2). The person running the session can turn over control of the session to you by clicking the Transfer Session button on the Session tab.

To join a support session in an assisting capacity, follow these steps:

1. **From the Support Center page, click the Assist Session link in the Provide Support menu.**

   The Assist Support Session in Progress page, as shown in Figure 10-6, appears.

2. **Enter the Support Session Number and then click Join.**

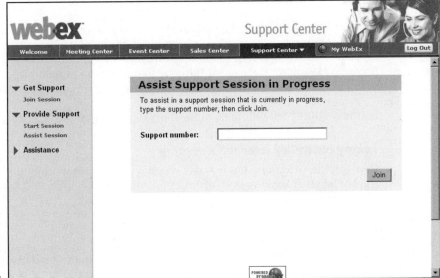

Figure 10-6: Fill in the session number to get into a session in progress.

Getting Supportive

It's time to sit down in a support session and see just what goes on. In a nutshell, here's what you can do:

- ✔ Share a desktop or applications, or transfer files.
- ✔ Take a look at your customer's system information; log in to, or reboot the customer's computer.
- ✔ Chat in an instant messaging format.

✔ Share a video feed with your customer.

✔ Record your support session.

Whether you're supporting a network or software application user or perhaps answering questions about a new procedure or product, you'll find that the tools offered in a support session are easy to use and effective.

Many of the features covered as an overview here are the same as those used in the Meeting Center although they are accessed in the support session environment. For more information about sharing and using other tools in an online WebEx environment, see Chapter 7.

Taking control

How often have you called a technical support person about a problem with your computer, only to spend many minutes explaining what you're seeing on your screen and trying to enact commands that this faceless phone voice provides? Wouldn't the easiest thing be to just let the person take control of your computer and do the troubleshooting firsthand? Of course it would.

In this section, I tell you the simple steps to gaining or giving such control.

Taking control of someone's desktop

Here are the two ways that you can share a desktop: View somebody's desktop (or let them view yours), or take control of somebody's desktop (or let them control yours).

When you control somebody's desktop, you can

✔ Work in the desktop as if you were sitting right in front of their computer.

✔ Annotate on the desktop by using a highlighter tool.

✔ Troubleshoot software problems without ever having to stir from your comfy chair.

To view or control a customer's desktop, in the support session window, perform the following steps:

1. **Click the Desktop tab to display it (see Figure 10-7).**

2. **Click Request View to view the customer's desktop, or click Request Control to view *and* control the customer's desktop.**

   No matter which button you click, a dialog box will tell the customer either that the support rep (you) would like to view her desktop or that you would like to control her desktop (see Figure 10-8). In either case, the customer simply either clicks OK to allow the sharing or clicks Cancel to deny the request.

3. The customer should click OK to accept.

The shared desktop appears. A little green button labeled Sharing appears in the upper-right corner (see Figure 10-9).

To end sharing, click the Stop Sharing icon from the floating icon tray.

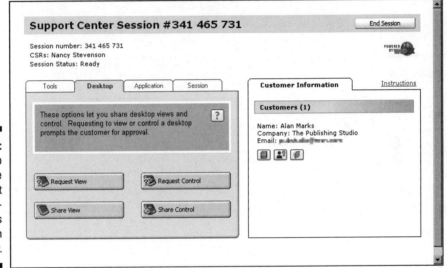

Figure 10-7: The Desktop tab of the support representative's session window.

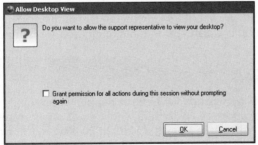

Figure 10-8: This message asks to let the representative view a customer's desktop.

Sharing menu

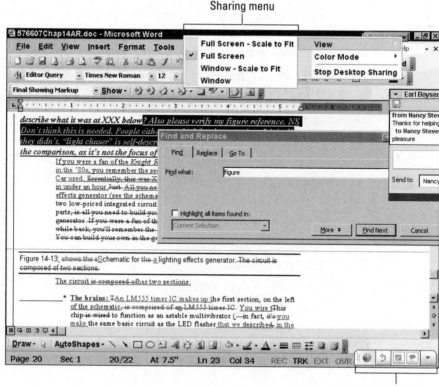

Figure 10-9:
A shared
desktop
with a word
processor
displayed
and the
Sharing
menu open.

WebEx toolbar

To switch control back and forth between you and the customer, just click the desktop, and control is given to the other person.

If your customer is a bit shy about giving you control of his desktop, you can request to view-only and use annotation tools to guide the customer through fixing the problem.

Sharing applications

Sharing applications is very handy for helping people understand how to use software features or supporting customers who are not comfortable sharing their entire desktops. You might also share an application to run a demo of a procedure or product to help a support-needy customer understand the features better.

Sharing applications is simple and very similar to the process for sharing a desktop. To share an application, follow these steps:

1. **Click the Application tab to display it (see Figure 10-10).**

Figure 10-10:
The
Application
tab in the
support
session
window.

2. **Click Request View to view the customer's application, or click Share View to provide a view of an application on your computer for the customer.**

   No matter which button you click, a dialog box appears to the customer that says you would like to view his application or that you would like to show him an application of yours (see Figure 10-11).

3. **The customer should click OK to accept.**

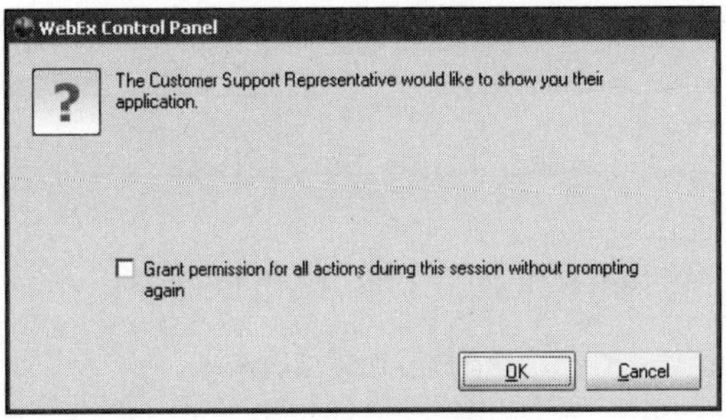

Figure 10-11:
Customers
must
confirm
the sharing
of an
application.

The Application View or Application Control dialog box appears, depending on the button that you choose in Step 2.

4. **Choose an application from the Share a Currently Running Application list and then click the Share button.**

TIP

If you want to share an application that's not currently running, click the New Application button in the Application View or the Application Control dialog box.

When sharing an application, you have access to a Sharing menu and WebEx tools, just as you do when sharing a desktop. Use these to annotate, change the view to full screen, change the color mode to higher resolution, or stop sharing.

Taking control of a customer's computer

Sometimes you need to delve deeper into a customer's computer system to troubleshoot a problem. Luckily, the support session window has a Customer Information section with three little tools, as shown in Figure 10-12. The little buttons in this section come in mighty handy. Here's what they do:

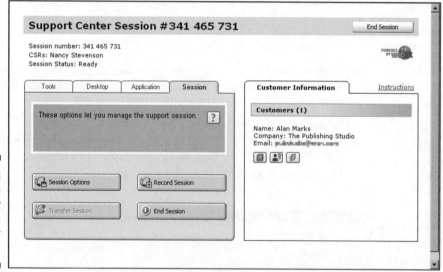

Figure 10-12:
The session window including Customer Information.

✔ The System Information tool on the far left displays information about the customer's computer system (see Figure 10-13), including hardware, installed software, browser, and running software.

✔ The Log On as a Different User button allows you to log on to the customer's system as a different user. For example, a network administrator might log on with her own account information to be able to use certain access rights to make a change to the customers system.

✔ The Reboot Computer button does just what it says: It requests that the customer give you permission to reboot his or her computer. This action might be required to put new settings on the customer's system into effect, for example.

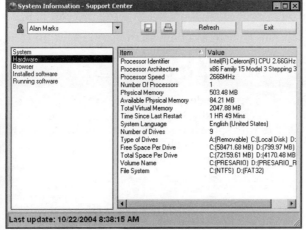

System Information - Support Center

Alan Marks ▼ | | | Refresh | Exit

System	Item	Value
Hardware	Processor Identifier	Intel(R) Celeron(R) CPU 2.66GHz
Browser	Processor Architecture	x86 Family 15 Model 3 Stepping 3
Installed software	Processor Speed	2666MHz
Running software	Number Of Processors	1
	Physical Memory	503.48 MB
	Available Physical Memory	84.21 MB
	Total Virtual Memory	2047.88 MB
	Time Since Last Restart	1 HR 49 Mins
	System Language	English (United States)
	Number of Drives	9
	Type of Drives	A:(Removable) C:(Local Disk) D:
	Free Space Per Drive	C:(58471.68 MB) D:(799.97 MB)
	Total Space Per Drive	C:(72159.61 MB) D:(4170.48 MB
	Volume Name	C:(PRESARIO) D:(PRESARIO_R
	File System	C:(NTFS) D:(FAT32)

Last update: 10/22/2004 8:38:15 AM

Figure 10-13:
Your customer's computer system information.

The Log On as a Different User and Reboot Computer buttons both present a dialog box to the customer, requesting permission for the action. The customer clicks OK, and the action is allowed.

You can also access network and mapped drives on yours and customer's computer if you need network information to solve a problem.

Transferring files

Error code #154-J? Ah . . . one of my favorites. I just happen to have a white paper on that error you should read. . . .

When it's time to share a file or document with a customer to show the steps necessary to meet a support need, just transfer the file to him while in a support session so he can be empowered to fix it himself in case the same problem happens again. Here's how:

1. **On the Tools area of the session window, click the Transfer Files button.**

   A dialog box appears, allowing you to choose between File Transfer Advanced and File Transfer Basic. File Transfer Advanced gives you a full view of all the file directories on your and customer's computer. File Transfer Basic allows you to select the files to transfer, keeping your file directories to yourself. You can also deliver files directly to a specific file directory or folder on your customer's computer, which is a really secure way to transfer files.

2. **Leaving the default Advanced setting, click OK to proceed.**

   An Allow File Transfers dialog box appears on the customer's screen.

3. **The customer should click OK to allow the transfer to proceed.**

   The WebEx File Transfer window, as shown in Figure 10-14, appears.

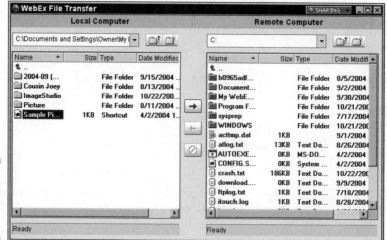

Figure 10-14:
Choosing
files to
transfer.

4. **If you are set up with advanced options, you can now go to the folder on the Remote Computer where you want to upload the file by clicking the Up One Level button or by double-clicking folders to open them.**

5. **Select the file that you want to transfer from in the Local Computer area and then click the right-pointing arrow to upload a copy of the file to the location on the remote computer that you select in Step 4.**

6. **To get a file from the remote computer and send it to your local computer, select the file from the Remote Computer area and click the left-pointing arrow.**

When you finish transferring files, click the Close button in the top-right corner of the window.

Note the Create New Folder button for both the local and remote computer, which you can use to place files in a folder that you create just for your files. You can also delete folders, delete files, and rename files.

You can also access network and mapped drives on your computer and the customer's computer.

Chatting

Chatting in a support session works just like chatting in any online meeting. (See Chapter 7 for more about chatting.) Both you and your customer have a chat button on your session page. When you or your customer clicks the Chat button, the floating Chat window appears (see Figure 10-15). Enter a comment and then click Send, and the window appears in the Chat window. The customer can then enter a comment, click Send, and so on, allowing you to happily chat back and forth.

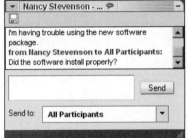

Figure 10-15: The support session chat window.

Chat in a support session can also be invoked from a shared application or shared desktop environment, so you can compare notes on what you're both looking at or make suggestions or provide information to each other. Use the Chat tool in the Floating Icon tray to do this.

To quickly save a chat, click the Save icon (it looks like a little computer disk) in the upper-left corner of the Chat window.

Getting personal with video

Nothing gets you up close and personal with a customer in need like a smile and a nod of encouragement. But how do you do that online? One word: video. With a simple Webcam setup, you can help your customer place a face with your words of support. Session Manager software automatically detects any Webcam connected to a participant's computer.

Note that the customer doesn't have to have a Webcam set up to watch you on video. Also, consider using video to show more than just yourself: Show products, procedures, or whatever you want!

Fine-tuning video

In the video window, you can find an Options button. Click it, and a dialog box offering several options appears. You can increase the video frame rate, which makes it feed faster but can degrade the quality. The Video Resolution setting allows for low, medium, and high resolution.

This setting can also have an impact on how smoothly the video appears to the viewer. An Advanced Options button opens a dialog box in which you can more finely control settings for your specific camera, such as brightness.

Both you and your customer have a Video button on your session window page (although, at first, your customer's is inaccessible). You initiate the video process by clicking your Video button, and two things happen: The Video window (see Figure 10-16) appears, and the Video button on your customer's window becomes available. In this way, you can share video of each other as long as you each have some sort of Webcam set up at your desks.

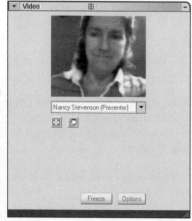

Figure 10-16: A Video window makes things up close and personal.

If you want the focus to be on your own talking head, click the Full Screen tool right under the video display. Click the View Session Window button to return to the floating window view.

Recording your session

A great support session can form the basis for training or helping other users or can simply be a useful archive in a frequently asked-questions (FAQ) library.

Recording a support session records all on-screen activity — such as video, shared applications or desktops, or chat — and is simplicity itself. The site administrator has to set up auto recording as an option for support sessions, so if the feature isn't working, give this guy or gal a jingle or ping.

If you want to capture audio, alas, it's not quite so simple. You have to attach a phone-recording adapter to your computer and phone. No network-based recording is available for Support Center.

Follow these steps to record a session:

1. **From the Tools tab on the session window, click Record Session.**

2. **An Allow Record message appears to the customer, asking for permission to record the session. Have the customer click OK.**

   The Save Record dialog box appears.

3. **Enter a filename for the session and click Save.**

   The Recorder Panel shown in Figure 10-17 appears. Use the tools here to begin, stop, or pause the recording.

Figure 10-17:
The Recorder Panel offers tools to control recording.

If the Recorder Panel disappears from view as your session proceeds, go back to the Session tab of the session window and click the Stop Record Session button to end recording.

Playing back a recorded session

To play back a recorded session, locate it with Windows Explorer and double-click it. The WebEx Recorder opens and begins playing the session back on your screen.

It's Been Swell . . .

Even the most productive support session must come to an end — hopefully, happily with a problem resolution. To end a session at any time, click the End Session button on the Tools tab of your session window. Your customer can also leave a session that's still in progress by clicking the Leave Session button on the customer's session page. When you end a session or a customer leaves a session and if your site administrator has set up the feedback feature, the feedback form shown in Figure 10-18 appears. Try to encourage your customers to fill out the feedback form to help you improve your support services in the future.

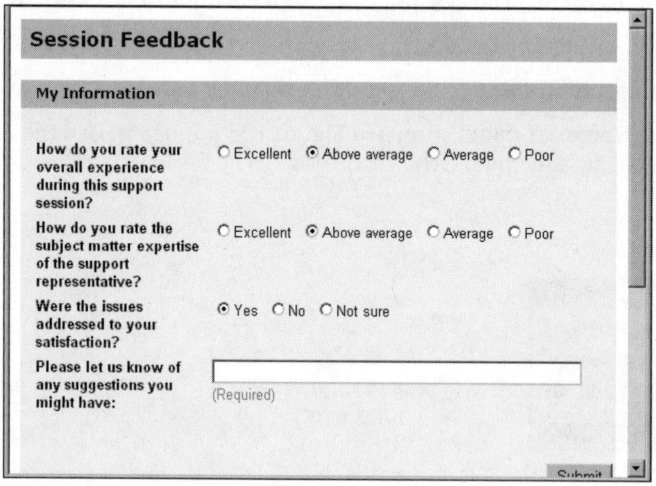

Figure 10-18:
Getting customer feedback on your support.

Session Feedback

My Information

How do you rate your overall experience during this support session? ○ Excellent ● Above average ○ Average ○ Poor

How do you rate the subject matter expertise of the support representative? ○ Excellent ● Above average ○ Average ○ Poor

Were the issues addressed to your satisfaction? ● Yes ○ No ○ Not sure

Please let us know of any suggestions you might have: (Required)

Submit

Chapter 11

Creating Virtual Classrooms with Training Center

*O*nline training is available in many forms on the Internet. From full-blown, interactive university courses to simple bullet-point presentations viewed at a student's leisure, the Internet allows individuals and organizations to cut training costs anddeliver a rich and engaging classroom experience over a Web browser.

With WebEx, training isn't simply another kind of online meeting. With WebEx Training Center and presentation applications such as Microsoft PowerPoint (see Chapter 6 for some tips on making great online presentations), you can design presentations, course materials, and tests as well as create a rich inter-active environment for student learning. You can even record training sessions so that others can access the content in the future. Finally, you'll find it useful to generate reports that tell you how effective your training efforts are.

And the best part of it all: You can deliver this training to your own employees, customers at home or abroad, or salespeople on the road. WebEx offers a secure and reliable online classroom that these folks can access from virtually anywhere. In this chapter, you discover the ins and outs of online training.

Getting Set Up for Training

Ever have one of those anxiety dreams in which you walk into a classroom full of people and begin teaching the class (perhaps naked) without a smidgen of preparation? Scary, huh?

It's the same in a virtual classroom: Preparation is key (although, oddly, you could attend naked if turn off your QuickCam). Before you run a training session using WebEx, you need to take care of one technical task, which is to download the *Training Manager* (a small client program that takes only a minute or two to download). In addition, you should tend to the task of preparing class materials and tests, just as you would for a physical classroom.

Downloading Training Manager

If you've used WebEx's Meeting Center to run or attend a meeting, you have already downloaded the software client called Meeting Manager. (It's downloaded automatically for you the first time you host or attend a meeting, as you can read about in Chapter 3.) Training Manager is a similar piece of software. These two client programs both enable your computer to connect to WebEx meetings or training sessions.

Training Manager is a small program and takes only moments to download by following these steps:

1. **Log in to your WebEx site and click the Training Center tab. If you don't have the Enterprise Edition, log in to your Training Center site.**

2. **Click the arrow to the left of the Set Up menu and then click the Training Manager link.**

    The screen in Figure 11-1 appears.

3. **Click the Set Up button.**

    A progress screen appears, followed by the screen shown in Figure 11-2 telling you that Training Manager has been installed.

Training Manager also automatically downloads when you first start or attend a training session. Also, even if you've preinstalled it (not a bad idea — you can get to your training without the delay), when you enter a session, a quick update installation might occur.

Figure 11-1:
The choices offered for downloading Training Manager.

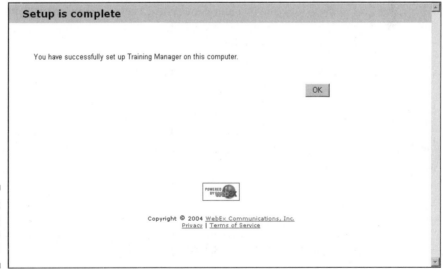

Figure 11-2:
Training Manager is installed!

Designing online training for success

WebEx provides a great interactive virtual classroom with all sorts of valuable tools for delivering information and working with students. However, a classroom won't do you a heck of a lot of good if you don't have anything to say. Creating course materials and tests prior to walking into the WebEx virtual classroom is your first step.

Does every training session require that you prepare course materials ahead of time? No. If you are a self-assured presenter, you can use Training Center to present a live video feed of yourself giving a lecture without prepackaged slides or other materials. You can also use Training Center to have an interactive brainstorming or discussion session with students via the whiteboard and Chat features. But for most sessions, you need to prepare audio, video, or slides, and you should get them done well ahead of time.

Creating course materials

A WebEx training session might consist of one or more live presenters, interactive chats, software demonstrations, delivery of student polls or tests, and presentation of course materials.

What form might course materials take? Well, as with offline classes, it varies. For example, you can use any and all of these items as course materials:

- Prerecorded video files
- PowerPoint slide presentations, including transitions, animations, sounds and narration, if you like
- Documents you can share, such as Excel worksheets or PDF brochures
- Graphics, such as an Excel chart or a CAD drawing
- Web content you can share by using the Sharing a Web Browser feature of WebEx
- Prerecorded events, such as a previously delivered live training lecture

You can also make hands-on labs available, in which you set up students with remote computers so that they can practice a software application or view self-paced tutorials on their own. See the section, "Reserving a hands-on lab," later in this chapter.

To prepare these materials, you first have to create them in whatever application you choose. For video, for example, you can set up a Webcam and use programs such as Adobe Premiere to record and edit your video. PowerPoint is the program of choice for bullet-point presentations and works seamlessly within a WebEx online session.

After you create these files, you should upload them to the My Files section of My WebEx. Follow these steps to do so:

1. **Log in to your WebEx site or Training Center and display the My WebEx tab.**

2. **Click the My Files menu.**

   The page shown in Figure 11-3 appears.

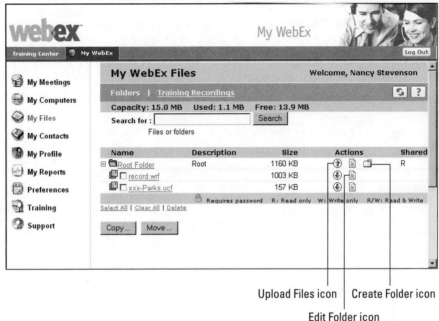

Figure 11-3:
The My
WebEx
Files page.

Upload Files icon | Create Folder icon
Edit Folder icon

3. **To create a new folder, click the Create Folder icon (located in the Root Folder Actions column and shaped like a little manila folder), enter a folder name, and click OK in the dialog box that appears.**

4. **To add a file to the Root or other folder, click the Upload Files icon in the Action column for that folder.**

   The Upload File dialog box, as shown in Figure 11-4, appears.

5. **Click one of the Browse buttons; the Choose File dialog box appears. Locate the file you wish to upload and click Open.**

6. **Repeat Step 5 for up to three files. When you're done, click the Upload button in the Upload File dialog box.**

7. **Click the Close button to close the My WebEx Files page when you're done.**

With the files you want to use uploaded, you can now use them as course materials when scheduling a training session. Links to those materials then appear on the Session Information page where students can go to download them before the session begins.

Chapter 6 gives you the lowdown on creating great presentation materials.

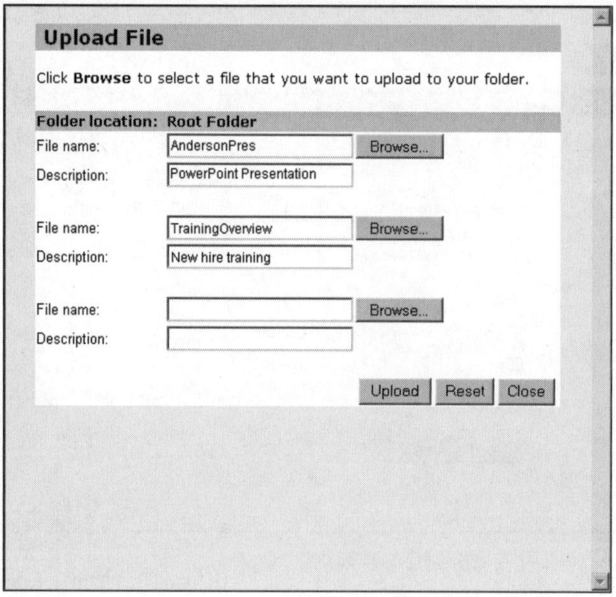

Figure 11-4:
Upload up to three files at a time from this dialog box.

Creating tests

If you're like me, there is no doubt a special place in your heart for tests. In school, you lived in fear of them for days beforehand, sweated as you tried to understand what the heck *x* and *y* had to do with the circumference of a swimming pool, and anxiously awaited your scores.

If you've ever been on the other side of the fence, as you are when you provide training using WebEx, you know that tests are simply one way to make sure that students are keeping up with the information that you provide. Tests help you gauge how effective your training is, pointing out where you might need to provide more coverage of a particular concept or skill.

You can deliver a test within a training session, or you can arrange for students to take a test outside of a training session. All tests that you create are saved in your Test Library, available on your WebEx site (if you have Enterprise Edition) or Training Center site.

To create a test, follow these steps:

1. **From the Training Center tab of Meeting Center, click the Test Library link under the Host a Session menu.**

   The Test Library page, as shown in Figure 11-5, appears.

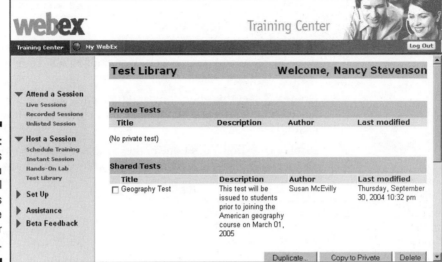

Figure 11-5:
Here's where you store all your tests for use in your training.

2. **Click the Create New Test button (near the bottom of the page).**

   The Create Test page, as shown in Figure 11-6, appears.

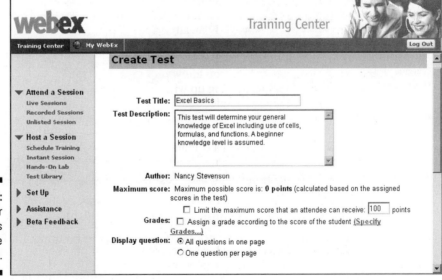

Figure 11-6:
Build your test in this easy-to-use form.

 3. **Enter a Test Title and Description in the first two text boxes.**

 4. **Customize the following settings:**

   • **Maximum Score:** Select the check box here to limit the maximum possible number of points a student can get, adjusting the default 100 points if you wish.

   • **Grades:** Select this check box and then click the Specify Grades link to set grade ranges in the page that appears, as shown in Figure 11-7.

   • **Display Question:** Select one of these radio buttons to either display all questions on a single page or display one question per page.

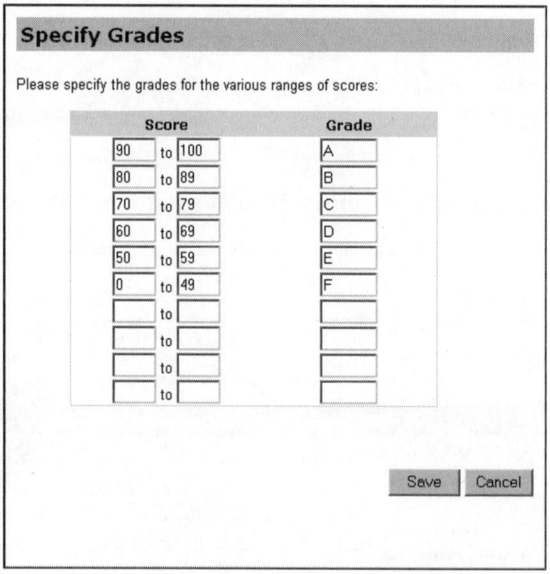

Figure 11-7: Set grade ranges in this dialog box.

 5. **Click the Insert Question link near the bottom of the form.**

   The Add Question dialog box, as shown in Figure 11-8, appears.

 6. **Click the arrow in the Question Type field and select one of the question types, such as multiple choice or fill-in-the-blank.**

 7. **Depending on the type of question that you're creating, fill in the required information.**

   For example, for true/false questions, complete the information shown in Figure 11-9; for fill-in-the-blank, enter the information shown in Figure 11-10.

 8. **Click Save to save the question.**

   On the Edit Test page, a scoring panel appears, as shown in Figure 11-11.

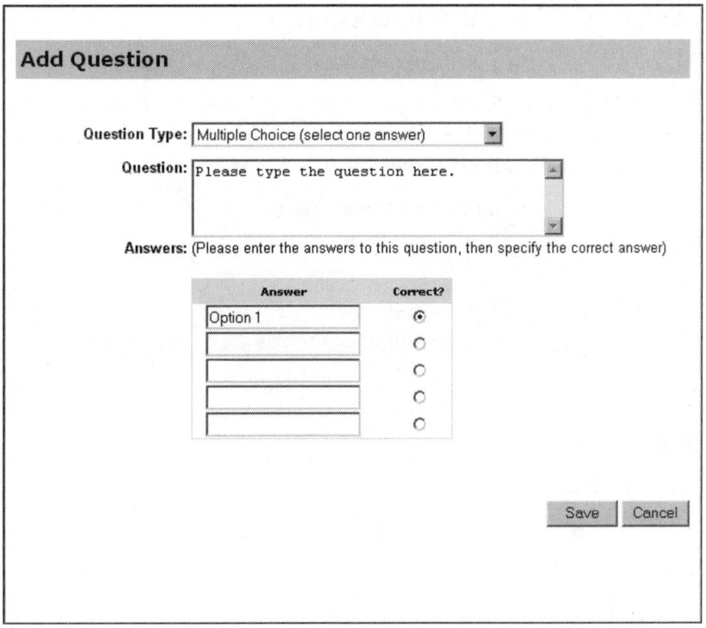

Add Question

Question Type: Multiple Choice (select one answer)

Question: Please type the question here.

Answers: (Please enter the answers to this question, then specify the correct answer)

Answer	Correct?
Option 1	●
	○
	○
	○
	○

Save   Cancel

Figure 11-8:
Create a
variety of
question
types from
this page.

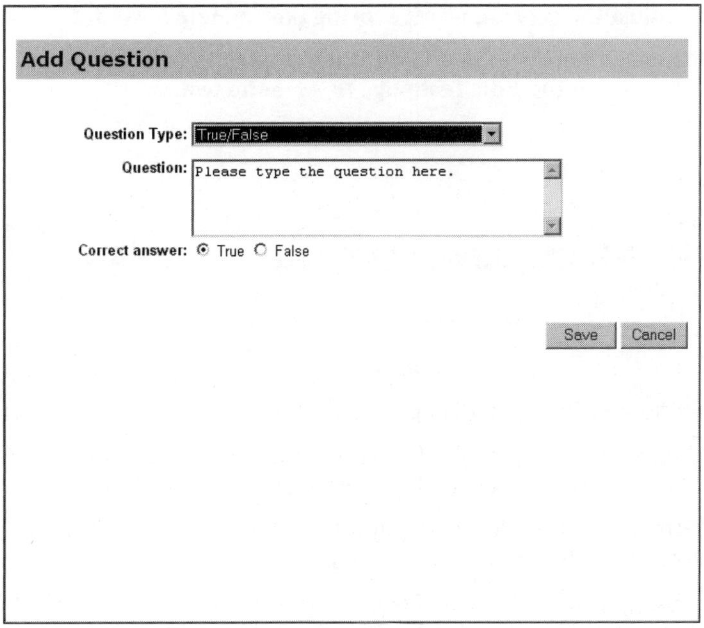

Add Question

Question Type: True/False

Question: Please type the question here.

Correct answer: ● True ○ False

Save   Cancel

Figure 11-9:
Specify the
choices for
a true/false
question.

Add Question

Question Type: [Fill in the blanks ▾]

Question: (Please type the fill in the blanks question, using [] as a blank, and enclose the correct answer within the []. You can have more than one blank in the question)

The capital of New York State is [Albany].

[Save] [Cancel]

Figure 11-10:
A fill-in-
the-blank
question.

9. **Adjust the scoring or set scoring parameters and then click Save.**

10. **Repeat Steps 5–9 to add additional questions, and then click the Save button on the Edit Test page to save the test.**

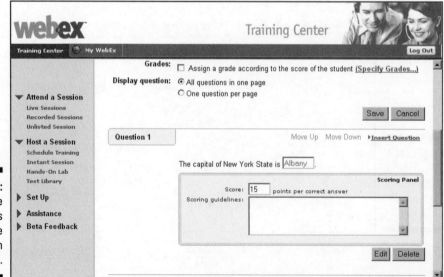

Figure 11-11:
Set score
parameters
for the
question
here.

Polls can provide another tool for judging how students are following the course. Generally, you use polls to gather attendee opinions or facts about them, such as previous training in the topic at hand. Tests are used to test understanding of information that you provide. Chapter 7 covers taking a poll in more detail.

Hosting a Training Session

At this point in the training planning process, you have all your course materials created and saved to your My WebEx Files; you've designed and saved tests to determine how learners are progressing; you might have created some notes for yourself for a live video presentation and perhaps even have lined up some guest presenters. What's next? The next step is to schedule the training and invite attendees.

WebEx has devised a form in which you personalize all the settings and enter all the information about your training session, including the when, where, and who. In this section, I go through that form so you know what's needed.

To access the form, from the Training Center tab of Meeting Center, open the Host a Session menu by clicking the arrow to the right of it. Then click the Schedule Training link. The form in Figure 11-12 appears, ready for you to begin entering information.

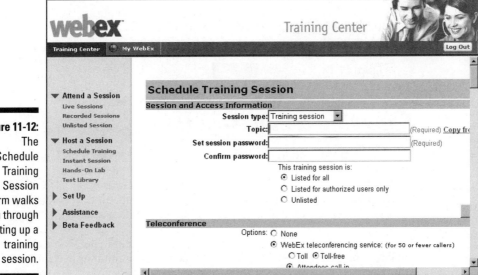

Figure 11-12: The Schedule Training Session form walks you through setting up a training session.

Scheduling the training session

The first three sections of this form deal with details such as the session title and password, teleconferencing options, and the date and time for the training. Here's what you enter:

- ✔ **Session and Access Information:** Choose a session type from the drop-down list and enter a topic for your training. (Your site administrator has the option of creating session types for your organization. These are predefined sets of features and options available for sessions. For example, a site administrator might create a session type that doesn't include video as an option. If you create that session type when scheduling a session, video will not be available. Setting a session password is required, so enter one and then confirm it by entering it again. Select a radio button to choose whether your meeting will be private, listed in your calendar of meetings on your WebEx site or unlisted. An unlisted session requires that attendees provide a session number to attend; you have to communicate the training session number to them, and they have to type it into a login form to join a session.

- ✔ **Teleconference:** Select one of these choices depending on whether you want to use WebEx's teleconferencing service, another service, or Internet Phone. Note that the None option can be used if you prefer that attendees merely view a presentation online rather than call into it. Also, note that the Internet Phone option requires attendees to have headphones or speakers connected to their computers. If they want to speak as well as listen, they also need a microphone.

- ✔ **Date and Time:** Enter information about the date, time, time zone, and duration of your training. If this course requires multiple sessions, select the Recurring Session or Multiple Session choice under Occurrence, and an additional section for setting multiple sessions appears, as shown in Figure 11-13.

Reserving a hands-on lab

A hands-on lab is essentially a remote computer set up with preloaded documents or tutorials for students to access. When you're setting up a training session, you can also set up students' access to a hands-on lab. Hands-on labs first have to be created by somebody with hands-on lab privileges before you can make them available to users when scheduling a session.

To schedule a lab, simply select the Reserve Computers check box, choose the lab from the adjacent drop-down list, and enter a number in the Number of Computers box. If you click the Check Availability button, you are told what hours are available for the day on which you're scheduling your session.

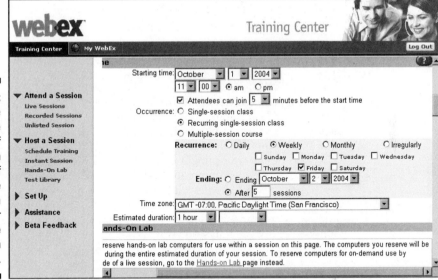

Figure 11-13:
The
Recurrence
section of
the form
appears if
you choose
either a
Recurring or
Multiple
session
setting.

When you click either the Schedule or Start Session buttons at the bottom of the scheduling form, your computers are reserved.

You can use hands-on labs outside of a training session. Use the Hands-On Lab link in the Host a Session menu of Training Center to do so.

Customizing the registration form

In the next section of the form, you can choose whether people are required to register for the class. I highly recommend that you register people for training, for several reasons:

- ✔ Registering people makes them feel they have a more sincere commitment to attend.

- ✔ A registration form is a valuable source of information about attendees that you can use to follow up after the session or to solicit attendance at future training.

- ✔ By using specific questions about student knowledge or experience, you can better prepare for your class by tailoring material to your students' needs.

If you select the Require Attendee Registration check box in this section of the scheduling form, you then follow these steps to customize the registration form:

1. **Click the Customize Form button.**

   The Customize Registration form, as shown in Figure 11-14, appears.

Customize Registration Form

Based on form: Default Form ▾ Load

Registration Options
Check the boxes of the following fields that you would like to appear in the registration form. Fields can be set to be optional or required.

Standard Options   ✓Include on form ®Required
✓ ®   ✓ ®
☑ ☑ First name   ☐ ☐ Address 1
☑ ☑ Last name   ☐ ☐ Address 2
☑ ☑ Email address   ☐ ☐ City
☐ ☐ Phone number   ☐ ☐ State/Province
☐ ☐ Fax number   ☐ ☐ ZIP/Postal code
☐ ☐ Company   ☐ ☐ Country/Region
☐ ☐ Title

My Custom Options

Select the options that you want to add on the registration form

Text Box   Check Boxes   Radio Buttons   Drop-Down List

2. **Select check boxes in the column labeled with a check mark to include various fields on the Registration Form, such as First Name, Last Name, Phone Number, and so on.**

3. **Select check boxes in the column labeled *R* to *require* that certain fields be completed in order to submit the form.**

4. **To create a custom question, click one of the buttons along the bottom of the page:**

   • **Text Box:** Clicking this option brings up the form shown in Figure 11-15, on which you can enter a label or prompt and size parameters for the text box.

   • **Check Boxes:** Here you enter a label for the group of check boxes as well as labels for each individual check box (see Figure 11-16).

   • **Radio Buttons:** Note that what appears when you click the Radio Buttons button is the same form that you see in Figure 11-16 for Check Boxes. The only difference is that the selection in the Type field is Radio Buttons. Radio buttons allow attendees to select only one choice; check boxes allow multiple choices.

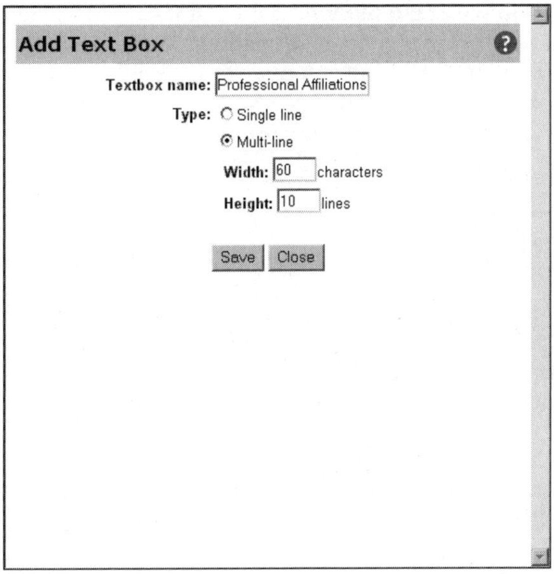

Figure 11-15:
The Add
Text Box
form.

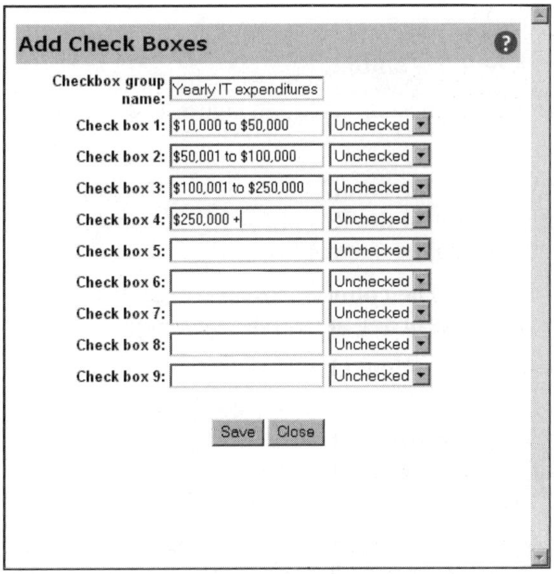

Figure 11-16:
Building a
check box
entry.

- **Drop-Down List:** Again, from the form shown in Figure 11-16, you can create a label for the list, entering as many items as you like in the Choice boxes. These appear when the arrow on the drop-down box is clicked.

5. **When you finish adding questions, you can use the two columns of check boxes to specify whether a question should be included on your registration form and whether an answer is required, as you did with the contact information check boxes in Steps 3 and 4.**

6. **Click OK on the Customize Registration form to save your changes.**

Inviting folks

If you set up a training session and nobody comes, is there any point? No. That's your next step: Getting students into your virtual classroom. You can invite both attendees and presenters to your class by using the next two sections of the Schedule Training Session form.

Note that you can also invite attendees on the fly to a meeting in progress by choosing Participant⇨Invite, entering an e-mail address, and clicking the Send Invitation button.

Scroll down to the Attendees section of the Schedule Training Session form. From there, to create a list of folks to invite to your training event, just follow these steps:

1. **Click the List Attendees button.**

The Invite Attendees page, as shown in Figure 11-17, appears.

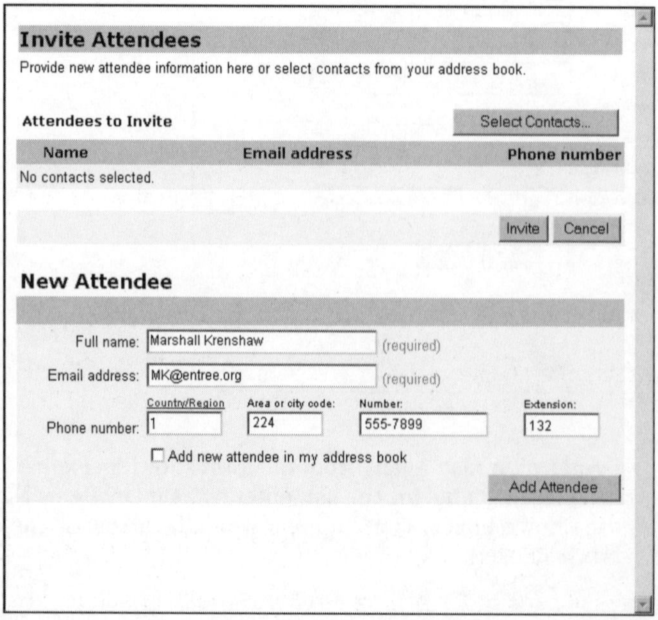

Invite Attendees

Provide new attendee information here or select contacts from your address book.

Attendees to Invite   Select Contacts...

Name	Email address	Phone number
No contacts selected.		

Invite   Cancel

New Attendee

Full name: Marshall Krenshaw   (required)

Email address: MK@entree.org   (required)

Phone number: Country/Region [1] Area or city code: [224] Number: [555-7899] Extension: [132]

☐ Add new attendee in my address book

Add Attendee

Figure 11-17: Enter attendee information here.

2. **Enter a New Attendee's name, e-mail address, and phone number in the appropriate boxes and then click the Add Attendee button. (Note that if you want to add this person to your Address Book, you should select the Add New Attendee in My Address Book check box before clicking this button.)**

3. **To choose an attendee from your Address Book, click the Select Contacts button.**

   Your Address Book is displayed (see Figure 11-18).

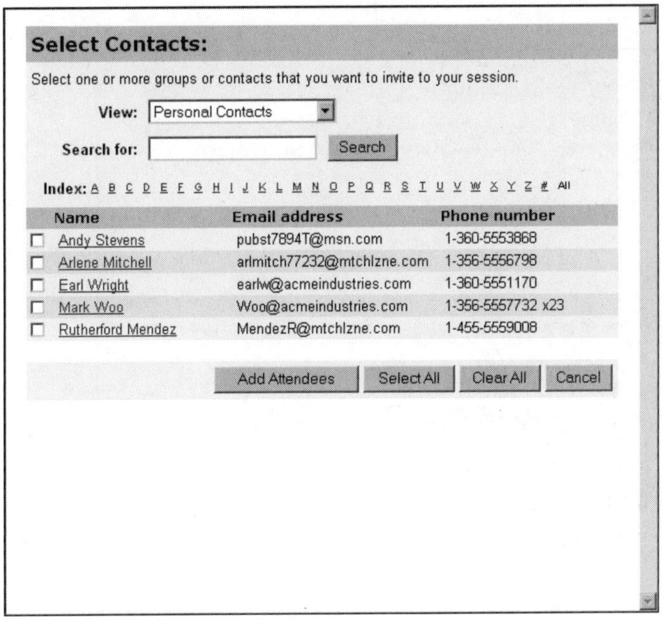

Select Contacts:

Select one or more groups or contacts that you want to invite to your session.

View: [Personal Contacts ▼]

Search for: [ ] [Search]

Index: A B C D E F G H I J K L M N O P Q R S T U V W X Y Z # All

Name	Email address	Phone number
☐ Andy Stevens	pubst7894T@msn.com	1-360-5553868
☐ Arlene Mitchell	arlmitch77232@mtchlzne.com	1-356-5556798
☐ Earl Wright	earlw@acmeindustries.com	1-360-5551170
☐ Mark Woo	Woo@acmeindustries.com	1-356-5557732 x23
☐ Rutherford Mendez	MendezR@mtchlzne.com	1-455-5559008

[Add Attendees] [Select All] [Clear All] [Cancel]

Figure 11-18:
The WebEx
Address
Book.

4. **Select the check boxes for all the people you want to invite, and then click the Add Attendees button.**

   They are all added to your invitation list with one click.

5. **Click the Invite button to finalize your invitation list.**

The next section in the form allows you to invite presenters. Frankly, it involves exactly the same steps given above to invite attendees, so feel free to give this one a try all by yourself.

Choosing your particular session options

Few things in life are under your control, but you'll be glad to hear that some of the settings for your WebEx training session are among them. In the next section of the Schedule Training Session form, you can take control of options, such as the privileges that your attendees have during your training session, security settings, the message that greets attendees, and a URL to send folks to after your session ends.

To adjust these settings, scroll to the Session Options section of the Schedule Training Session form and follow these steps:

1. **Click the Edit Options button.**

   The form shown in Figure 11-19 appears.

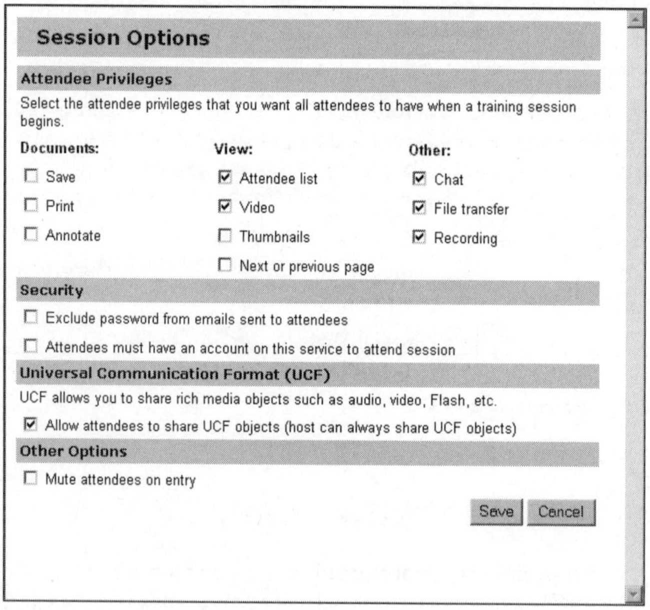

Figure 11-19:
The Session Options form is where you control attendee privileges.

Session Options

Attendee Privileges
Select the attendee privileges that you want all attendees to have when a training session begins.

Documents:	View:	Other:
☐ Save	☑ Attendee list	☑ Chat
☐ Print	☑ Video	☑ File transfer
☐ Annotate	☐ Thumbnails	☑ Recording
	☐ Next or previous page	

Security
☐ Exclude password from emails sent to attendees
☐ Attendees must have an account on this service to attend session

Universal Communication Format (UCF)
UCF allows you to share rich media objects such as audio, video, Flash, etc.
☑ Allow attendees to share UCF objects (host can always share UCF objects)

Other Options
☐ Mute attendees on entry

Save   Cancel

2. **In the Session Options dialog box, you can tweak the following settings and then click Save:**

   • **Attendee Privileges:** Select the check boxes for the things that you want attendees to be able to do during a session, such as saving, printing, and chatting.

   • **Security:** You have two options here: You can keep the password from being included in the e-mail sent to invite attendees to the session, and you can require that attendees have an account on your WebEx site to attend. You might exclude a password from the e-mail if you'd rather provide the password in some other fashion, such as by phone or carrier pigeon. If any attendees are likely to be outside of your organization, be sure that you don't select the Attendees Must Have an Account check box, or they might not be able to get in. (There is a feature that allows you to turn on attendee accounts for folks outside of your organization so they can join your session even if this option is selected — but only if you purchase this option.)

- **Universal Communications Format (UCF):** This is the format that WebEx uses for sharing multimedia files. If you want attendees to be able to share their own UCF files, select this check box.

- **Preventing interruptions:** If you want to mute attendees when they enter the meeting so they won't interrupt, select the check box in this section. This option is available only if you use integrated WebEx teleconferencing and not a third-party service.

3. **Back in the Session Options section, if you like, enter a URL that you want attendees to be directed to at the end of the session. This can be your organization's Web site or a site where you've set up a hands-on lab, for example. This way your students can keep on working even after your live session is over.**

4. **In the Entry and Exit Tone field, choose Beep, Announce Name, or No Tone from the drop-down list.**

5. **To set a customized greeting to your training session, click the Customize Greeting Message When Attendee Joins link, enter your message, and click OK.**

E-mailing automatic reminders

In the Email Options section of the scheduling form, you can customize certain settings for the messages that will be sent to attendees and presenters, including Invitations, Updates, Registrations, and Reminders. In each of these sections, you can choose the types of automatic e-mails that you'd like to send (such as a notification sent out if the session is rescheduled or cancelled) and the timing schedule for those e-mails (see Figure 11-20).

Use the check boxes and drop-down lists to select the e-mail items that you want to send as well as when you want them to go.

By default, the e-mails are sent from the address associated with your WebEx user account; if you want your e-mails to be sent from another unique e-mail account, just enter that address in the Via E-mail Address text box.

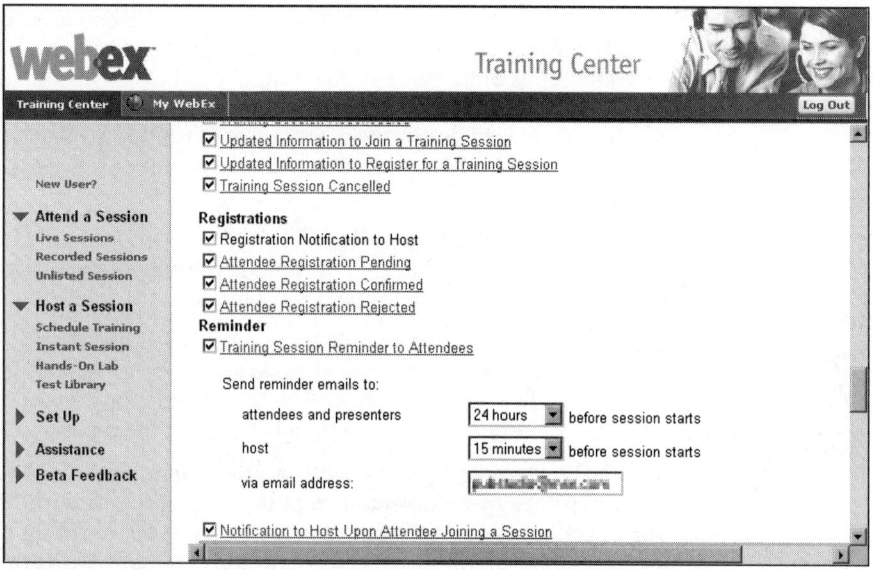

Figure 11-20:
E-mail
options you
control.

Adding an agenda to keep things on track

The information page for your course appears when people first try to join your session. The information that you can add here includes an agenda, a description, and a graphic (your organization logo, a photo of the main presenter, or an ice-breaking cartoon relevant to the topic come to mind).

In the Session Information section of the Schedule Training Session form (see Figure 11-21), you can choose to display information in Plain Text or HTML, and then enter your agenda and description in the appropriate boxes. You can cut and paste these from elsewhere, if you like.

The benefit of using HTML text is that it's nicer looking, but some browsers don't read it very well. Plain text can be read by one and all.

To add a graphic to the information page, follow these steps:

1. **Click the Import Picture button.**

   The Upload Your Picture dialog box, as shown in Figure 11-22, appears.

2. **Click the Browse button; in the Choose File dialog box that opens, select the file you want to upload and then click Open.**

3. **Click the Import button to upload it to WebEx.**

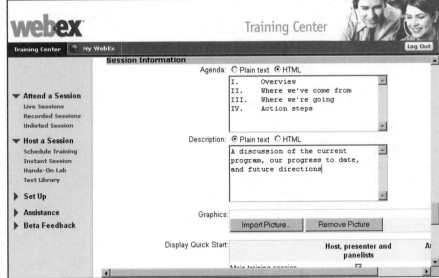

Figure 11-21:
An agenda is always a good idea to keep a session on track.

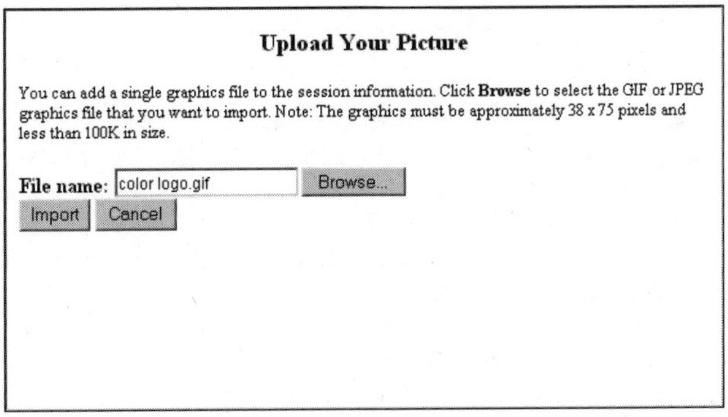

Figure 11-22:
Upload a picture from your hard drive or a removable disc.

The final option in the Session Information section is whether you will display the Quick Start panel during the session. You can display it for the host and presenters only or also for attendees. (You can't display it only for attendees.) The Quick Start panel contains a set of shortcuts that you can click to access features, such as the whiteboard.

Uploading course materials and tests

Earlier in this chapter, in the section "Creating course materials," I tell you how to place files in your WebEx Files. I had a reason to suggest you do that before I had you start scheduling a session: When you hit the Course Materials portion of this form, you simply click Add Course Material and the Add Course Material page shown in Figure 11-23 appears, with all the files in My Folders displayed. Select the check boxes of the various files and then click the Select button to include them as course material.

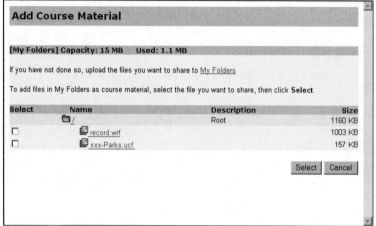

Figure 11-23:
Course materials you've placed in your My Folders file are all available here.

Did you skip the section in this chapter on creating course materials? Did you forget one teensy file when you added course materials? Not to worry; you can add materials for your class while you fill out the scheduling form simply by clicking the My Files link on the page shown in Figure 11-23. This takes you to My Files, where you can upload additional files; then go back to the course materials dialog box and select them.

You can add tests after you click the Schedule button at the bottom of the scheduling form. You can create a new test on the confirmation screen that appears (see the earlier section, "Creating tests," to find out how to do this) or copy a test that you already created. You can also set options for starting the test with a live session or delivering it via a Web site.

Final steps — all set up!

Scroll to the bottom of the Scheduling form, and you find three buttons. One is labeled Cancel, which would be a shame given all the input that you just made (but things change, so if you must, you must). The other two are much more productive choices. Click Start Session, and your session begins instantly. Click Schedule, and a Session Scheduled page appears (see Figure 11-24).

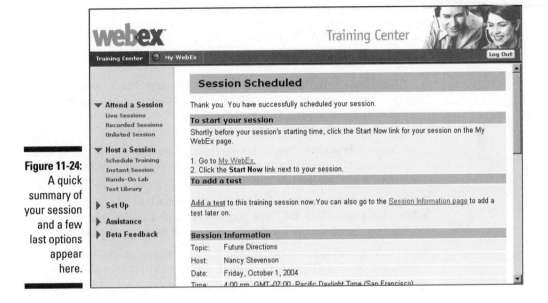

Figure 11-24:
A quick summary of your session and a few last options appear here.

To add tests to your course from the page in Figure 11-24, follow these steps:

1. **Click the Add a Test link.**

   The Add Test page, as shown in Figure 11-25, appears.

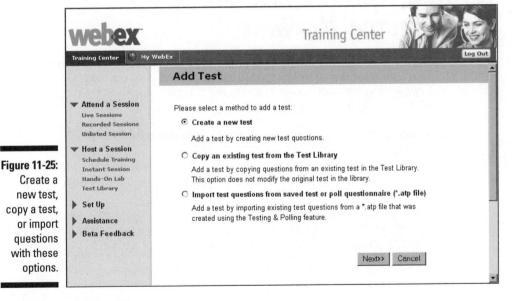

Figure 11-25:
Create a new test, copy a test, or import questions with these options.

2. **Select one of the three options presented:**

   • **Create a New Test:** This option takes you to the page discussed in the earlier section of this chapter, "Creating tests." Follow the steps in that section to create a new test.

   • **Copy an Existing Test from the Test Library:** This option takes you to the page shown in Figure 11-26, where you can select a test and then click Next. You're given an opportunity to edit the test; then you click Save to save the test for this session.

   • **Import Test Questions:** Choose this option if you used a Test and Poll questionnaire during a previous session and saved it; it will be converted into test format.

3. **After you make your choice in Step 2, you return to the Session Scheduled page. Click OK, and you are returned to the Training Center Live Sessions view with all scheduled courses displayed.**

   Your course now appears on the list of training sessions in WebEx (assuming you didn't make it private), and appropriate e-mail invitations are on their way.

You can now start your session by going to your My Meetings page in My WebEx and clicking the Start link in the Status column for the meeting that you want to begin.

Turning Training into an E-Commerce Machine

What if you're in the business of providing training for a fee, or you want to have each division in your company pay for their own training? Good news: Training Center allows your customers to pay you for their training conveniently by using credit cards.

Training Center E-commerce includes the following two features:

✔ **Fee-based training (for attendees).** With this feature attendees pay a fee for attending your sessions. (For details, see the next section, "Setting up fee-based training.")

✔ **Pay-per-use training (for hosts).** This feature requires hosts to pay before they can start each training session. (See the section, "Setting up pay-per-use training," for more about this.)

Setting up fee-based training

When you use fee-based training, attendees pay a fee to attend your sessions. A fee-based training session requires that attendees register and provide credit card information.

To require a session fee for a training session, type a U.S. dollar amount in the Session Fee text box on the Schedule Training Session page.

Setting up pay-per-use training

Pay-per-use requires that hosts pay up front, before they can start each training session. Pay-per-use is designed for organizations that do not want to deal with billing for every training session conducted on their Training Center Web sites.

For example, an organization that allocates a training budget for each division can now ask individual divisions to cover their own expenses for conducting training on the organization's Training Center Web site. Then the organization can reimburse the costs. To turn on this E-commerce feature, just contact your WebEx account manager.

To set up a pay-per-use training session:

1. **Click Start Session or Schedule on the Schedule Training Session page after you finish specifying options.**

   The Estimated Session Cost page appears. This page displays the estimated cost of the session based on the number of people minutes, teleconferencing minutes, and the rate per minute. The number of people minutes is the meeting duration multiplied by the number of computers connected in the session. The number of teleconferencing minutes is the session duration multiplied by the number of computers connected in the teleconference.

2. **Modify session settings (this is optional), and then click Change.**

3. **To return to the Estimated Session Cost page, click Start Session or Schedule.**

4. **Enter your credit card information as instructed.**

Setting Up an Instant Session

Although the Schedule Training Session form covered in the previous sections of this chapter is easy to complete, it does take some time. If you're the instant coffee, instant ramen, instant gratification kind of person, you might want a shortcut to starting a training session. That's where Instant Sessions come in.

From the Training Center tab of your WebEx site, follow these simple steps to start an Instant Session:

1. **In the Host a Session menu on the left, click the Instant Session link.**

   The Start an Instant Training Session form, as shown in Figure 11-26, appears.

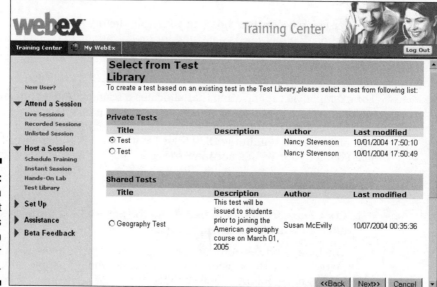

Figure 11-26:
You're just a few short entries away from your session.

2. **Enter the session topic and a password with confirmation.**

3. **Choose whether to make this an unlisted meeting and whether to use teleconferencing.**

4. **Click the Start Session button.**

   The Teleconference page, as shown in Figure 11-27, appears.

5. **If you chose to use teleconferencing in Step 3, on the screen that appears choose None, the WebEx teleconference service, another service, or Internet Phone, and then click OK.**

That's it. The session begins. Now you can invite attendees from within the training session by choosing Participant➪Invite and choosing either voice or e-mail as your method.

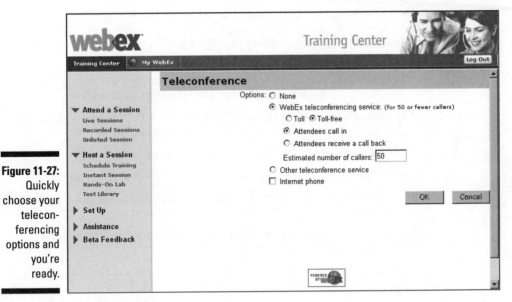

Figure 11-27:
Quickly
choose your
teleconferencing
options and
you're
ready.

For advice about participating in distance learning (learning via your computer), I recommend that you buy *Distance Learning Online For Dummies* (Wiley). Why, you ask? It helps you understand the world of online learning and how to get the most out of it. Oh, and I wrote it. . . .

Using Training Tools

Many of the tools available in a training session are identical to the ones that you use in any meeting. I cover these in Chapter 8, so I won't repeat myself here. However, I do want to provide a few tips about how to use these tools specifically in a training environment as well as how to administer course materials and tests.

Maximizing WebEx for training

Some of the WebEx meeting features discussed in the earlier chapters of this book are also available within WebEx Training Center. The features that you use in one way to meet with a client or project team can be used in other ways for teaching in a training environment.

In WebEx Training Center, you can

✔ Train people on computer applications via the shared applications feature.

✔ Demonstrate how to set up a computer operating system or make settings for your network by sharing your desktop with students.

✔ Use the whiteboard to sketch out concepts and processes and have students try their own hands at making refinements.

✔ Administer tests to check on student progress.

✔ Generate reports on everything from attendance to test scores.

✔ Use the Chat feature to hold lively online discussions about course material that students have read prior to the session.

✔ Offer prepackaged, self-paced training modules by recording training sessions for later playback.

✔ Set up hands-on computer labs that can be accessed remotely at any time, even during a training session.

In short, just about any bell or whistle that an online distance-learning designer can create, you can mimic in a WebEx training session.

WebEx's unique trainer's dashboard

The Training Center environment offers several tools adapted specifically to classroom needs that trainers and students can use to interact. Several feedback tools are located on the Participants panel, as shown in Figure 11-28.

Use these tools to do the following:

✔ Raise Hand allows a participant to alert the trainer that he or she has a question or wants to stop the proceedings.

✔ Yes and No buttons allow students to reply instantly to an instructor's question, such as "Did everybody get that?"

✔ The Go Faster and Go Slower buttons are a way for students to give an instructor an instant signal that things are lagging behind or rushing way too fast for them. If one of these buttons is clicked, the corresponding symbol appears next to the name of that student, but only on the trainer's dashboard.

✔ The Emoticon drop-down list allows attendees to click on their name in the Participants panel and add an emoticon (such as Surprise!, or Satisfied, or Have a Break) next to their name in the participant list.

✔ The Feedback Results drop-down list lets an instructor instantly see how many people have responded to a question that requires the Yes and No buttons.

✔ The Clear tool lets you clear all icons (Yes, No, Go Faster, Go Slower, and Emoticons) from participants' Feedback columns.

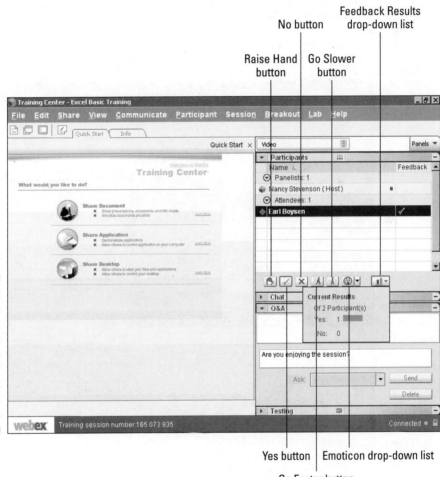

Figure 11-28:
The tools available to participants and the trainer during a training session.

Don't forget the Pointer tool that appears on the Training Session toolbar when you're sharing a page, slide, or the whiteboard. Click it (it's a big right-facing arrow icon) and then move your mouse around a document or presentation to cause an arrow with your name in it to appear on your students' computer screens. This helps you draw attention to important information on the topic at hand.

Sharing course materials

When people register for your test, the course materials that you assign during the scheduling process appear as links. The attendee can click those links to download the files.

When you're actually running the session, the course material that you add when scheduling the session is displayed automatically when the session starts. If you uploaded several course material files, there will be a tab for each file (see Figure 11-29); click the tab to display that file.

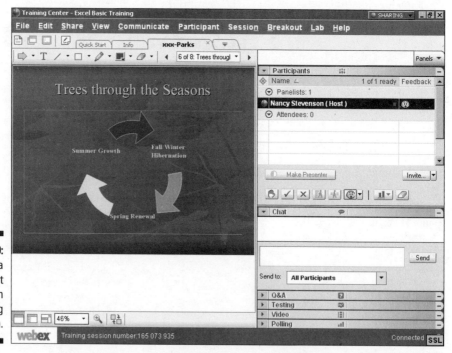

Figure 11-29: Displaying a PowerPoint presentation in a training session.

If you are running an Instant Session and want to show materials, choose Share⇨Presentation or Document, select the document that you want to share, and click the Open button. The document or presentation is displayed.

Using Hands-on Lab

Starting a hands-on lab from within a training session is simplicity itself. Choose Lab⇨Start Hands-on Lab. If you want to record what students do during the lab, choose Lab⇨Hands-on Lab Options, select the Record Remote Computers Automatically When Participants Connect check box, and click OK.

If you start your meeting outside of the time when you originally scheduled it and you try to start a hands-on lab, you get a message that tells you that you reserved the lab for a different time. You have to access the lab at the originally scheduled time, or end your meeting, and schedule a new one with the lab starting right now, then start the meeting again.

Time for a test!

When you enter a training session, one of the panels is labeled Testing. To start a test, open this panel (see Figure 11-30), click a test that you want to start, and click the Launch for All button.

Figure 11-30:
The Testing
panel.

> ▼ Testing
> | Title | Status |
> |---|---|
> | **Geography Test** | **Not started** |
>
> Refresh for All   Launch for All

The instructor sees the screen shown in Figure 11-31, with various control options. The student sees the test (see Figure 11-32).

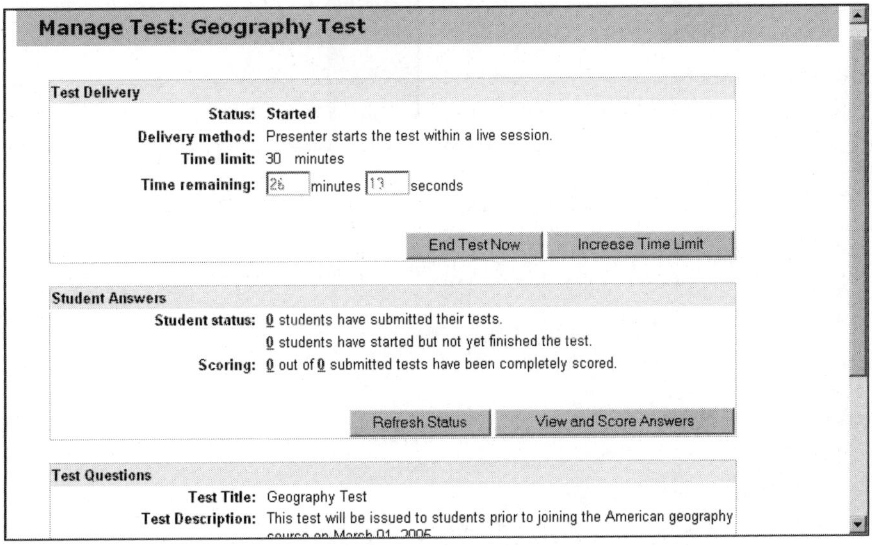

Figure 11-31:
The test
from the
instructor's
point of
view.

> **Manage Test: Geography Test**
>
> **Test Delivery**
> Status: Started
> Delivery method: Presenter starts the test within a live session.
> Time limit: 30 minutes
> Time remaining: 26 minutes 13 seconds
>
> End Test Now   Increase Time Limit
>
> **Student Answers**
> Student status: 0 students have submitted their tests.
> 0 students have started but not yet finished the test.
> Scoring: 0 out of 0 submitted tests have been completely scored.
>
> Refresh Status   View and Score Answers
>
> **Test Questions**
> Test Title: Geography Test
> Test Description: This test will be issued to students prior to joining the American geography
> course on March 01, 2005.

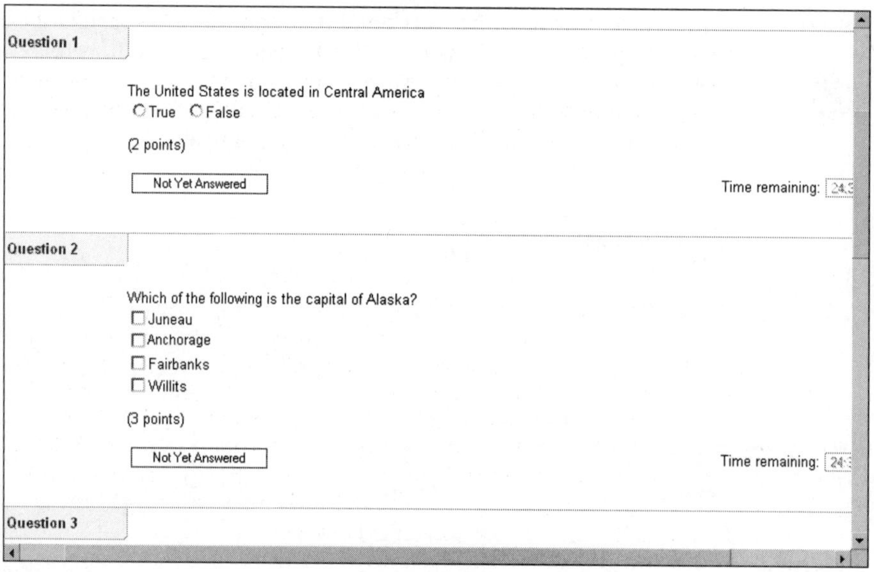

Figure 11-32:
The test
from the
student's
point of
view.

When a student finishes, he clicks the Save Answers button and then the Submit Test button. The instructor can select a student and then click the View and Score Answers button to view submitted tests (see Figure 11-33). The instructor can also enter overall comments in a text box provided at the top of the test.

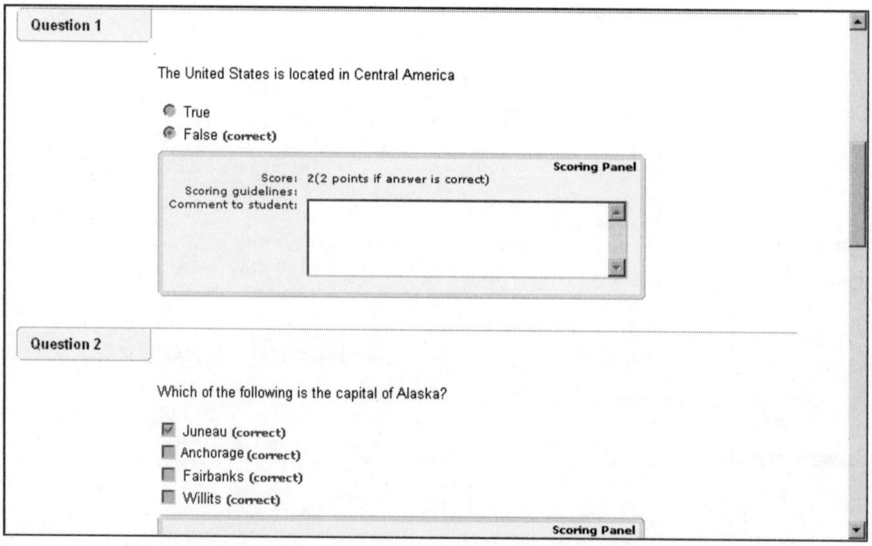

Figure 11-33:
An
individual
student's
test results.

Don't forget to use WebEx's reporting capabilities to put your training on target. Reports can help you track attendance, results of tests, and registration information to spot trends and help you modify to your promotion or content accordingly. You can also integrate data from reports with learning management systems that you might have in place. See Chapter 12 for all the details about reporting with WebEx.

Recording Sessions for Posterity

Chapter 8 (a hotbed of information) covers the process of recording a session. This is an especially good idea for training. Recorded training sessions become self-paced training for those who weren't around for the live session. You can add recorded sessions to the recorded sessions library by using My Files. Over time, you can build up a library of prerecorded training sessions. These can be accessed through the Training Center by clicking the Recorded Sessions link on the Attend a Session menu.

Self-paced training can become out of date, so keep track of when sessions were recorded. If the information presented gets slightly out of date, you can always supplement the recording with a page of printed updates. When it gets too out of date, just record a more recent session and ditch the old one by going to My Files from My WebEx, selecting the file, and deleting it.

Part V
Taking WebEx Further

The 5th Wave   By Rich Tennant

"You know I'm pretty sure the WebEx meeting comes with volume control."

In this part . . .

They say that one's reach should always exceed one's grasp. So why should you stop at the basic ins and outs of using WebEx? Once you have the knack for scheduling and holding meetings and events online with WebEx, you might want to consider a few advanced topics.

This part is about two topics: generating and using reports about your WebEx activities; and administering your WebEx site, including setting up user accounts, handling security issues, and configuring general site settings.

Chapter 12

Making the Most of Reports

So your department has jumped on the WebEx bandwagon in a big way and been happily using it to meet and support customers for several months. Your boss pulls you aside after a long, boring offline meeting and asks how productive WebEx is for your team. You promise to get back to him with specific information the next day.

You now have three choices:

1. Run around to everybody in your department and ask them whether they remember exactly how many WebEx meetings they attended in the last few months, how many people attended, what kind of feedback they got from support sessions, and on and on. (This will produce a lot of pained looks from your staff, I guarantee you.)

2. Have your assistant tell your boss you were abducted by aliens and therefore can't get back to him about this.

3. Run a few WebEx reports.

Call me crazy, but I vote for Number 3. Here, then, are the ins and outs of the WebEx report feature.

Who's Reporting Whom?

Reports in WebEx come in two flavors: the reports that any meeting host can generate through My WebEx, and the more sophisticated performance reports that a WebEx site administrator can generate to monitor enterprise-wide use of WebEx through an add-on product called GlobalWatch.

This chapter covers both types of reporting. The first two sections deal with host-level reports; the section "Meet GlobalWatch" gives you the lowdown on administrator-level reporting.

Eyeing the Reporting Landscape

Depending on which WebEx applications your company is using, you have different reports available to you as someone who hosts WebEx meetings. If, for example, you use Sales Center and Meeting Center, you have sales reports and some usage and attendance reports available. If you use the Support Center, you can generate a log of support sessions, and so on.

Generally speaking, whatever WebEx applications you bought, reports available in your WebEx site cover certain key information at varying levels of detail:

- **Usage:** How many meetings you have run of a certain type, how long they were, and so on.

- **Enrollment and Attendance:** How many people registered, and how many attended? You can also get details about attendees in this type of report.

- **Access Anywhere:** If you use Access Anywhere to connect with remote computers (see Chapter 5 for details), you can get some information about that activity through reports.

- **Details:** A few reports also show details about online meetings or sessions, such as attendee details or archived files accessed.

Often, when a report is displayed, some items in it are formatted as links. Click these links to see more details. For example, in a report listing meetings that you ran in a certain timeframe, click a particular meeting's link, and details about that meeting appear.

Let's Make a Report!

If you're the type who hosts meetings, generating a report in WebEx is simplicity itself. The information is all in there, and you don't have much control over the report design. You just pick the report that you want to run, specify information such as attendee name or a date range, and that's it.

Where you find meeting host reports

Reports live in the My WebEx area of your WebEx site if your site administrator has turned this option on for your account. Go to the My WebEx page and click My Reports to display a list of available reports, similar to the one shown in Figure 12-1.

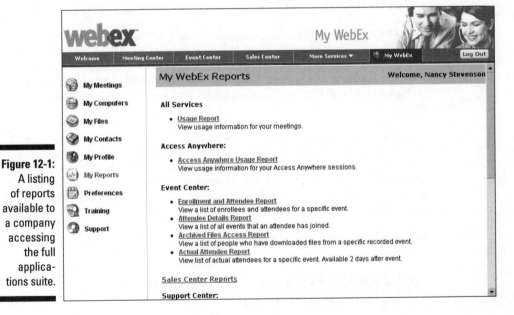

Figure 12-1:
A listing
of reports
available to
a company
accessing
the full
applications suite.

What is available to you differs depending on the WebEx services that you purchased. But if you went for the full enchilada (WebEx Enterprise Edition with all the available services), you have the following report features available to you:

   ✔ **All Services, Usage Report** shows you the usage across any services
   that you purchased.

   ✔ **WebEx Access Anywhere** provides reports on access of remote
   computers. (See Chapter 5 for the lowdown on Access Anywhere.)

   ✔ Event Center includes four types of reports about marketing events:
   **Enrollment and Attendee Report, Attendee Details Report, Archived
   Files Access Report,** and **Actual Attendee Report.**

   ✔ The link to Sales Center Reports accesses a **Sales Meeting Report.**

   ✔ Support Center provides a **Customer Service Representative (CSR)
   Activity Log Query.**

   ✔ The Training Center offers both the Live Training Usage Report and
   Recorded Training Access Report.

Running a report

If you haven't done anything with your WebEx account since you signed up,
reports won't do you much good because they provide information about
your WebEx activity. But, assuming that you've been working with WebEx
even a bit, you've unknowingly (and from this point on, knowingly) generated
information about your meetings, events, and sessions that could come in
very handy.

Creating most reports requires similar steps: You find the report by going to
the My Reports page, clicking the report, identifying a date range or other
information, and then running the report. I'll step you through one so you get
the feel for it. A Usage Report for all services that you have available is a
good candidate for a dry run because it will be available no matter what combination of services you have chosen.

To run a Usage Report for all the services your company has access to, follow
these steps:

   1. **Go to the My WebEx page of your WebEx site.**

   2. **Choose the My Reports menu.**

   3. **Under All Services, click the Usage Report link.**

      The Usage Report page, as shown in Figure 12-2, appears.

   4. **Using the drop-down lists in the From and To fields, specify the date
      range for the report.**

   5. **(Optional) If you want to narrow it down to meetings on a certain
      topic, enter the relevant word or words in the Topic field.**

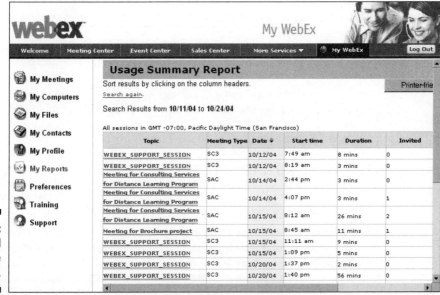

Figure 12-2:
Here's
where you
designate
the date
range for
the report.

Usage Report

View usage information for your meetings.
Note: Report can only be generated for dates up to three months prior to today.

From: October ▾ 18 ▾ 2004 ▾
To: October ▾ 24 ▾ 2004 ▾
Topic: [   ] (optional)
Sort results by: Date ▾ [Display Report]

Copyright © 2004 WebEx Communications, Inc.
Privacy | Terms of Service

Figure 12-2:
Here's where you designate the date range for the report.

6. **Click the arrow on the Sort Results By field if you want to sort by date, topic, username, or start time.**

7. **That's it! Click the Display Report button, and your report appears (see Figure 12-3).**

Usage Summary Report

Sort results by clicking on the column headers.
Search again.

Search Results from **10/11/04** to **10/24/04**

All sessions in GMT -07:00, Pacific Daylight Time (San Francisco)

Topic	Meeting Type	Date ⇕	Start time	Duration	Invited
WEBEX_SUPPORT_SESSION	SC3	10/12/04	7:49 am	8 mins	0
WEBEX_SUPPORT_SESSION	SC3	10/12/04	8:19 am	3 mins	0
Meeting for Consulting Services for Distance Learning Program	SAC	10/14/04	2:44 pm	3 mins	0
Meeting for Consulting Services for Distance Learning Program	SAC	10/14/04	4:07 pm	3 mins	1
Meeting for Consulting Services for Distance Learning Program	SAC	10/15/04	8:12 am	26 mins	2
Meeting for Brochure project	SAC	10/15/04	8:45 am	11 mins	1
WEBEX_SUPPORT_SESSION	SC3	10/15/04	11:11 am	9 mins	0
WEBEX_SUPPORT_SESSION	SC3	10/15/04	1:09 pm	5 mins	0
WEBEX_SUPPORT_SESSION	SC3	10/20/04	1:37 pm	2 mins	0
WEBEX_SUPPORT_SESSION	SC3	10/20/04	1:40 pm	56 mins	0

Printer-frie

Figure 12-3:
A typical Usage Report.

Some typical reports

The preceding section was like an appetizer: It showed you how to generate one report, but left you wanting more. Generating any WebEx report is equally simple. But so I don't leave you hungry, I'll give you a taste of some of the other reports that you might have at your disposal.

Figure 12-4 shows a Live Training Usage Summary, and Figure 12-5 shows a CSR Activity Log Query. Here's the type of information that you find in these reports:

Figure 12-4:
A Live
Training
Usage
Summary
report.

✔ The **Live Training Usage Summary** appropriately summarizes live training through Training Center versus activity involving playback of recorded training sessions for self-paced training. You generate this report by entering a date range. The report contains information on session topics; start time; duration; and attendees, including how many were invited, how many registered, the total number who attended, and the number who were absent. If you click any specific meeting's link, you get a more detailed report for that meeting, with each participant listed so you can see exactly who registered, attended, and so on.

✔ The **CSR Activity Log Query** gives you information on support sessions that you ran using Support Center. You generate this report by entering some criteria such as Support Session Number, company name, or satisfaction rating, as well as a date range. If you prefer, you can search by date only or by criteria only. The report shows the date and time of each session. Click a session link to see more detailed information (see Figure 12-6), such as a customer's name, e-mail address, and feedback on the session.

Figure 12-5: A CSR Activity Log Query.

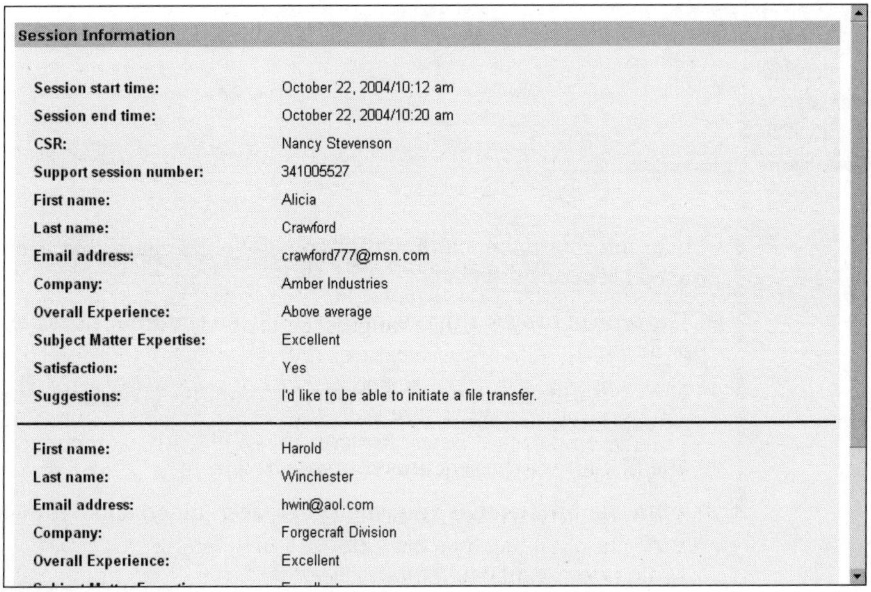

Figure 12-6: A detail of a Customer Support Session report.

Meet WebEx GlobalWatch™

GlobalWatch takes reporting into the realm of your system administrator. *GlobalWatch* is an add-on service to WebEx that gives your site administrator a comprehensive view of the performance of your WebEx meeting service. GlobalWatch provides your site administrator with real-time and historical performance information (which networking-inclined types refer to as *latency*) for each meeting and each individual attendee who came to your meeting. (See Figure 12-7.) GlobalWatch provides the following detailed meeting information:

Figure 12-7:
A Global-
Watch
view of the
detailed
user latency
(delay).

- ✔ User information, including the type of WebEx client that each person used (Java or Active-X).
- ✔ The type of browser that each person used (Internet Explorer, Netscape, or Firefox).
- ✔ The operating system on each user's computer (Windows, Mac OS, Linux, Unix).
- ✔ The IP address that each user connected from.
- ✔ A timestamp that tells you when each user joined and left the meeting.

✔ An overview of all the services that were used during your WebEx session. These services might have included presentation sharing, application or desktop sharing, WebEx audio conferencing, or WebEx video conferencing.

✔ The average delay, measured in five-minute intervals, between the WebEx meeting switch and the individual attendee's computer.

GlobalWatch also provides your site administrators with

✔ An overview of all pending and resolved *trouble tickets*. Trouble tickets are records of support calls customers make.

✔ Detailed reports of usage across your company and by department. This includes statistical information about the total number of meetings, attendees, and duration. Your site administrator can also run an exception report that includes all meetings that experienced a high latency (more than 1,000 milliseconds).

✔ The ability to proactively monitor the availability of the WebEx meeting service and to measure the performance from specific locations on the customer's network back to WebEx.

GlobalWatch empowers your site administrator by providing many proactive tools that can be used to better manage and control your WebEx meeting site.

Now I Have a Report: What Do I Do With It?

The whole point of putting all this information at your fingertips is for you to make use of it (and show your boss how much money you're saving by using online meetings). Here are some of the ways how you might use the reporting features of WebEx and GlobalWatch:

✔ Examine or calculate ROI of online meetings by generating regular reports of usage (see Figure 12-8).

✔ Review attendance figures to ensure that regular sessions or meetings you're running are being promoted adequately.

✔ Compare those who enroll for events with those who attend to see whether you should generate more meeting reminders to draw people in.

✔ Identify departments that are not taking advantage of more frequent online communications by scanning usage reports for underutilization.

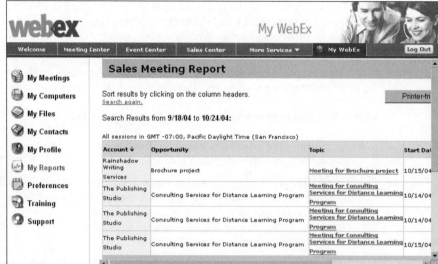

Figure 12-8:
A Sales
Center
report
showing
activity.

✔ Look at the archived files that are being most often accessed to identify areas of training that many people need help with.

✔ Use department coding features in GlobalWatch to charge costs of meetings to departments or customers.

✔ Review meeting and attendee performance information in GlobalWatch so that you can better support your end-user base and shorten the time to resolution of problems reported by your end users.

As with any report data, the significance is directly related to your needs and business strategies. But if you think that you could use some data about your WebEx account activity, odds are that WebEx has anticipated that need either in its built-in reporting or through GlobalWatch.

The specific reports available are likely to be changed or added to over time. Check the My Reports menu on your My WebEx site to explore all the reports available to you.

Chapter 13

Administering WebEx Made Easy

*T*he comprehensive suite of on-demand applications that WebEx offers for functions such as online meetings, marketing events, customer support, training, and sales is a boon to your business, it's true. But just who is going to manage this thing? (All eyes slowly turn toward the IT guy/gal, knowing that he/she will take care of everything.) Well, overworked IT guy/gal: This chapter's for you.

Just what is your company letting itself in for if it sets up a WebEx account? If you've bought into more than a pay-per-use solution from WebEx, you need to designate a site administrator who can set up user accounts, track your WebEx activity, manage security settings, and set up and maintain a company list of contacts. If your company is small and holds only a few meetings, an administrative assistant might be a good choice for your site administrator. If your company is larger or more meeting-active, the role probably ought to belong to somebody in the IT department.

In this chapter, I take a look at some of the common practices that site administrators must perform. Many other options and configurations in site administration are not covered here. But don't worry: As usual, WebEx documentation and support resources take you by the hand and give you training and documentation of specific procedures and practices when you sign up. And, thankfully, online help is available to guide you through all the options. Just click the Help link in the navigation bar on your administration site.

What Do WebEx Administrators Do?

WebEx Site Administration (see Figure 13-1) provides tools that help you easily manage your organization's WebEx service site.

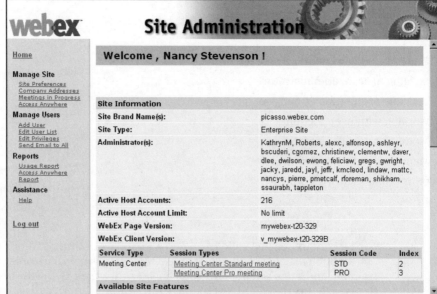

Figure 13-1: The WebEx Site Administration environment.

You can use Site Administration to

- ✔ View information about your organization's WebEx service, including its configuration and features.

- ✔ Add, modify, or deactivate user accounts.

- ✔ Maintain a company address book that includes contact information that all users can use when inviting attendees to meetings.

- ✔ Process requests to sign up for an account on your WebEx service site (if your site includes the signup option).

- ✔ Customize templates for e-mail messages that your WebEx service sends to users (if your site has the e-mail templates option).

- ✔ Manage Access Anywhere (if your site includes the Access Anywhere option).

- ✔ Manage security options for your WebEx service, including password requirements.

- ✔ Set up tracking codes that let you track usage of your WebEx service.

- ✔ Customize the Navigation bars on your WebEx service site.

- ✔ Specify configuration preferences for your organization's WebEx service site.

- ✔ Manage options for the specific services that your WebEx site includes.

- ✔ View a list of meetings, training sessions, support sessions, events, or Access Anywhere sessions in progress on your WebEx service site.

- ✔ View a list of remote computers that users have set up for Access Anywhere, and determine which computers users are currently accessing remotely.

- ✔ View detailed usage reports.

First Things First: Logging In and Out

To log in to Site Administration, you must first have an administrator account. WebEx creates an initial administrator account for your organization when you sign up.

Confused about your account? If you have any questions about administrator accounts, just contact your WebEx account manager.

Follow these steps to log in to Site Administration:

1. **Enter your Site Administration URL in your browser address bar.**

   The URL for Site Administration is in this format:

   ```
   http://your_company.webex.com/your_company/admin.php
   ```

   where *your_company* is the brand name for your WebEx service.

2. **On the page that appears (see Figure 13-2), type your user name in the User Name box.**

3. **Type your password in the Password box.**

4. **Click the Log In button.**

   The Home page appears (refer to Figure 13-1), showing information about your organization's WebEx service.

To log out of Site Administration, click Log Out on the Navigation bar.

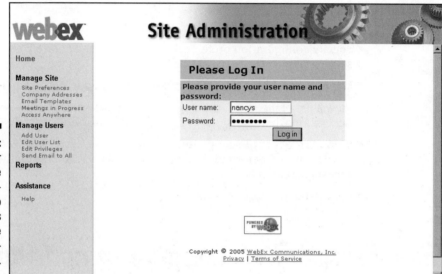

Figure 13-2:
Enter your
user name
and pass-
word to
gain access
to Site
Adminis-
tration.

If your company has the Enterprise Edition of WebEx, after you log into your WebEx site, you can see a button in the horizontal navigation bar that takes you to the Site Administration page. If there is no room on the navigation bar, this button appears in the More Services menu.

To use Site Administration, your WebEx user account must have the Site Administrator privilege. If your account has full administrative privileges, you can go to town and change any settings in Site Administration you like. If your account has read-only administrative privileges, you can view all information and settings in Site Administration, but you can't change any settings.

Taking a Look at Your Site's Information

Information is any administrator's lifeblood. You need to be able to quickly review your site's settings to know who your users are and what WebEx features your organization is taking advantage of.

You can view the following information about your organization's WebEx service site on your site administration home page:

  ✔ The brand name for your WebEx service Web site

  ✔ The type of WebEx service for which your organization has an account

  ✔ The user names of the administrators for your site

  ✔ The number of users who have accounts on your organization's WebEx service site

  ✔ The version of your WebEx service

  ✔ The types of meetings that users can host using your organization's WebEx service site

  ✔ The features that are available with your organization's WebEx service site (as shown in Figure 13-3)

This information appears when you first log on to the site. To view the information at any time, click the Home button on the Navigation bar. The Home page appears, showing you all the bells and whistles of your WebEx service.

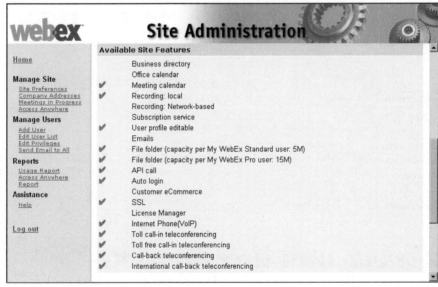

Figure 13-3: The site features with check marks are yours to use.

You can also take a peek at who's doing what by viewing a list of meetings, training sessions, support sessions, events, or Access Anywhere sessions that are currently in progress on your WebEx service site.

For each meeting, you can see the

- ✔ Topic
- ✔ Host's name
- ✔ Starting time

To view a list of meetings in progress, just click Meetings in Progress on the Navigation bar, under Manage Site. The Meetings in Progress page appears (see Figure 13-4), showing any meetings, training sessions, support sessions, events, or Access Anywhere sessions that are currently in progress.

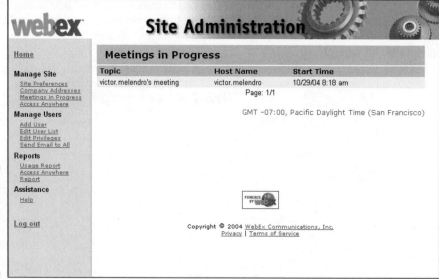

Figure 13-4: Scope out all your user meetings in progress here.

Working with User Accounts

Users come in all shapes and sizes, from your IT manager and the CEO to the company receptionist and field sales person. Each of these folks needs different things from your WebEx service. The roles that they play in meetings typically determine what kind of user accounts they should get as well as what sorts of privileges.

Who's who?

You can add any number of user accounts, but your organization's contract with WebEx usually limits the number of users who can actually host or attend meetings, training sessions, support sessions, or events, or access remote computers at any one time.

Users don't have to have user accounts to attend meetings, training sessions, support sessions, or events *unless* a host selects the option that a user account is required to attend when setting the meeting up.

Here's a rundown of the various types of user accounts:

✔ **Host only:** This specifies that the user can use your organization's WebEx service site to host meetings, training sessions, support sessions, or events, depending on your site type.

✔ **Site Admin:** This is the user who can use your organization's WebEx service as a host and use Site Administration to administer your WebEx service. In other words, this is probably you.

Because a Site Administrator can manage user accounts, handle registration requests, and specify preferences for your organization's WebEx service, WebEx recommends that you have only one or two Site Administrator accounts to avoid confusion.

✔ **Site Admin - View Only:** This is like Site Admin Lite. If you specify this option when setting up an account, the user can use your organization's WebEx service as a host and use Site Administration to view user account information, registration requests, and WebEx configuration and preferences. However, a site administrator with view-only privileges can't make changes to user account information or change settings for your organization's site.

✔ **Attendee only:** If the Attendee accounts option is enabled on your site, this user can log in to your WebEx service Web site to attend meetings, but that's it. The user can use My WebEx to maintain his or her profile and to view a list of meetings to which he or she is invited but can't actually host meetings on your site.

Adding a user account

You can either add user accounts one at a time or add multiple user accounts simultaneously, using a batch process.

If your organization's WebEx service site includes the account signup option, you can also add users by accepting requests to signup for an account on your site. This feature is available for both Host accounts and Attendee accounts. Usually, attendees just set up their own Attendee account through the account signup option.

Follow these steps to add a user account:

1. On the Navigation bar, under Manage Users, click Add User.

The Add User page appears (see Figure 13-5).

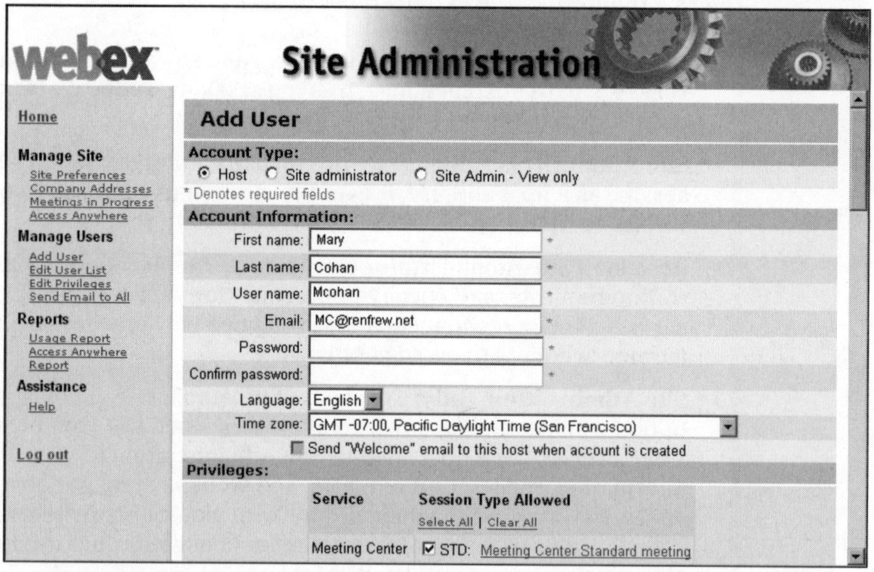

Figure 13-5:
The Add
User page.

2. Specify account information as follows:

a. Select an option at the top of the page to designate the account type.

b. Specify the user's first name, last name, user name, password, and e-mail address.

c. To automatically notify a user that an account has been created, select the Send "Welcome" Email to This Host When Account Is Created check box.

d. Set the appropriate privileges, such as the services for which the user is allowed to host meetings and the session types for each

WebEx service. Set the account's privileges for WebEx Telephony options, such as Call-in, Call-back third-party teleconferencing, and Internet Phone (VoIP). You can enable General tools, such as the Recording Editor, as well as service-specific options, such as the Hands-on Lab Admin for Training Center, or Sales Rep for Sales Center.

 e. In the My WebEx section of the form, you can allocate additional storage space on your WebEx site for a user by entering a value in MB in the Additional Storage field.

 f. Other information — such as the user's phone number, address, language, and time zone — is optional.

3. Click Add.

Site Administration adds the user account to the list of accounts on the Edit User List.

Specifying privileges for user accounts

We're not all born with the same privileges. Some people come complete with silver spoons dangling from their mouths; others aren't so lucky. But in the world of WebEx, it's the Site Administrator who decides who gets what privileges.

You can change the privilege assignments for a user account at any time by specifying the following:

✓ **The types of meetings that a user can host on your WebEx site.** Session types determine which services and features a user can use.

✓ **Whether a user can use My WebEx Standard or My WebEx Pro features.** To see the features available for each type, click the link at the head of the STD or PRO columns in the Edit User List page, which you can display by scrolling to the right from the screen you can see in Figure 13-6)

✓ **Which teleconferencing services a user can take advantage of** during a meeting or training session, such as toll-free call-in or call-back.

✓ **You can temporarily deactivate a user account at any time.** While a user account is deactivated, the user cannot host meetings using your organization's WebEx service site. You can reactivate a deactivated user account at any time. This can be useful when you want to set up new users but not activate their accounts until they are approved by management.

You can change the privileges for either all user accounts simultaneously or only specific user accounts. However, if you change privileges for all accounts, you can still modify those privileges for specific accounts.

1. **On the Navigation bar, under Manage Users, click Edit User List.**

   The Edit User List page, as shown in Figure 13-6, appears.

Figure 13-6: Here's where you can pick a user to make changes to privileges.

2. **Locate the user account in the list.**

   To quickly locate a user account, do one of the following:

   • Type the user's user name in the User Name box and click Search.

   • Type the user's e-mail address in the Email box and click Search.

   • In the Index, click the letter that corresponds to the first character in the user name.

   • In the Index, click # to list any user names that begin with a number.

3. **To make a user account active or inactive, select or clear (respectively) the Active check box for the account; then click Submit.**

4. **To change the session types that a user can host, or the features of MyWebEx (Standard or Pro) the user has access to, select or clear the check boxes in the Session Types and My WebEx columns. Then click Submit.**

5. **To edit details about a user account, click the link for the account under Name.**

   The Edit User page, as shown in Figure 13-7, appears.

6. **Specify new account information.**

7. **Click Update to save your changes.**

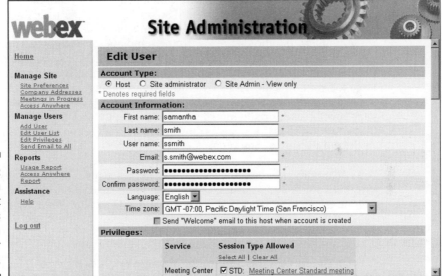

Figure 13-7:
Here you can edit details about a single user account.

To make it easier to find an individual user, you can sort the list of users by selecting an option in the Sort List By drop-down list. You can sort the list in ascending order according to user first names or last names, e-mail domains (that is, the text that follows the @ symbol in an e-mail address), or the time when you created the account.

Finally, note that you cannot remove a user account from your WebEx service site by using Site Administration. However, you can make an account inactive (see the previous steps), change the information about the account, or assign it to another user.

Managing E-Mail Templates

Your WebEx service is designed to save you time and effort. One of the ways how it does this is to automatically send e-mail messages to meeting or session attendees, invitees, and hosts when certain events happen. For example, if a host invites attendees when she schedules a meeting, your WebEx service automatically sends a nice little invitation e-mail message to each invited attendee. If she also chooses to, she can specify that a reminder e-mail should go out a day before the meeting, and so on.

Site Administration holds the key to the template for each e-mail message that your WebEx service sends out. If the option to edit e-mail templates is enabled on your site, you can change the default messages to customize them for your specific needs by editing, rearranging, or deleting the text and *variables* (code text that your WebEx service recognizes and substitutes with your specific user or site information). But don't worry if you decide later that you want to be more generic: You can also revert any e-mail template to its default version at any time.

You can modify the template for any e-mail messages that your WebEx service automatically sends to users, but keep in mind that Site Administration might include e-mail templates that are not applicable to your WebEx service.

To modify an e-mail template, follow these steps:

1. **On the Navigation bar, under Manage Site, click Email Templates.**

   The E-mail Templates page appears, showing a list of all e-mail templates that are available for your WebEx service.

2. **If your WebEx site has multiple services, under Existing Email Templates For, select the service for which you want to modify e-mail templates.**

3. **Under Email Name, click the link for the template that you want to modify.**

   The Edit Email Message page appears, showing the content and variables in the e-mail message.

4. **Modify the text and remove or rearrange variables as necessary.**

   Be sure that you don't modify the text code for variables and that a percent sign (%) precedes and follows all variables.

5. **Click Update.**

Maintaining Company Contacts

When folks set up meetings, sessions, and events via WebEx, they have to designate who will attend. This can include attendees, presenters, or in-support-sessions people to assist in the session. The host can choose these folks from a company address book when the meeting is being set up. Guess who gets to set up the company address book and populate it with contacts?

(Yup. You.)

Importing contacts

I just know that for years, your company has been storing contact information somewhere on your network, and you groan at the thought of having to reenter all that information into yet another online Address Book. Never fear: You can import lists of contacts from Microsoft Outlook or any comma-delimited file. A *comma-separated-values files (CSV)* is a kind of data file in which commas are used to separate fields of data. You might save an Excel spreadsheet of contact information as a comma-delimited file and import that file into WebEx's Address Book, for example.

Note that you control the company address book, but individual users can also create personal contact lists from their My WebEx pages.

Follow these steps to import a list of contacts from Outlook:

1. **In the Navigation bar of the Site Administration site, click the Company Addresses link.**

   The Company Address Book page, as shown in Figure 13-8, appears.

2. **Click the Import button.**

3. **In the Batch Import Contacts page that appears (see Figure 13-9) choose Microsoft Outlook in the Method 1 drop-down list.**

   The other options in this list are Exchange, which offers more advanced options only for those who feel expert at importing data tasks, and `.csv` file import. (See the upcoming Tip for more about this option.)

4. **Click the Import button.**

   A message appears: `Importing Outlook Address Book.` Just relax and chant your mantra while your computer does its thing — it could take a few moments, depending on just how many contacts you've stuffed into Outlook.

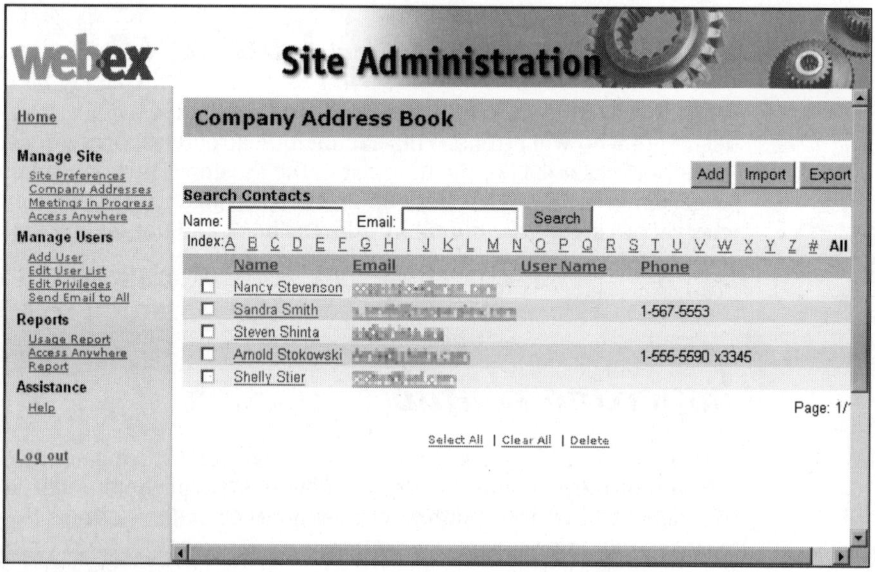

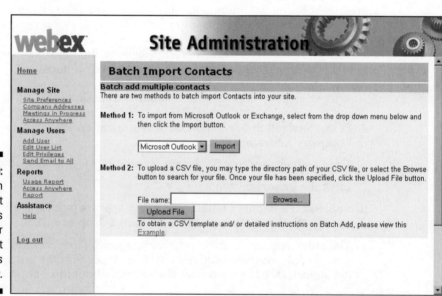

Figure 13-8:
Manage
your
contacts
in the
Company
Address
Book.

Figure 13-9:
The Batch
Import
Contacts
page for
getting a lot
of contacts
fast.

If your company doesn't use Outlook, you can use the comma-delimited file option. To import a comma-delimited file of contacts (such as an Excel spreadsheet saved as a comma-delimited file), enter a filename in the Method 2 field shown in Figure 13-9 and proceed with your import.

Adding contacts one by one

After you get the bulk of your contacts into WebEx, from time to time, you'll want to add a new contact. You can easily add a contact to WebEx from the Company Address Book page (refer to Figure 13-8) by following these steps:

1. **Click the Add button.**

   The form shown in Figure 13-10 appears.

2. **Fill in whatever fields you want to include; the required Full Name and Email Address fields are enough to invite somebody to a meeting, but everything else is optional.**

3. **Click the Add button. That's it!**

Figure 13-10: Enter a new contact's information.

webex — **Site Administration**

Company Address Book

Get Map...

Home

Manage Site
Site Preferences
Company Addresses
Meetings in Progress
Access Anywhere

Manage Users
Add User
Edit User List
Edit Privileges
Send Email to All

Reports
Usage Report
Access Anywhere Report

Assistance
Help

Log out

New Contact

| Full name: | Ephraim Pike | (Required) |

| Email address: | Epike@publicets.org | (Required) |

| Company: | Public ETS Group |

| Job title: | Chief Administrator |

| URL: | www.publicets.org | (if known) |

Phone number:

| Country/Region | Area or city code: | Number: | Extension: |
| 1 | 987 | 555-9090 | |

Phone number for mobile device:

| Country/Region | Area or city code: | Number: | Extension: |
| 1 | | | |

Fax number:

| Country/Region | Area or city code: | Number: | Extension: |
| 1 | | | |

Editing contacts

Charlie used to work at Apex Toys but moved to Toys Is We; Mary got married, and now her last name is Dipplewithe; Claude changed his cellphone provider. . . .

You get the idea: Nothing is forever. In our hurly-burly world, contact information for people is often as changeable as the weather in spring. Here, then, are the simple steps involved in editing a contact to get his or her information up to date.

1. **With the Company Address Book page displayed, click the name of the contact that you want to edit.**

   The person's contact information is displayed. (This is the page shown in Figure 13-10.)

2. **Change the contents of any field you wish to change and then click the Update button.**

Exporting contacts

After you spend all this time getting contacts into your WebEx Address Book, you shouldn't have to duplicate the effort to get that data in Excel. Well, good news. You don't have to. Here's how to export your WebEx contact list to Excel:

1. **From the Company Address Book page, click the Export button.**

2. **In the File Download dialog box that appears (see Figure 13-11), click Save.**

   The Save As dialog box appears.

Figure 13-11:
You can
open or
save the
Address
Book
contents.

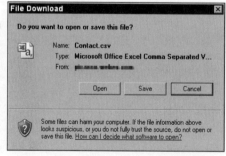

3. **Select a location to save the file to, and then click Save.**

   The file is saved in the comma-separated-value format in the specified location.

Now use the Import feature in Excel to import this file of contacts.

Deleting contacts

Time for something easy. To delete a contact, select the check box in front of it on the Company Address Book page and click the Delete link. Bye-bye, contact!

It's All about Security

Security is a hot topic these days, near and dear to any administrator's heart. You'll be happy to hear that you can use Site Administration to provide security for your WebEx service site.

What's in your control

By adjusting various settings, you can require any of the following:

- ✓ Users have to specify a password for any meetings that they host. No password, no meeting.

- ✓ All meeting passwords must be in a strict password format that you specify and cannot contain any specified text strings or words.

- ✓ All user account passwords must be in a strict password format that you specify.

- ✓ All meetings must be unlisted — that is, they must not appear on your site's public calendar. This provides additional security for your meetings because meeting information is not displayed publicly. To join an unlisted meeting, attendees have to provide a unique meeting number that they get from the host.

- ✓ All attendees must provide their e-mail addresses to join a meeting.

- ✓ All requests to send a forgotten user password must be approved.

- ✓ All users must log in to your WebEx service site. If you choose this option, all users must have a user account and log in to view anything on your site. This effectively makes your site a private meeting site.

✔ With Site Administration, you can provide security for your WebEx service site by requiring restrictions for the following:

- Access to your WebEx service site

- Access to meetings on your WebEx service site

- User names and passwords for accounts

- The length and format in which users can specify passwords

- Access to a user's shared folders or Personal Meeting Room page

- The access code for access to remote computers through Access Anywhere

Specifying security options

Site Administration provides you with several options for preventing unauthorized folks from accessing or using your WebEx service site. These options let you choose the ideal level of security for your service.

To specify security options:

1. On the Navigation bar, under Manage Site, click Site Preferences.

The Site Preferences page, as shown in Figure 13-12, appears.

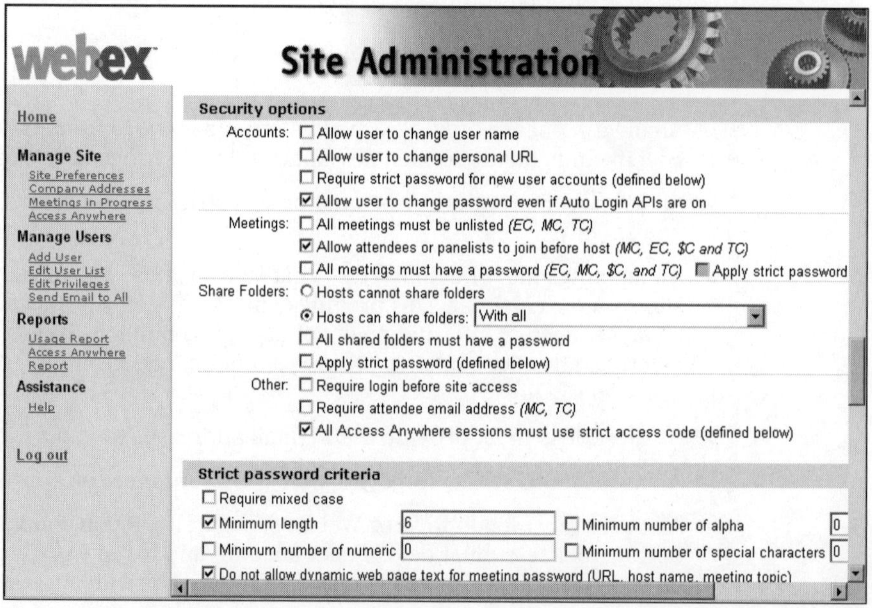

Figure 13-12:
The security section of your preferences: Control Central for security settings.

A word about password protection

The All Meetings Must Have a Password item in the Security Options on the Site Preferences page is an important item. WebEx strongly recommends that you activate this option if it's not already to help ensure the security of meetings on your site. If you also select the Apply Strict Password check box, you can use additional settings in the Strict Password Criteria section that follows to control passwords more tightly.

Here are some of the criteria that you can manage in the Strict Password Criteria section:

✔ The password length; by default this must be at least six characters, but you can specify a different minimum length.

✔ The password cannot contain any text that appears on the Meeting Calendar page, such as the host's name or the meeting topic.

✔ The password cannot be an easy-to-guess word, such as *meeting* or *password*. You include such words in the Do Not Allow Meeting Passwords from This List section.

Note that these criteria apply only to the Meeting Center, Training Center, Event Center, and Sales Center sites. Support Center is the odd man out here.

2. **Under Security Options, select the check boxes or radio buttons for any security limitations that you wish to impose on your site.**

3. **Click Update to save your changes.**

Part VI
The Part of Tens

The 5th Wave — By Rich Tennant

BEFORE WebEX....

"GET READY, I THINK THEY'RE STARTING TO DRIFT."

In this part . . .

Ten ways to skin a cat. Ten things we love about Raymond. Ten . . . well, you get the idea. Lists of ten seem to be popular, so I've provided you with four of them in this part.

Chapter 14 tells you ten neat things to explore if you use WebEx throughout a larger enterprise. Chapter 15 is where I pass on tips about customers' most frequently asked questions, with answers straight from the mouths (or keyboards) of WebEx's own support folks. Chapter 16 offers ten ideas about how small businesses can get the most out of WebEx.

Chapter 14

Ten Things WebEx Can Do for Your Enterprise

. . . .

In This Chapter

▶ Discovering what WebEx Enterprise Edition has to offer

▶ Exploring ideas for increasing your enterprise's productivity with WebEx

▶ Understanding how WebEx optimizes the online event experience for enterprises

. . . .

*W*hen does a company become an enterprise? The day you don't get to say good morning to everybody in the company because some of them are a five-minute walk or five-hour flight away might just be the day you've crossed into the realm of an enterprise. That's the day you're big enough to have to make a special effort to ensure that everybody is on the same page about things like company goals and policies, order status, new product announcements, and so on.

When you cross that enterprise line, you need extra help facilitating state-of-the-art communications to prevent chaos. WebEx can be a big part of your enterprise communications strategy, and the Enterprise Edition will become your new best friend.

In this chapter, you discover some of the features that make WebEx a perfect fit for any enterprise. Some of the features that help your enterprise come with your garden-variety WebEx account, and some are strictly available in the Enterprise Edition. Talk to your WebEx account manager to figure out how to get set up to take advantage of the ones you need.

Security, Security, Security

Security is of special concern to enterprises, which typically have to share information between geographically diverse departments, offices, vendors, and customers in safe ways.

The MediaTone Network, owned by WebEx, doesn't involve any third-party folks in transmitting data, so you don't have to worry about information going astray. And what goes on in your meeting is never stored, only transmitted.

Finally, you can experience media-rich presentations both inside and outside your own corporate firewall and you can define and enforce your own security policies for online meetings.

Things Change: Scalability

Because WebEx is a Web service, it grows or shrinks along with your needs. You don't have to invest in server and software maintenance, so if more employees need to participate in online meetings, there's no new IT investment.

Tailored packages can offer savings with unlimited product training services, including access to self-paced modules, unlimited Service Assist sessions, and cost-effective meeting access packages.

Through My WebEx, users in your enterprise can access whatever WebEx services they need from a single place with a single login.

We Just Opened Our 500th Branch Office

If your enterprise is located all over the map, WebEx is a perfect solution for your communication needs. As long as people have a computer with Internet access they can access meetings, files, support, and training. Whether you want to provide consistent training to thousands of employees around the world, or effective support to customers from Tangiers to Tallahassee, this centralized online service helps you keep your many offices, people in the field, vendors, and customers connected.

Supporting protocols

MediaTone technology, which underlies all of WebEx's offerings, is built to deliver rich-media content to a huge number of customer devices, so your CEO can get into a meeting via his cell phone, and your CFO can dial in via Internet Phone. (If what follows is geek to you, just hand this page to your IT team — they'll thank you for it.)

Supported standards include

- ✔ H.323, the leading protocol for Voice over Internet Protocol (VoIP)

- ✔ Session Initiation Protocol (SIP), used for conferencing via Internet Protocol (IP) phone or instant messenger devices

- ✔ Lightweight Directory Access Protocol (LDAP), a vendor-independent network directory protocol that provides directory server integration for WebEx services

- ✔ Extensible Markup Language (XML)

- ✔ Secure Sockets Layer (SSL)

- ✔ Aviation Industry CBT Committee (AICC) protocol

- ✔ Sharable Content Object Reference Model (SCORM)

Getting Decision Makers What They Need

The ability to initiate One-Click Meetings and share documents and applications means that people who make decisions can get together instantly and access the information they need.

If you're a bean counter who must make decisions about your online meeting solution, use WebEx usage history and recorded access history to see just how much your people are getting out of the service.

Enterprise-Powered Collaboration

Everybody, from project teams to department workgroups, can use WebEx to enhance collaboration. Being able to pull the team together wherever they are through an online meeting can be a powerful tool for efficiency. In addition, the ability to share applications, such as a project management software package with up-to-the minute project data, and files, such as a spreadsheet with budget data, enables teams and workgroups to stay on the same page.

WebEx meeting features, such as the Whiteboard for group brainstorming and annotation tools to mark up shared documents, offer the possibility of an interactive environment that goes far beyond sketching ideas on paper.

As reported in *Fortune* magazine's November 29, 2004 issue, many large companies like ChevronTexaco, Sun Life Financial and Georgia-Pacific are taking advantage of the Internet to run brainstorming sessions that allow people in far-flung locations to meet and brainstorm online.

Speaking the Language: Localized Versions

Today, business is not confined to any geographical borders. Increasingly, companies must broaden their borders to encompass employees, vendors, and customers around the world.

When in Rome, do as the Romans do, right? Well, what if you're French, German, Swedish, Chinese, Japanese, or Korean? No problem. Enterprise Edition has localized Meeting Center versions in all those languages. Instant Global Village!

Teleconferencing Your Way

You say you're already set up with your own teleconferencing system and don't want to rock the boat by switching to WebEx for teleconferencing services? No problem. WebEx lets you use either its teleconferencing services or your existing teleconferencing solution. It's up to you.

Lowering Your Costs

Using WebEx can save you money in more ways than I have time to explore here. But if you've got an enterprise, consider these typical ways you can save money. With WebEx you can

- Accelerate and streamline processes used to deliver and support products and services.
- Reduce costs associated with lost cycles, deferred decisions, and unnecessary travel and facility expenses.
- Have control over online meeting costs because of usage-based cost allocations that enterprise subscription pricing offers.

✔ Provide ongoing training at a much reduced cost. Bottom line: A better-trained workforce means more profits.

✔ Purchase subscription minutes that you can use for any WebEx service. That means you just pick and choose the right tool for any job without worrying about the costs.

✔ Give your accounting folks a way to manage costs and control accountability by using integrated tracking numbers.

✔ Experience rapid deployment of WebEx, made possible because you don't have to install hardware or software on site. You usually don't have to configure or integrate enterprise software or firewalls, either.

Getting Dedicated Support

If your enterprise is large, you could have employees meeting 24 hours a day, seven days a week, in various parts of the world. You can't afford to lose your online meeting support for even an hour. That's why WebEx provides premium support services for enterprises.

Enterprise Edition users get

✔ A dedicated 800 number for anytime access

✔ A single Service Level Agreement (SLA)

✔ Unlimited Service Assist sessions

Integration Rules!

Enterprise. . . the word conjures up images of *Star Trek*. . . I mean, Enterprise Resource Planning (ERP), right? So if you are utilizing enterprise solutions in your organization, you'll be glad to hear that your enterprise can easily integrate WebEx services within existing corporate applications for accounting, CRM (Customer Resource Management), ERP, human resources, and others. WebEx fits within your business processes that you already know and love. This means that you can run any enterprise software application to share data with employees, provide demos to customers, or offer training to employees without ever leaving the original application.

Beam me up, Scotty!

One more feature enterprise types will like: You can configure WebEx services to reflect your corporate look, extending branding across your enterprise.

Chapter 15

Top Nine Frequently Asked Questions from WebEx Tech Support

*W*hen you want advice about something, I say go right to the source. So I tapped into WebEx's own customer support reps, and they shared their most frequently asked customer questions (and answers) with me. And because I like you, I'm going to share those answers with you.

Many of these questions relate to procedures I've covered in more detail elsewhere in this book, but because the questions come up so frequently on the tech support lines, this chapter provides a handy common-problem solution list. Perhaps one of these items will help you in your learning curve as you explore all WebEx has to offer.

You can connect with these nice folks yourself by going to www.webex.com and choosing Customer Care⇨Technical Support.

How Do I Share a Presentation or Document?

First things first: You have to have started a meeting or session of some sort (such as a training session) to do this. Then, from within your meeting window, choose Share⇨Presentation or Document. An Open dialog box is displayed; select the file you want to share and click Open.

See Chapter 8 for more about sharing things with others during a meeting.

Where Can I Locate WebEx Security Information?

Enter this URL in your browser to go to the WebEx Knowledge Base: `http://kb.webex.com`. Enter the term "security" in the search box and click the Search button. Then just click the link for the topic you're interested in to display information about that topic.

If you need help with security questions, call Technical Support at 1-866-229-3239 and choose Option 4. To find international support numbers, go to `www.webex.com/customercare/phone-numbers.html`.

How Do I Join a Meeting?

You can join two types of WebEx meetings: listed and unlisted. A listed meeting appears on the public meeting calendar. An unlisted meeting (logically enough) doesn't.

To join a listed meeting, follow these steps:

1. **Go to the WebEx URL provided by the meeting host (usually** `company_name.webex.com`**).**

2. **Click the Join link next to the meeting you want to join.**

3. **Enter your name, e-mail address, and password, if the host assigned one.**

4. **Click OK.**

   You'll now be connected.

If there is no Join link next to your meeting, it could be because you're too early and the meeting hasn't started. Click the Refresh button on your browser to check again in a minute or two. Be sure you've got the time zone for the meeting time right; there is time zone information near the top of the meeting listing page. Finally, if you've been clicking Refresh for what seems like hours, you might just want to call the meeting host and make sure the meeting hasn't been cancelled.

To join an unlisted meeting, follow these steps:

1. **Go to the WebEx URL provided by the host.**

2. **On the left side of the Navigation bar, click the Unlisted link.**

3. **Enter the meeting number, which is required to join an unlisted meeting. (Your host should provide this to you.)**

4. **Enter your name, e-mail address, and password, if any.**

5. **Click OK.**

   You are now connected.

Read more about joining and participating in meetings in Chapter 8.

How Do I Share Remote Control of My Desktop?

Sharing control of your desktop is a great way to provide technical support for a software product or to let your customer view a graphic, animated demo, or document on your computer.

First you have to start a meeting, session, or event. Then follow these steps to share your desktop:

1. **Choose Share⇨Desktop.**

2. **Select a user you want to share control with.**

3. **Click OK.**

You can read more details about working within a shared desktop in Chapter 7.

How Do I Distribute a WebEx Recording File?

When you record a WebEx meeting or presentation, it's saved in WebEx Recording File (`.wrf`) format. You have a few options for saving or sending these files to others. You can save the file, along with the WebEx Player, which is required in order to play `.wrf` files, on a CD, or send the file by e-mail.

To send a `.wrf` file to CD, first download the WebEx Player from your WebEx site by choosing Support and scrolling to the Record/Playback section of the page. Add the `.wrf` files and player executable file to your CD.

To send a `.wrf` file by e-mail, follow these steps:

1. **Create a new e-mail and include in the body the message that recipients will have to install the WebEx Player to view the files.**

2. **Include a link to the WebEx Player on your company's WebEx site so the recipients can go there to download it.**

3. **Using the Attach feature of your e-mail program, attach the `.wrf` files.**

The link to download the WebEx Player typically looks something like this: `company_name.webex.com/client/latest/atplay.exe`.

How Do I Invite Attendees from within a WebEx Meeting?

Sometimes you're in the middle of a meeting and you realize Bob Whatshisname from Accounting really should have been invited. What to do? Invite him. You can do it during a meeting easily by following these steps:

1. **Choose Participant⇨Invite.**

2. **Select the By E-mail option.**

3. **Enter the invitee's e-mail address in the dialog box that appears and click the Send Invitation button.**

Can I Start a Meeting before the Scheduled Start Time?

This one's easy, but apparently the question occurs to folks frequently enough that technical support would like you to know the answer. Yes, a host can start a meeting at any time before the scheduled start time. There are two possibilities here:

✔ If starting the meeting a significant amount of time before the scheduled start time, for example the day before or an hour before, once the host starts the meeting, only then will attendees have the option to join it. Basically it's like the host unlocking the meeting room door prior to the meeting for attendees to enter on their own accord.

✔ If the host has allowed people to join, say, 15 minutes ahead of the scheduled start time in setting the meeting up, people can join early, but no earlier than the time increment the host has designated (in this example, 15 minutes before schedule start time).

Why Did My Connection Get Interrupted?

WebEx provides a *really* reliable connection thanks to the WebEx MediaTone network, so you might have to take the blame if you lost a connection. Doing any of these things could interrupt your connection:

✔ Refreshing the Web page

✔ Typing in another URL

✔ Clicking the Back or Forward buttons

The bad news: If you do one of these actions and your connection is lost, you'll have to close all open browser windows and join the meeting all over again. The good news: This only takes a minute or so to do.

What Is the Difference between a Call In and Call Out Teleconference?

Essentially, getting involved in a teleconference can happen in a couple of ways. A participant can call a number to access an online meeting, or the WebEx service can call out to attendees to hook them up with the meeting. The host makes this choice when scheduling a meeting. (Chapter 8 covers the various ways to get connected to a meeting.)

Chapter 16

Ten Ideas for Small Businesses to Maximize Success

In This Chapter

▶ Exploring how to become more productive with WebEx

▶ Growing your business with WebEx's help

▶ Maximizing your resources with WebEx

Some would say that small businesses are the backbone of our economy. Mom and pop stores of yesteryear have become Joe and Charlene start-ups. Startups have a way of growing and changing all the time. (Think Bill Gates in his garage, or Mary Kay at her kitchen table.)

If you're running a small business, you have your own unique needs. What kinds of needs? Well, for one thing, everybody who works for you wears so many hats you probably have a ten-tiered hat stand in every office. Money is not exactly growing on trees in your reception area. And you can't wait years for sales to close. (Stop me if this sounds familiar.)

In this chapter, I take a look at some of the ways that any small business can take advantage of WebEx to raise productivity, become more efficient, and save money.

Start Sharing!

If you work for a small business, you have to share things. You share the stapler, the coffee-making duties, and the three phone lines. So the sharing capabilities of WebEx are a natural fit for you.

Here are just a few ways WebEx can help you share things to help you save money:

- ✓ **Maximize software spending with shared applications.** For example, if you want to see what your staff thinks of an application you're considering buying, let them play around with it in an online environment before you buy multiple copies.

- ✓ **Save on overnight charges by finding other ways to share documents.** You don't have to make ten copies of your budget before the meeting. Share the budget document file during the online meeting and save the copy costs.

- ✓ **Share your desktop to demonstrate a new process.** It's quick and easy training that saves you from having to go to each person's desk and teach him or her the latest scheduler or e-mail client.

Grow Beyond Your Office

Three cubicles, a reception area, and two manager's offices in an industrial park in Oshkosh may be a fine place to work, but to grow beyond your own office walls you need a way to connect with the world at large. Here's how WebEx helps you do that:

- ✓ **Global reach:** Even a small business can land a client with an office in England or Rome. To communicate with international offices via traditional phone services is cost prohibitive. To connect via e-mail is too impersonal. Use WebEx video playback or video conferencing features to make more direct connections and stay competitive with the big guys who have in-house video-conferencing facilities or huge travel budgets.

- ✓ **Collaborate more powerfully than you can with a conference call:** Let's face it: There are limitations to conference calls. You can't dazzle customers with multimedia presentations, share documents, or even see their reactions to your presentation. Using WebEx, you can incorporate rich media presentations, file sharing, and even inexpensive video into your meetings.

David and Goliath: You versus the Competition

Your greatest competitor is three times bigger than you. You're sick of walking away from sales pitch meetings with the sinking feeling that you've been sideswiped by that competitor because it is able to offer a glitzier sales pre-sentation, even though you know you can beat its pants off when it comes to your product or service. What to do?

In a word, WebEx. With WebEx, you can

- ✔ Meet with customers more often, ensuring that they never forget who you are, what you can offer, and how service-oriented you are

- ✔ Solve problems instantly to retain hard-won customers

- ✔ Provide world-class support and training with a small investment

Start Where You Want, Grow When You're Ready

What you do with WebEx is up to you. The ability to start with a few Pay-Per-Use meetings, then move to a simple WebEx Express package or a small business package, and then finally to grow into a tailored solution is a power-ful tool. If you land a huge contract and experience astronomical growth leaps, WebEx will be there to help you make those leaps successfully.

As a Web-based service, WebEx saves you the investment in hardware or software that other options require.

IT Guy . . . What IT Guy?

Large companies have IT staffs. Small businesses often don't have much more than an assistant who is pretty good with computers (mostly because he lives on computer games when he's not at work). If this sounds like you, you'll be glad to hear that WebEx comes with a staff of people who are there to ensure you have productive online meetings. Meeting Center Assists, which provide a live helper to get you through your learning curve, help you get comfortable right off the bat.

And WebEx's easy-to-use interface and online documentation and training provide your folks with all they need to be successful with WebEx.

Small Business Packages for Added Value

WebEx recognizes that small businesses are a large part of its customer base. That's why it offers specially tailored small-business packages that help you succeed. Here are the two small business packages offered as of this writing (but be sure to check the latest offerings when you're ready to shop WebEx):

✔ **The Small Business Value Package:** This package was designed to help you increase the number of leads you get and to help you grow your business. It includes

- WebEx Meeting Center for interactive meetings
- WebEx Event Center
- WebEx Meeting Assist to provide hand-holding support while you're learning your way around online meetings
- Production Services to monitor your online event and provide real-time assistance
- Integrated Audio Conferencing

✔ **The Small Business Premium Package:** This includes everything in the Value Package, plus

- The WebEx Sales Center for high-quality sales demos and presentations
- WebEx Training Center, which offers a dynamic virtual training classroom
- WebEx Support Center for remote online support service

Travel Budget? Ha!

Your competition has a dedicated phone line to its travel agency, as well as massive corporate discounts. You access an online discount travel service that you pray will give you an airfare to Detroit under $10,000 when you have to get to your customer's site with only a day's notice.

If the words "travel budget" cause your accountant to react with a serious twitch, relax. Using WebEx means that you can save on travel costs for sales calls, product demos, customer training, problem solving, and just about anything else you can think of. Just do them all online!

Looking Like the Big Guys

Napoleon didn't let size hold him back; neither should you. If you're currently small, but think big, you can use WebEx to do things that make your company look bigger and totally professional, such as

- **Professional-looking seminars to boost sales:** Give potential customers information and training to educate them about why your service or product is useful and you've won half the sales battle.

- **Customer training and support:** You may not have a huge customer support or training organization, but does your customer have to know that? Of course not! Deliver training and support via WebEx and you've got all the tools the huge competitors have, at a fraction of the cost.

- **Snazzy presentations:** You could e-mail a PowerPoint presentation to your customer, but how much more effective would it be to host an online presentation, annotating the presentation as you go, allowing your customer to ask questions and get answers right then, and sharing documents? Cool, huh?

- **Product demos:** Why limit yourself to simple canned demos? Let your customers play around with your desktop or applications. And you don't even have to travel to their offices — just set up a session through Sales Center, and that's it!

Many Hats, Many Training Dollars

When your business is small, everyone wears a lot of hats, so you have to train each employee in more than one role. Trust me, this can get expensive.

Ease the cost of this training by using WebEx. You can provide self-paced or instructor-led training to help new employees get up to speed on company procedures, or train folks to use new software you've adopted or learn how to use a new selling system that will help you defeat the competition.

Oops . . . We Slowed Down

It happens: You lose a big contract, your industry or the economy slows down, and a small business sometimes can't support all its costs in lean times as a large business is able to.

WebEx gives you the flexibility to move to a smaller package when you need to, and then shift to one with more features when things get going again. Just keep in mind that most packages have a three-month minimum, but if you fulfill that, WebEx can help you make changes to accommodate both your growth and the lean times.

Chapter 17

Ten Ways That Companies Get the Most Out of WebEx

*W*ebEx doesn't offer a one size fits all approach to Web-based interaction. In fact, WebEx provides a pretty customizable suite of Web-based meeting solutions, which means that the combination of applications you purchase and the way you use them in your business can vary. Some companies go for every bell and whistle, some get big results from implementing just a meeting and training solution, or a support or sales solution. (Of course the beauty of all this flexibility is that whatever combination you choose, it's easy and fast to deploy because all your people need is a browser and Internet connection).

In this chapter I give you a glimpse of the many ways that real world companies (small and large) are using WebEx applications. I hope that these case studies give you ideas for how best to implement WebEx in your organization. Then you can take those ideas and talk to your WebEx account manager to discuss the best options for your needs.

StratX Jumps on the Remote Learning Bandwagon

StratX is a global marketing and strategy development consultancy that helps Fortune 500 companies design and deploy simulation based, interactive seminars. Two years ago the business decided to expand its use of computerized conferencing systems, specifically to enhance it's e-learning offerings. However they had clients who were cautious about allowing them to install applications on their computer systems.

They took a look at WebEx and liked what they saw. "It's a light program on the client side, it takes minutes to set up, and it's very firewall friendly," says StratX's director of e-learning solutions, Delphone Parmenter. StatX takes advantage of the capacity to share documents, software applications, and a whiteboard in real time to teach market-focused strategies to classes of individuals in remote locations. They use various WebEx tools such as polling to interact with and keep the attention of attendees. They even customized their online classroom to provide access to their computerized business games and to make the environment more intuitive for their users.

The results? The total number of StratX customer being taught online has moved up from 200 to 600 in the last year. And, the percentage of people who complete the courses has soared from only 70 percent, to an impressive 92.5 percent.

Iowa Foundation for Medical Care Increases Productivity

With over 500 employees, the IFMC works with government agencies and healthcare providers in all 50 states to improve the quality of medical care. With seven offices of their own and three major divisions, they were challenged to provide their contingency with quality support for processing of Medicare and Medicaid benefits.

An important part of the foundation's requirements was the need to comply with security requirements of federal reporting agencies. WebEx's offerings supported SSL encryption, support for all firewalls, and security features that were important in a medical reporting setting. Now IFMC uses WebEx Training Center to deliver training, Meeting Center to hold online meetings, and assist their Help Desk staff via Support Center. Using Support Center, for example, they can observe clients entering information into their software and see where mistakes are occurring.

Epicor Beefs Up Customer Support

Epicor is in the business of delivering integrated enterprise software for mid-sized companies. They needed a way to share and use the users' screens and use remote control to diagnose, troubleshoot, and resolve issues with their software at client sites from a distance.

Epicor had already implemented WebEx Meeting Center in their sales organization. When they added Support Center to their operations, they found that they reduced customer call resolution times by 50% or more. In certain cases issues that were taking 4 hours to resolve were now resolved in 30 minutes or less. In just one support center they experienced savings of 100 call time hours a month.

Epicor also uses WebEx to remotely implement customized software solutions for customers, saving time and money in travel costs.

CHT R. Beitlich Gets Technical Support Going

This German textile manufacturer has operations in approximately 50 countries. Their challenge was to provide their satellite offices with technical support and maintenance. Support Center allows them to provide real time diagnoses and resolution of problems over the Internet. Instant sessions, remote patch downloads, and interactive desktop sharing have proved to be most valuable tools in supporting their offices. They can even do entire systems installations at remote sites without ever traveling there.

DSM Cuts Travel Costs and Time to Market

No stranger to international operations, DSM is a global leader in the chemicals industry with 200 offices and 40 production sites worldwide. The cost and time involved with collaborating via physical meetings was taking its toll on DSM.

As part of the chemical/pharmaceutical industry, DSM was especially concerned with security. The security features offered by SSL and the WebEx Mediatone Network, where a client's information is never stored but switched in real time, were very attractive to this kind of company. Also, interactive features such as sharing documents and applications proved useful.

DSM has even integrated the WebEx Meeting Center service with its calendaring program, allowing users to schedule and attend meetings from within their calendars.

The result of this improved collaboration has been savings in time, money, and faster cycles to get product to market.

Emory University Saves Busy Students Time

Emory University serves some 11,000+ students. To help these students be the most productive they implemented WebEx Training Center, creating virtual classrooms students could log into from their home PC.

The Whiteboard feature provided handy for discussions of case studies and strategies. PowerPoint presentations with annotation capabilities enhances teacher-student interaction. Student study teams also use WebEx features to collaborate on projects.

Faculty have even instituted virtual office hours, where students can stop by and talk without having to hike across campus or across town. An added benefit is the ability of faculty to network with colleagues around the world, even inviting other academic experts to participate in virtual classroom sessions.

InfoGenesis Gets Smart with SMARTtech

When your focus is on hospital information technology, your efficiency can be a matter of life and death. InfoGenesis provides software, hardware, installation, and training to the hospital and food services industries. Providing great customer support is a key concern of the company. They need to constantly provide updates, patches, and refinements to their customers.

InfoGenesis also had a need to make connections between its data center and customers over Virtual Private Networks. With other online remote access solutions direct network connections were required that were impossible to achieve with VPNs. The seamless connection provided by WebEx through any firewall was an elegant answer to this challenge.

WebEx's SMARTtech remote access technology was the solution InfoGenesis needed. They use a third party software to manage downloads of patches and updates to customers. Technicians can use WebEx sessions to access a remote system and take remote control to view log files and use SMARTtech technology to transfer files between systems.

Mindspeed Lowers the Cost of Sales Training

Mindspeed provides semiconductor networking solutions, which they work with some of the movers and shakers in the wireless industry as well as others. Mindspeed's sales reps and channel partners are located around the globe. When new products launch they have to provide rapid, cost-effective training on semiconductor-related issues, which, trust me, is pretty complex technology.

Videoconferencing services just cost too much to make them practical. Enter WebEx. Mindspeed's strategy is now to hold weekly updates, rather than inundating salespeople and channel partners with a day or two of training every few months. This has worked well, because people get the information in smaller chunks, and are not overwhelmed by the technology. This small chunk of training model also means salespeople spend less time off the road, and more time out there selling. The result is that Mindspeed has reduced its training delivery costs by 96 percent.

But training isn't the only use MindSpeed has for WebEx applications. Their product designers in diversely located design centers brainstorm and collaborate on shared designs online. Because of WebEx, sharing large-scale schematics has become easy to do.

Fidelity Trains over 5,000 People

Fidelity Information Services is a division of Fidelity National Financial. They have clients in more than 50 countries to whom they provide application software, information processing management, and outsourcing services for the financial services industry.

With over 5,000 staff members to train worldwide, Fidelity's training group needed a cost-effective solution to training. Though they had used various online training solutions in the past, they found that WebEx Training Center worked better with their Learning Content Management System (LCMS). They got the flexibility to use all the training content tools they had in place, and the bandwidth to deliver them through WebEx.

Air Liquide Keeps Employees Off the Road

Air Liquide leads the pack when it comes to industrial and medical gases. Next time you get oxygen when you're in the hospital, there's a good chance these folks supplied it.

So, what were their meeting challenges? With 30,800 employees located in more than 65 countries you can imagine the communication challenges. Add to that a decentralized model that allows each subsidiary a certain amount of autonomy, a proliferation of collaboration tools resulted. As this became more and more unwieldy, Air Liquide management looked for a more unified solution.

What tipped the balance in this situation were the incidents of September 11, 2001. International travel now became more than an inconvenience, it became fraught with difficulties and actual danger. The company made the leap to meeting with WebEx. The result was increased interaction among teams, savings of travel time and costs, and added safety for employees who no longer had to be on the road to physical meetings.

And, because all a user needs is a Web browser to access WebEx meetings, they could extend the communication channel to individuals outside the company, including suppliers, customers, and consultants.

Appendix

Frequently Asked Questions

● ●

*T*he thing about frequently asked questions (FAQs to you) is, they exist because enough people wondered about something to ask. Therefore, they usually answer about 99.9999% of the things people need to know.

You can find some of these answers on WebEx's Web site, but I have compiled them here for you. The questions and answers are organized by the WebEx Center you need more information about. Look for the info you need to know here, and then go to www.webex.com to check into what additional updated information they provide there.

Frequently Asked Questions about WebEx Event Center

Event Center, formerly known as OnStage, is a WebEx meeting service that is tailored specifically for Web-based seminars of 25 to 3000 participants. When you've got an audience of a few thousand people, you want to get things right. Here, then, are some FAQs designed to help you do just that.

How does Event Center differ from other services?

Here are some key differences between Event Center and other WebEx services. Event Center:

- ✔ Provides extensive automation of invitations, enrollment, approvals, reminders, and thank-yous.

- ✔ Includes lead-source tracking ID's and automated lead scoring so you can rank your leads for follow-up.

- ✔ Supports a team of "panelists" that manage hosting, presenting, polling, text Q&A, integrated audio, and attendee support.

- ✔ Includes a calendar of scheduled events that is formatted specifically for listing Web-based events.

✔ Automatically installs the Event Manager plug-in whenever an attendee enrolls in an event, then installs any necessary updates once an attendee joins the event.

✔ Supports customized HTML invitations.

✔ Allows an event host to publish recorded events on an Event Center Web site.

✔ Prohibits attendees from remotely controlling shared applications, Web browsers, or desktops.

✔ Allows an event host to generate custom reports at any time before or after an event.

✔ Allows XML and API integration with CRM, SFA and Marketing Automation systems.

Can I use Event Manager for Windows if I am a restricted user running Windows NT, Windows 2000, or Windows XP?

Yes, administrator privileges are not required to install Event Manager.

What do I need to host or attend events on Microsoft Windows?

Here's a rundown of the minimum requirements to host or attend fully interactive events using Event Manager for Windows:

✔ Windows 98, Me, NT, 2000, or XP

✔ Intel x86 (Pentium 400MHZ +) or compatible processor

✔ 128 MB RAM

✔ Microsoft Internet Explorer 5, 6, Mozilla 1.6 or later, or Netscape 4.7, 7.x

✔ JavaScript and cookies enabled in the browser

✔ 56K or faster Internet connection

✔ A localized version of Windows is required to host or attend fully interactive events on Asian versions of Event Center (Japanese, Traditional Chinese, and Simplified Chinese).

What do I need to host or attend events on Mac OS?

Are you a Mac devotee? No problem. Minimum requirements to host or attend fully interactive events for Mac OS:

✔ Mac OS 10.2.x or later

✔ Internet Explorer 5.2 or Safari 1.1 or later

✔ JavaScript and cookies enabled for the browser

✔ Java 1.3.1 or later

What do I need to host or attend events using Solaris*?

Here are the minimum requirements to host or attend fully interactive events using Event Manager for Solaris:

- ✔ Solaris 8 or 9
- ✔ Java Plug-In 1.3.1 or later
- ✔ UltraSPARC or SPARC processor
- ✔ 512 MB RAM
- ✔ Netscape 7, or Mozilla 1.6 or later
- ✔ JavaScript and cookies enabled in the browser
- ✔ 16-bit or better video display
- ✔ CDE
- ✔ 56K or faster Internet connection

What do I need to host or attend events using Linux*?

When you open source types wan to host or attend fully interactive events using Event Manager for Linux, you must have either Red Hat Enterprise Linux, Red Hat Desktop, or SuSE Linux.

Other Linux distributions may work if you're are using:

- ✔ Linux Kernel 2.4+
- ✔ Java Plug-In 1.4.1 or later
- ✔ Xfree86
- ✔ Intel x86 (Pentium 400MHZ +) or compatible processor
- ✔ 128 MB RAM
- ✔ Netscape 7 or Mozilla 1.6 or later
- ✔ JavaScript and cookies enabled in the browser
- ✔ GNOME, KDE, or other compatible desktop manager
- ✔ 56K or faster Internet connection

I see that you support Mozilla; can I use Mozilla's Firefox browser?

Although not officially supported by WebEx at this time, Mozilla users can use Firefox to join and host an event.

How come I can't join a meeting with Mozilla browser, when it's supposed to be supported?

If you are using Mozilla as your browser on a UNIX based operating system such as Solaris or Linux or Apple's Mac OS X platform, you have to make sure that the Java plug-in is installed on your workstation. Mozilla does not ship with the Java Plug-In by default on these platforms. The following Web sites provide instructions for their individual operating systems:

- Linux: `http://plugindoc.mozdev.org/linux.html#Java`
- Solaris: `http://plugindoc.mozdev.org/solaris.html#Java`
- Mac OS X: `http://plugindoc.mozdev.org/OSX.html#Java`

On UNIX-based systems, you have to use a symbolic link (if you don't know what this is, ask your administrator). The example below is based on a Red Hat Linux environment:

```
$ cd /usr/local/mozilla/plugins
$ ln -s /usr/java/j2sdk1.4.2_04/plugin/i386/ns610-gcc32/libjavaplugin_oji.so
            libjavaplugin_oji.so
```

I really like the new look and features of WebEx, how come I don't have any of the new floating panels and new color themes from my Mac, Linux or Solaris machine?

The new user interface you see on a Windows platform contains WebEx's newest set of improvements based on user experience. Currently, the new look and feel, as well as new features, is not available on any other operating system. However, users on non-Windows operating systems can still host and attend the same events as their Windows counterparts. The new look and features are being planned for Mac, Solaris and Linux operating systems in a future release. (If you buy this book a year or so after the lastest WebEx interface is released, these products may all be available and you won't even have to ask this question!).

Is branding available for Event Center Web sites?

Yes, if you purchase a Subscription service. Talk to your account manager to discover more about this.

What does the Event Center Production Services offer?

The Event Center Production Services is a team of experts who help you produce your Web-based events — from start to finish. Production Services provides the following:

- Design and setup for your event
- Management of all technical aspects of your event
- Event rehearsals and dry-runs
- Training and coaching to presenters

✔ Consultation on preparing presentations and conducting effective events

✔ Technical support before and during an event

✔ Event recordings

✔ Recorded event archives for up to 90 days

✔ Coordination and set up of teleconferencing services

✔ Generation of follow-up reports after an event

What are public, private, and unlisted events?

When scheduling an event, you can specify the event to be public, private, or unlisted. Here's how these break down:

✔ **Public event** — Appears on the Upcoming Events page and the Recorded Events page, if the event host makes the recording public. On the Upcoming Events page, an **Enroll** button appears for the event until the host starts the event.

✔ **Private event** — Appears on the Upcoming Events page and the Recorded Events page, if the event host makes the recording public. On the Upcoming Events page, the text **Private** appears instead of an **Enroll** button. Once you're within 15 minutes of the event's scheduled starting time, and the host starts the event, a **Join** button appears.

✔ **Unlisted event** — Does not appear on the Upcoming Events page. However, it appears on the Recorded Events page if the event host makes the recording public.

How do I customize email messages for event invitees, enrollees and attendees?

When you schedule an event, you can customize any of the email messages that Event Center sends to event invitees, enrollees and attendees. First, on the Schedule an Event page, select the check box for the email messages that you want to send:

✔ Enrollment Pending

✔ Enrollment Approved

✔ Enrollment Rejected

✔ Reminder

✔ Thank You for Attending

✔ Absentee Follow-up

Next, click the link for the email message to open the Edit Email Message window.

When customizing the content of an email message, you can use several variables, which Event Center automatically replaces with information about the event when sending the message. For example, you can use the variable %Topic%, which Event Center automatically replaces with the event name specified on the Schedule an Event page. You can also restore an email template by clicking the **Restore to Default** button.

I already started the event, but attendees do not see the Join button on the Upcoming Events page. Why?

If you haven't enabled the join-before-host feature for an event, then the Join button appears on the Upcoming Event page only if both of the following are true:

- ✔ The event host has already started the event.
- ✔ The current time is within 15 minutes of the event's scheduled starting time.

How many attendees can Event Center accommodate?

Event Center is developed based on a highly scalable platform. Event Center can accommodate up to 3,000 concurrent attendees in a single event for document sharing. When application sharing is used in an event, the recommended event size is 1,000 concurrent attendees.

Can an event be recorded?

Yes. Using WebEx Recorder, subscription customers can record their own events, or the Event Center Production Team can record events for customers. Recorded events can be published on an Event Center Web site, where others can play them.

What is the recommended size for a VoIP event?

WebEx recommends keeping a VoIP event to less than 500 attendees with the following activities: document sharing, chat, and Q&A. You should minimize application-sharing usage when you're running a VoIP event.

What are WebEx teleconferencing offerings?

WebEx offers several types of teleconferencing services: Toll, and toll-free reservation-less or operator-assisted.

What is WebEx reservation-less teleconferencing, and when should I use it?

Reservation-less teleconferencing is on-demand teleconferencing, which you can schedule using the Schedule an Event page. With reservation-less, you can optionally choose to prompt attendees for their phone number and the system will call them back. This option is appropriate for events with fewer than 125 participants for which you don't need:

✔ Operator assistance

✔ *0 option for question-and-answer (Q & A) sessions

✔ Side conferences or sub-conferencing to allow the presentation team preparation or technical support time

WebEx recommends reservation-less teleconferencing for:

✔ Dry runs

✔ Practice sessions

✔ Smaller, less formal events for which you do don't need the help of an operator

How do I get WebEx reservation-less teleconferencing?

You can contact your Client Service manager to enable this service on your site.

What is WebEx operator-assisted teleconferencing, and when should I use it?

You must schedule a WebEx operator-assisted teleconference before the event's starting time. An operator-assisted teleconference provides the following features:

✔ Operator-assisted audio

✔ A *0 option, which participants can dial to speak to an operator

✔ Support for side conferences for presentation team preparation or technical support

✔ Support for online question-and-answer (Q & A) sessions

I recommend operator-assisted teleconferencing for events with more than 125 participants when you need formal and personalized service.

How do I schedule a WebEx operator-assisted teleconference?

To schedule a WebEx operator-assisted teleconference, dial 1-866-389-3239 (toll-free) or 1-916-851-8501.You can also schedule a teleconference by sending an email message to the following address: ecproductionservices@webex.com.

Can I use my own teleconferencing vendor?

Yes, you can always use your own teleconferencing service provider for your events.

Frequently Asked Questions About WebEx Sales Center

Sales Center is a WebEx meeting service that is tailored specifically for delivering live, interactive sales demos over the Web. Using Sales Center, your organization can maximize selling time, shorten sales cycles, land more sales, and reduce your travel costs. Sales Center leverages the performance, reliability, and security of the WebEx Mediatone Network to provide a world-class, collaborative sales platform.

Can you give me some ideas of what can I do with WebEx Sales Center?

WebEx Sales Center has all the capabilities that your sales organization needs to implement an online selling. With WebEx Sales Center, your sales reps can create online sales calls to:

- ✔ Develop likely suspects into prospects
- ✔ Provide online demonstrations and sales presentations
- ✔ Meet with customer stakeholders worldwide
- ✔ Work jointly on proposals
- ✔ Negotiate terms and conditions for contracts
- ✔ Close the sale and position the customer for future opportunities

What can my sales reps and team do with WebEx Sales Center?

The online sales process enabled by WebEx Sales Center makes it possible for sales reps to:

- ✔ Generate more qualified leads
- ✔ Create and distribute online collateral
- ✔ Reduce the complexity of the sales process
- ✔ Use online team meetings to work important issues
- ✔ Turn online meetings into decision-making sessions
- ✔ Reduce travel time and expense
- ✔ Accelerate the sales cycle

What does WebEx Sales Center do for my sales management?

WebEx Sales Center has the following benefits:

For sales managers, moving from the traditional sales process to the tech-driven sales process:

✔ Makes the sales pipeline more transparent to management

✔ Allows sales management to have a greater impact

✔ Creates an environment that encourages teamwork

✔ Reduces the overall cost of the average sale

✔ Increases average revenue and profit per sale

How does WebEx Sales Center reduce selling costs?

Two of the biggest expenses in sales are prospecting for qualified leads and making sales calls at customer sites. Fortunately, these are the exact two areas where WebEx Sales Center can have the most positive financial impact.

✔ **Saving Money on Prospecting:** Prospecting gets more expensive every year. In many sales environments, a successful lead developed from tele-marketing can cost $15 or more. Magazine advertising can be even more expensive. Unless advertising is highly targeted to a particular audience, it's not unusual for companies to spend up to $100 per qualified lead. Special sales events can be even pricier. It's not unusual for a company to spend $10,000 on a special event, only to end up with ten real prospects. That's $1,000 per lead!

With WebEx Sales Center, a sales organization can use online events to prospect for qualified leads. Such events typically cost a small fraction of special events at hotels and trade shows, and can be even more effective.

✔ **Saving Money on Sales Calls:** Because WebEx Sales Center reduces the need for sales-oriented business travel, WebEx Sales Center radically reduces the cost of closing business. Even without counting travel, it cost a company an average of $1,000 per sales call to have a sales rep conduct needs analysis, present a solution, and conduct follow-up activities. If the customer is located remotely, it can cost an addition $1,000 (on average) in travel expenses per sales call. Since it takes, on average, four sales call to close a sale, that's $8,000 that must be spent before a sale is even made! And that doesn't count the lost opportunity cost of business travel. If the average sales rep spends a day every week travel-ing, it's the equivalent of paying a "tax" of 20 percent on all sales activities!

WebEx Sales Center completely changes that equation. While the intellec-tual effort of moving the sale forward remains constant, travel expenses and lost opportunity costs are minimized. This can have an enormous impact. If a sales force of 100, for example, uses WebEx Sales Center to avoid a day of travel per week, that's the equivalent of adding 20 more sales reps to the staff – at no extra expense. In addition, at $1,000 a trip, WebEx Sales Center would be saving a whopping $5 million in travel expenses (50 weeks*100 reps* $1,000).

Furthermore, conducting online sales calls can give you and your prospects the flexibility to meet more often, which can significantly reduce the sales cycle.

How does Sales Center differ from Meeting Center?

Sales Center includes all the major features in Meeting Center Professional, as well as the following additional features:

- Sales Management
  - Silent Monitoring
  - Team Roles
  - Sales Meeting Reports
  - Account/ Opportunity
  - Sales Force Automation
- Team Selling
  - Attention Indicator
  - Subject Matter Experts
  - Private Chat
- Prospect Experience
  - Simplified Prospect View
  - Join as a Group
  - Prospect Portal
- Personalized Selling
  - Sales Team Picture
  - Customized Emails
  - Role-based Invitation

What do I need to host or attend events on Microsoft Windows?

Minimum requirements to host or attend fully interactive events using WebEx Sales Center for Windows:

- Windows 98, Me, NT, 2000, or XP
- Intel x86 (Pentium 400MHZ +) or compatible processor
- Microsoft Internet Explorer 5, 6, Mozilla 1.6 or later, or Netscape 4.7, 7.x
- JavaScript and cookies enabled in the browser
- 56K or faster Internet connection

Is branding available for Event Center Web sites?

Yes, if you purchase a Subscription service.

What does the WebEx Sales Center Assist Services offer?

The WebEx Sales Center Assist Services is a team of experts who help customers produce their entire Web-based online sales call — from start to finish. Assist Services provides the following:

- ✔ Training and coaching to presenters
- ✔ Consultation on preparing presentations and conducting effective online sales calls
- ✔ Technical support before and during an event
- ✔ Recording and editing of your online sales call to create best practices or sales training materials
- ✔ Coordination and sets up of teleconferencing services

How do I schedule meetings using Microsoft Outlook?

You can download the installer from the Support page, and install it. You will need administrative privileges to install it on Windows NT, 2000, and XP. You can then use Outlook to schedule WebEx meetings, invite attendees, and start WebEx meetings. Your invited attendees can easily join the meeting from their Outlook Calendars.

What happens if I invite people who are not using Outlook or are not in my organization?

These invitees receive a normal invitation email message, which contains a link that they can click to join the meeting.

Do I have to download software to host a meeting?

To use all of the interactive features in a meeting, you must run Meeting Manager on your computer. Meeting Manager lets you or anyone in the meeting share most types of documents or applications. Unlike installing software from a disk or downloading it over the Internet and installing it manually, your meeting service automatically downloads and sets up Meeting Manager for you. Each time you participate in a meeting, Meeting Manager maintains itself by checking for the latest version and automatically updating itself, as necessary.

For first-time users, the Meeting Manager for Windows download is approximately 1.0 MB. Meeting Manager then downloads updates as appropriate.

Can I use Meeting Manager for Windows if I am a restricted user running Windows NT, Windows 2000, or Windows XP?

Yes, administrator privileges are not required to install Meeting Manager.

How do I install the fully interactive Meeting Manager manually?

Instructions for manually installing the fully interactive Meeting Manager are available in Chapter 3.

How do I uninstall Meeting Manager?

To uninstall Meeting Manager for Windows, use Add/Remove Programs in the Control Panel.

To uninstall Meeting Manager for Mac OS, double-click the installer, then, on the Easy Install menu, choose Uninstall.

To uninstall Meeting Manager, run `wbxsetup`, as described on the WebEx Support page. Then follow the instructions on your screen to uninstall the software.

To uninstall Meeting Manager for Palm, refer to your WebEx site's Palm Support page.

What affects the performance of my online sales calls?

Because WebEx online sales calls provide real-time collaboration and sharing over the Internet, performance depends on both the Internet itself and the WebEx service. WebEx constantly monitors service and network performance, and continually enhances its infrastructure to keep WebEx meeting services available and reliable.

Some of the factors that affect performance are the following:

- ✓ The speed of your computer's connection to the Internet
- ✓ The performance of your Internet service provider
- ✓ Overall Internet traffic on your routed connection to the WebEx server
- ✓ Performance of firewall and proxy servers, if your computer is behind a company firewall

I have a high-speed Internet connection. Does that help my sales call performance?

Although you may have a high-speed connection to the Internet, there can often be congestion or packet loss (data that is dropped during transmission) on the Internet, between you and the WebEx servers on the WebEx Interactive Network. You usually can't do much about this, other than to inform your network administrator or Internet service provider. Problems are often of short duration and resolve themselves over time. However, you should report serious, persistent problems. Of course, more bandwidth usually allows more throughput — but not always. For example, a clear 56K modem connection can perform well, while a congested "high speed" T1 connection can cause you sleepless nights and significant hair loss.

Furthermore, a good connection won't help you if you're an attendee in a meeting and the presenter has a poor connection. Thus, it's most critical that the presenter have a connection that's up to snuff.

What can I do to speed things up?

First, get the fastest connection that you can. ISPs are rapidly deploying DSL, cable modem, and T1 connections. Dial-up modems can do the job, but anything less than 56K is probably too slow. Even with a 56K modem, your actual connection speed may vary.

Next, try using document and presentation sharing instead of application or desktop sharing, because document and presentation sharing uses less bandwidth. Also, sharing documents or presentations that contain fewer graphics can improve the performance.

Also make sure the presenter has a fast connection. It doesn't help the attendees to all have T1 connections if the presenter is on a slow modem connection.

How can I test performance?

The Trace Route utility on your Windows computer can help you to determine where problems are occurring between your computer and the WebEx server. On Windows' Accessories menu, open a DOS prompt or a Command prompt window, then type

```
tracert your_siteURL
```

where your_site_URL is the address for your WebEx meeting service Web site. Be sure that you include a space after tracert.

When running Trace Route, your computer sends packets of information across your connection to measure the amount of time it takes to for the packets to reach the meeting server. Ideally, packets should take between 1-60 ms to reach the server. If packets take between 60-100 ms to reach the server, your connection is slow and you'll feel the consequences in a WebEx meeting. Times longer than 100 ms are likely to seem unacceptably slow. If you continue to experience poor performance, ping your network administrator.

What's the difference between document sharing and application sharing?

Document sharing uses a printer driver (the WebEx Document Loader) to create an image of your document, which is then presented for review and markup in the Meeting Manager content viewer. This image is a lot like a printed document or fax — that is , you can't edit it, you can just admire it. This image requires relatively little bandwidth and so it works well at slower connection speeds.

On the other hand, application sharing sends images of the application in real-time, allowing you to edit documents as well as show all of an application's features, such as menus and tools. This type of sharing is much more powerful and requires more bandwidth.

What types of files or applications can I share?

You can share virtually any document or application. However, applications with streaming content may not work well, because this kind of content is not streaming directly from the source to attendees. However, if you want to share a Web page with streaming content, you can use Web content sharing, which opens a window on each attendee's computer and streams the content directly from its source.

Does everyone in a meeting need the file or application that I want to share?

No. Only the presenter in the meeting must have the file or application on his or her computer.

How can I modify documents that I'm sharing?

In document sharing, you can annotate documents, but not edit them, because the content is an image like you view in a PDF document or fax. However, you can use application sharing to edit documents as you share them in a meeting, and save the final version in the native application format (the format the document was originally created in). Application sharing lets all the attendees see the changes that you make, or edit the document themselves, if you grant them remote control.

Can I share more than one document or presentation at a time?

Yes, you can share as many documents or presentations as you like in the content viewer. Each document or presentation that you open appears on its own tab in the content viewer. Because Meeting Manager automatically labels each tab with the title or name of the document or presentation, you can quickly locate the document or presentation that you want to share with attendees.

Can I save annotated documents or presentations and view them offline?

In a word, yes. To save any document or presentation in a file on your computer, choose **Save** on the **File** menu. To view the saved file offline, simply double-click it. The document or presentation appears in the WebEx Document Viewer, which is part of Meeting Manager.

Can I save annotations made during application sharing or desktop sharing?

Yes. To do this, you can record your meeting. A recording captures all annotations and other actions that you make during application or desktop sharing.

Can I show animations and slide transitions in presentations?

Sure. If you share a Microsoft PowerPoint presentation, attendees can see animations and slide transitions in their content viewers. Alternatively, you can show animations and slide transitions by using application sharing to share your slide-authoring application, then open the slides in that application.

What happens if people in a meeting have displays of different sizes or resolutions?

In a WebEx meeting, all of the attendees' views automatically display the meeting content, even if they have different display resolutions. No matter which resolution attendees' monitors are set to, attendees' views automatically follow the presenter's mouse pointer. Thus, the presenter should always keep the mouse pointer near the content under discussion. For best results, the presenter should set his or her monitor to 800 x 600 pixels, because this resolution is the most common. To change your monitor's display resolution for Windows, use the **Settings** tab in the Display Control Panel. For Mac OS, use the Monitors Control Panel.

Why do attendees sometimes see a yellow crosshatched pattern during application sharing?

The crosshatched pattern is the shadow of a dialog box or window that is in front of the shared application on the presenter's screen. Once the presenter closes this dialog box or window, the pattern disappears.

Can I use my keyboard keys to remotely control an application that is running on a different platform?

Yes. If you are remotely controlling a presenter's application, desktop, or Web browser and your computer's operating system is not the same as the presenter's, Meeting Manager automatically maps your keyboard keys to the presenter's keys. For details, look up *"keyboard shortcuts, using to remotely control software"* in the Index in the online Help for your WebEx meeting service Web site.

Which video cameras does WebEx Meeting Center support?

You can generally use any video camera, or webcam, that connects to either a USB or parallel port on your computer.

WebEx has tested the following video cameras for Windows and says they work just fine with Meeting Manager for Windows:

- 3Com Home Connect
- Creative Lab PD0040
- Creative webcam plus
- D-Link WebCam
- Epson type SW
- EZonics EZCam USB
- IBM PC Camera (Black)
- IBM PC Camera Pro (White)
- iBOT FireWire Desktop
- Intel PC Camera Pro
- Logitech QuickCam Home (USB)
- Logitech QuickCam VC (Parallel)
- Omiga CD370 Camera
- Video Camera (1394)
- Vista Imaging Vi Cam LPT
- Vista Imaging Vi Cam USB

WebEx has also tested the following video cameras for Mac OS and found them to be compatible with Meeting Manager for Mac OS:

- iBOT
- iREZ
- iSight

Why can't I bookmark some pages on my WebEx meeting service Web site?

Your meeting service Web site dynamically generates many of its pages, which you cannot bookmark. Therefore, you can only bookmark your home page.

How can I prevent uninvited attendees from joining my meeting?

The following are several ways that you can prevent uninvited attendees from joining your meeting:

✔ Specify a password for your meeting. Your meeting service automatically includes the password for your meeting in an invitation email message to each invited attendee.

✔ Schedule an unlisted meeting. On the Schedule a Meeting page, you can select the Unlisted meeting check box to prevent your meeting from appearing on the meeting calendar. Only attendees who have the meeting number can join the meeting.

✔ Restrict access to your meeting. Once all invited attendees have joined the meeting, you can choose Restrict Access on the Meeting menu to prevent others from joining the meeting.

✔ Expel any uninvited attendee from your meeting, by choosing Expel on the Participant menu.

Why don't email notifications show the meeting time in the attendee's time zone?

In email notifications, Meeting times automatically appear in the host's time zone. A host can change his or her time zone on the Preferences page. Although your meeting service can't figure out each attendee's time zone and adjust it automatically for each email notification, attendees can easily view meeting times in their time zones on your meeting service Web site by selecting a different time zone on the Preferences page.

Frequently Asked Questions about Support Center

Support Center is a super place to get one-on-one with customers or employees. Here are some oft-asked questions to help you get the most of Support Center.

What do I need to host or attend a support session on Microsoft Window?

Minimum requirements to host or attend a support session for Microsoft Windows are as follows:

✔ Windows 98, Me, NT, 2000, or XP

✔ Intel x86 (Pentium 400 MHz +) or compatible Processor

✔ 128 MB RAM

✔ Microsoft Internet Explorer 5, 6, Mozilla 1.6 or later, or Netscape 4.7, 7.x

✔ JavaScript and cookies enabled in the browser

✔ 56K or faster Internet connection

If you're a global type of company, you should know that you have to have a localized version of Windows to start or attend fully interactive support sessions on Asian versions of Support Center (Japanese, Traditional Chinese, and Simplified Chinese).

What do I need to host or attend a Support session on Mac OS?

Minimum requirements to host or attend fully interactive Support Sessions for Mac OS are as follows:

- ✔ Mac OS 10.2.x or later
- ✔ Internet Explorer 5.2 or Safari 1.1 or later, **Mozilla 1.4.1**
- ✔ JavaScript and cookies enabled for the browser
- ✔ Java 1.3.1 or later

What do I need to host or attend a Support Session using Solaris?

Minimum requirements to host or attend fully interactive meetings using Meeting Manager for Solaris are as follows:

- ✔ Solaris 8 or 9
- ✔ Java Plug-In 1.3.1 or later
- ✔ UltraSPARC or SPARC processor
- ✔ 512 MB RAM
- ✔ Netscape 7, or Mozilla 1.6 or later
- ✔ JavaScript and cookies enabled in the browser
- ✔ 16-bit or better video display
- ✔ CDE
- ✔ 56K or faster Internet connection

What do I need to host or attend Support Sessions using Linux?

For you open source folks, to host or attend fully interactive Support sessions using Linux, you must have Red Hat Enterprise Linux , Red Hat Desktop, or SuSE Linux.

Other Linux distributions may work if you are using:

- ✔ Linux Kernel 2.4+
- ✔ Java Plug-In 1.4.1 or later
- ✔ Xfree86
- ✔ Intel x86 (Pentium 400MHZ +) or compatible processor

✔ 128 MB RAM

✔ Netscape 7 or Mozilla 1.6 or later

✔ JavaScript and cookies enabled in the browser

✔ GNOME, KDE, or other compatible desktop manager

✔ 56K or faster Internet connection

What do I need to host or attend a Support Session using Citrix?

Minimum requirements to host or attend fully interactive Support session via Citrix include:

✔ Platforms supported: Windows XP SP1 and Windows 2000 SP4

✔ Browsers supported: Internet Explorer 5 or higher, Mozilla 1.4.1 or higher, Netscape 4.7 or higher

How come I can't join a Support Session with Mozilla browser, when it's supposed to be supported?

If you are using Mozilla as your browser on a UNIX based operating system such as Solaris or Linux or Apple's Mac OS X platform, you will need to make sure that the Java plug-in is installed on your workstation. Mozilla does not ship with the Java Plug-In by default on these platforms. The following web sites provide instructions for the associated operating system:

✔ Linux: `http://plugindoc.mozdev.org/linux.html#Java`

✔ Solaris: `http://plugindoc.mozdev.org/solaris.html#Java`

✔ Mac OS X: `http://plugindoc.mozdev.org/OSX.html#Java`

On UNIX based systems, there is a symbolic link that is required. The example below is based on a Red Hat Linux environment:

```
$ cd /usr/local/mozilla/plugins
$ ln -s /usr/java/j2sdk1.4.2_04/plugin/i386/ns610-gcc32/libjavaplugin_oji.so
              libjavaplugin_oji.so
```

How come I don't have any of the floating panels and new color themes from my Mac, Linux or Solaris machine?

The latest WebEx user interface you see on a Windows platform contains WebEx's newest set of user experience improvements. As of this writing, the new look and feel as well as new features, is not available on any other operating system. However, users on non-Windows operating systems can still host and attend the same meetings as their Windows counterparts. The new look and features are being planned for Mac, Solaris, and Linux operating systems in a future release.

Do I have to download software to start a support session?

WebEx Support Center service automatically downloads and sets up Support Manager for you. In fact, each time you start a support session, Support Manager saves you the trouble and maintains itself by checking for the latest version and automatically updating itself, as necessary.

For first-time users, the Support Manager for Windows download is approximately 2.5 MB. Support Manager subsequently downloads only updated components as needed.

Can I use Support Manager for Windows if I am a non-administrative Windows NT, Windows 2000 or Windows XP user?

Yes, administrator privileges are not required to install Support Manager.

How do I uninstall Support Manager?

To uninstall Support Manager for Windows, use Add/Remove Programs in the Control Panel.

As a customer attending the Support session are there any cool hot keys available to me?

Hot keys available to you are as follows:

- Ctrl + F10 = leave session
- Ctrl + F8 = start Chat session
- Ctrl + F3 = close chat window
- Ctrl + F7 = close file transfer
- Ctrl + F9 = close Application/Desktop sharing window
- Ctrl+Shift+F3 = focus on chat window

What affects the performance of support sessions?

Because WebEx support sessions provide real-time collaboration over the Internet, performance depends on both the Internet itself and the WebEx service. WebEx constantly monitors service and network performance, and continually enhances its infrastructure to keep WebEx meeting services available and reliable.

Some of the factors that affect performance are the following:

✔ the speed of your computer's connection to the Internet

✔ the performance of your Internet service provider

✔ overall Internet traffic on your routed connection to the WebEx server

✔ performance of firewall and proxy servers, if your computer is behind a company firewall

I have a high-speed Internet connection. Does that help?

Although you may have a high-speed connection to the Internet, there can often be congestion or packet loss on the Internet, between you and the WebEx servers on the WebEx Interactive Network. Much as you'd like to, you usually can't do much about this, other than to inform your network administrator or Internet service provider. Problems are often temporary and work themselves out over time. However, you should report serious, persistent problems. Of course, more bandwidth usually allows more throughput — but not always. For example, a clear 56K modem connection can perform well, while a congested "high speed" T1 connection can ruin your whole day.

How can I test performance?

The Trace Route utility on your computer can help you to determine where problems are occurring between your computer and the WebEx server. On the Windows Accessories menu, open a DOS prompt or a Command prompt window, then type

```
tracert your_site_URL
```

where your_site_URL is the address for your meeting service Web site. Ensure that you include a space after tracert.

When running Trace Route, your computer sends packets of information across your connection to measure the amount of time it takes to for the packets to reach the meeting server. Ideally, packets should take between 1-60 ms to reach the server. If packets take between 60-100 ms to reach the server, your connection is slow and may be noticeable in a WebEx meeting. Times longer than 100 ms are likely to seem unacceptably slow. If you continue to experience poor performance, give a shout to your network administrator.

What types of applications can I view or control?

You can view or control virtually any application running on a customer's computer.

Do I need to have the application that I want to view or control?

No, the application that you want to view or control does not need to be installed on your computer.

Sometimes images of a customer's desktop or application don't look so good. Why?

You may see degradation in the quality of some images as the WebEx compression algorithm scurries to automatically compensate for slow connections.

What happens if a customer has a display of a different size or resolution?

In a support session, Support Manager automatically displays the customer's desktop or application, even if the customer's monitor is set to a different display resolution. For best results, however, you should set your monitor to 800 x 600 pixels, because this resolution is the most common. To change your monitor's display resolution for Windows, use the Settings tab in the Display Control Panel.

Why do I sometimes see a yellow crosshatched pattern when viewing or controlling a customer's application?

The crosshatched pattern is the shadow of a dialog box or window that is in front of the shared application on the customer's screen. Once the customer closes this dialog box or window, the pattern goes away.

Which video cameras are supported?

You can generally use any video camera, or webcam, that connects to either a USB or parallel port on your computer.

WebEx has tested the following video cameras for Windows and found them to be compatible with Support Manager for Windows:

- 3Com Home Connect
- Creative Lab PD0040
- Creative webcam plus
- D-Link WebCam
- Epson type SW
- EZonics EZCam USB
- IBM PC Camera (Black)
- IBM PC Camera Pro (White)
- iBOT FireWire Desktop

- ✔ Intel PC Camera Pro
- ✔ Logitech QuickCam Home (USB)
- ✔ Logitech QuickCam VC (Parallel)
- ✔ Omiga CD370 Camera
- ✔ Video Camera (1394)
- ✔ Vista Imaging Vi Cam LPT
- ✔ Vista Imaging Vi Cam USB

Why can't I bookmark some pages on my Support Center Web site?

Your Support Center Web site dynamically generates many of its pages, which you cannot bookmark. You can therefore bookmark only the home page.

Glossary

Access Anywhere: An optional service on your WebEx site that allows you to access a computer from a remote location.

Access Anywhere Agent: Software that you can install on a computer, to allow you to remotely access the computer's desktop or applications.

annotation tools: In a WebEx meeting, tools that allow you to draw shapes, type text, and use pointers on shared documents, presentations, whiteboards, applications, desktops, or Web browsers.

application sharing: The act of sharing an application on your computer during a WebEx meeting. All participants can view the shared application, which appears in a sharing window on their screens. Participants can see all of your activity in the application.

Attendee: A participant in a WebEx meeting who primarily views information that a presenter shares in the meeting. An attendee also can perform other tasks according to his or her meeting privileges.

breakout session: In WebEx Training Center, a private application or desktop sharing session, away from the main training session, which allows participants to collaborate and interact with presenters or other students in smaller groups.

call-back teleconference: A telephone conference in which a participant provides his or her phone number when joining a WebEx meeting. The teleconferencing service calls the participant back, and a voice-response system instructs the participant on how to join the teleconference.

call-in teleconference: A telephone conference in which a participant calls a phone number when joining a meeting. When a participant calls the phone number, a voice response system guides the participant through the process of joining the teleconference.

company address book: A list of contacts in your personal address book that your WebEx site administrator maintains for your WebEx site.

content viewer: In a WebEx meeting, the content area in which a shared document, presentation, or whiteboard appears.

CSR dashboard: In WebEx Support Center, the window that provides a customer support representative with tools to provide remote support to a customer.

desktop sharing: The act of sharing your computer desktop during a WebEx meeting. All participants can view the shared desktop, which appears in a sharing window on their screens. Participants can see all of your activity on your desktop.

document and presentation sharing: Refers to sharing any type of document or presentation in the content viewer during a WebEx meeting.

Emoticons: In WebEx Training Center, icons that participants can use to convey voice inflections, facial expressions, and gestures during a training session.

Enterprise Edition: A WebEx site that includes two or more WebEx services, including Meeting Center, Event Center, Training Center, Support Center, and Sales Center.

Event Center: A WebEx service specifically designed for conducting large online events, such as marketing presentations.

Event Manager: In WebEx Event Center, client software that provides the Event window and sharing windows during an event.

Event window: In WebEx Event Center, the user interface with which participants interact during an event. The Meeting window is a component of the Event Manager software.

Feedback: In WebEx Event Center and Training Center, a feature that allows presenters to obtain quick yes-or-no attendee responses to questions that they ask, or to receive attendees' feedback on the pace of their presentations.

floating icon tray: A small toolbar that appears when you share an application, desktop, or Web browser. On the floating icon tray, icons represent minimized panels that you can open during the sharing session, without having to return to the main Meeting window.

G.723: An international standard for compressing audio data and defining the data format. Available in WebEx Recorder.

Hands-on Lab: In WebEx Training Center, sessions within a training session that simulate a physical computer lab, allowing participants to use computers remotely for hands-on learning and practice.

Host: A participant in a WebEx meeting who is primarily responsible for scheduling, starting, controlling access to, and ending a meeting.

host indicator: The text *(host)* , which appears in the participants list, to the right of the host's name in a WebEx meeting.

icon tray: The area above the panels in the Meeting window. On the icon tray, icons represent minimized panels that you can open.

Info tab: A standard tab that appears by default in the content viewer. The Info tab contains basic information about a meeting and its teleconference.

instant meeting: An impromptu meeting that you start immediately, without scheduling it first. Instant meetings require fewer setup options than scheduled meetings.

integrated teleconference: A teleconferencing service that is included with your WebEx service, rather than a third-party teleconferencing service. An integrated teleconference can be either a call-in or call-back teleconference.

Internet phone: A type of voice conference that allows participants to communicate over the Internet using voice over IP (VOIP) and a computer with a sound card, speakers, and a microphone.

local computer: In WebEx Access Anywhere, the computer that you use to access a remote computer during a remote access session.

MediaTone: WebEx technologies that enhance the multimedia capabilities of your WebEx service. For example, MediaTone includes the Universal Communications Format (UCF), Access Anywhere, and multiple document sharing capabilities.

MediaTone Network: A globally distributed, carrier-class information-switching architecture that delivers optimal performance by routing communications across several WebEx switching centers, or hubs.

MediaTone Platform: A distributed software architecture for Web-based communications services, which is deployed over the MediaTone Network. The MediaTone Platform supports the full range of data, voice, and video communications needed to simulate the full spontaneity and productivity of face-to-face meetings.

meeting calendar: In Meeting Center and Sales Center, a calendar on your WebEx site that provides a list of meetings that you or other users have scheduled or started.

Meeting Center: A WebEx service that you can use to conduct general, day-to-day online meetings.

Meeting Manager: In Meeting Center and Sales Center, software that provides the Meeting window and sharing windows during a meeting.

meeting number: A unique number that your WebEx service assigns to a meeting. For an unlisted meeting, participants must provide the meeting number to attend the meeting.

Meeting window: In Meeting Center and Sales Center, the user interface with which participants interact during a meeting. The Meeting window is a component of the Meeting Manager software.

multipoint video: A video mode in which the presenter and up to three other meeting participants can send video images simultaneously. Up to four video images can appear at once on the *Video* panel.

My WebEx: An area on your WebEX site in which you can access various user account features, such as your user profile, list of meetings, online address book, personal folders, One-Click Meetings, and Access Anywhere.

One-Click Meeting: A session that you can start at any time, as often as you want, by clicking a shortcut on your computer. To set up a One-Click Meeting, use the One-Click Meeting Wizard, which is available in the My WebEx area of your service Web site.

Panel: A group of controls that resides in an area of the Meeting window, to the right of the content viewer–for example, the *Participants* panel, the *Chat* panel, and the *Video* panel.

Panelist: In Event Center and Training Center, a participant who can present information, responds to chat messages, annotate shared documents, open and close polls, and view and answer attendees' questions in a Q & A session.

Participant: Refers collectively to all individuals in a meeting, including the host, presenter, and attendees.

participants list: The list of participants on the *Participants* panel in the Meeting window.

PCM: Abbreviation for pulse-coded modulation. The audio format standard for CD-ROM. Available in WebEx Recorder.

personal address book: An online address book that you maintain on your WebEx site. Your personal address book can contain a personal contacts list, contact groups, and a company address book.

personal folders: Storage space for your files on your WebEx site. If you store files in your folders, you can access them from any computer that is connected to the Internet. You can also share your folders so visitors to your Personal Meeting Room page can access the files in your folders.

Personal Meeting Room: A page on your WebEx site that lists only the meetings for which you are the host. If you provide others with the personal URL for this page, they can obtain information about your scheduled meetings, join your meetings in progress, and share the files in your personal folders to which you provide access.

Presenter: In a WebEx meeting, a participant who can share documents, presentations, and applications; conduct a poll, and so on.

presenter indicator: A green and blue symbol of a ball, which appears in the participants list, to the left of the name of the participant who is the current presenter.

Privileges: A user's capabilities to use specific features during a WebEx meeting. The host, presenter, and attendees have different privileges in a meeting.

Program: In WebEx Event Center, the grouping of live events or recorded events for a specific project, product, or audience.

question-and-answer (Q & A) session: In WebEx Event Center and Training Center, a feature that allows participants to ask questions and receive answers from the host, presenter, or panelists.

remote computer: In WebEx Access Anywhere, computer on which you have installed the Access Anywhere Agent, allowing you to access the computer over the Internet, using a local computer.

remote control: Refers to a WebEx meeting participant's ability to control an application, desktop, or Web browser that a presenter is sharing on his or her computer.

Sales Center: A WebEx service specifically designed for conducting sales meetings with prospects.

Session window: In Training Center, the user interface with which participants interact during a training session. The Session window is a component of the Training Manager software.

sharing window: In a WebEx meeting, a window that opens on participants' screens, in which a shared application, desktop, or Web browser appears.

single-point video: A video mode in which only the presenter, or a participant selected by the presenter, can send video images during a WebEx meeting.

site administrator: An employee of a company who administers that company's WebEx meeting service. A site administrator can add, modify, and remove user accounts; specify security options, maintain a company address book; and so on.

speaker indicator: In a WebEx meeting, a symbol of a phone or microphone, which appears in the participants list, to the left of the name of a participant who is connected in an integrated teleconference or Internet phone conference.

Support Center: A WebEx service specifically designed for providing technical support to customers remotely.

Support Manager: In Support Center, software that provides the CSR dashboard and sharing windows during a support session.

third-party teleconferencing service: Any teleconferencing service other than the teleconferencing service that your WebEx service provides.

thumbnail viewer: In a WebEx meeting, an area that a presenter can display on the left side of the Meeting window. The thumbnail viewer contains miniature images, or thumbnails, of each page in a shared document, presentation, or whiteboard.

training calendar: In Training Center, a calendar that lists training sessions either in progress or scheduled.

Training Center: A WebEx service simulates a classroom environment, specifically designed for conducting online training sessions.

Training Manager: In Training Center, software that provides the Session window and sharing windows during a training session.

UCF: See Universal Communications Format (UCF).

UCF media file: A media file type that you can play in the content viewer during a meeting, including WebEx Recording Format (WRF), audio, video, Flash, and Web page files. You can insert media files into a Microsoft PowerPoint presentation, using the WebEx Universal Communications Toolkit.

UCF multimedia presentation: A Microsoft PowerPoint presentation that contains UCF media files. You can share or view a UCF multimedia presentation in the content viewer, and play the media files for attendees. You can create a UCF multimedia presentation using the WebEx Universal Communications Toolkit.

UCF rich media: Refers to the following types of UCF media files: WebEx Recording Format (WRF), audio, video, and Flash.

Universal Communications Format (UCF): A WebEx file type that lets you do the following in the content viewer or the standalone Document Manager:

- ✔ Share multiple documents simultaneously
- ✔ Display slide transitions and animations in Microsoft PowerPoint presentations
- ✔ Share and play standalone UCF media files
- ✔ Share UCF multimedia presentations, in which you can play UCF media files

Universal Communications Toolkit: An add-in program for Microsoft PowerPoint that lets you insert media files into a PowerPoint presentation. You can play the media files while sharing the presentation in a WebEx meeting.

unlisted meeting: A scheduled meeting that does not appear on your WebEx site or on the host's Personal Meeting Room page. To join an unlisted meeting, attendees must provide a meeting number.

voice over IP (VOIP): A real-time voice communications technology by which computers send voice information in digital form over the Internet, rather than through the traditional public telephone system.

Web browser sharing: The act of sharing your Web browser during a WebEx meeting. All participants can view the shared Web browser, which appears in a sharing window on their screens. As you navigate to other Web pages in your browser, all participants "follow along" in their sharing windows.

Webcam: A video camera that you can attach to your computer. You can use a Webcam to send live video during a WebEx meeting.

WebEx Player: A WebEx product that plays back recordings that you make using the WebEx Recorder.

WebEx Recorder: A WebEx product that records all screen activity during a WebEx meeting or in any application outside of a meeting.

WebEx Recording Editor: A WebEx product that allows you to edit any recording that was made using WebEx Recorder. Using WebEx Recorder, you can add, delete, or rearrange recorded data; or dub audio.

WebEx Recording Format (WRF): A file format that comprises audio and images of user actions on a computer screen. A user can create a WRF file using WebEx Recorder and edit a WRF file using WebEx Recording Editor. A WRF file has a .wrf extension.

Whiteboard: In a WebEx meeting, a workspace that allows participants to draw and type simultaneously.

Index

• *T* •